Christ Meets Culture

Christ Meets Culture

The Influence of Sociocultural Factors
on the Translation of the Gospel in Brazil

Jair Fernandes de Melo Santos

Introduction by Daniel R. Sanchez

WIPF & STOCK · Eugene, Oregon

CHRIST MEETS CULTURE
The Influence of Sociocultural Factors on the Translation of the Gospel in Brazil

Copyright © 2020 Jair Fernandes de Melo Santos. All rights reserved. Except for brief quotations in critical publications or reviews, no part of this book may be reproduced in any manner without prior written permission from the publisher. Write: Permissions, Wipf and Stock Publishers, 199 W. 8th Ave., Suite 3, Eugene, OR 97401.

Wipf & Stock
An Imprint of Wipf and Stock Publishers
199 W. 8th Ave., Suite 3
Eugene, OR 97401

www.wipfandstock.com

PAPERBACK ISBN: 978-1-7252-7459-4
HARDCOVER ISBN: 978-1-7252-7460-0
EBOOK ISBN: 978-1-7252-7461-7

Manufactured in the U.S.A.   06/30/20

To Letícia, *Meu Amor*, to Efraim and Marília, *nosso tesouro*, to our parents, family members, churches, sponsors, and friends whose support and encouragement helped us to finish this journey, for the glory of Jesus Christ, to whom I ultimately dedicate this dissertation (Rom 11:33–36).

Contents

Introduction | ix
Abstract | xi
Abbreviations | xiii
Figures | xiv
Tables | xv
Preface | xvii

1. Christ Meets Culture: The Influence of Sociocultural Factors on the Translation of the Gospel in Brazil | 1
2. Christ Engages Culture: Biblical, Theological, and World Christian Studies Terms Defined and Applied | 32
3. Christ Changes Culture: A Critique of the Quantitative and Qualitative Growth of Evangelical Christianity in Brazil | 49
4. Christ Challenges Culture: Towards a Brazilian Baptist Theology of Evangelism and Discipleship | 71
5. Christ Dialogues with Culture: BBC Leaders Refining Gospel Translation from a Biblically Sound Angle | 96
6. Christ Interacts with Culture: Bridges and Barriers in the Major Traits as Viewed by BBC Leaders | 123
7. Christ Bridges Cultures: Brazilian Baptist Pathways in an Era of World Christianity | 160

Appendix: Barriers Turned into Bridges: Interviewees' Strategies for Engaging and Transforming the Culture | 173
Bibliography | 177

Introduction

I AM PLEASED TO write a letter of recommendation for this publication. What is unique about this dissertation is that it engages in scholarly research of key sociological factors in the Brazilian culture that contributed toward the translation of the gospel in that context. This has implications not only for an accurate historical understanding of the manner in which the early Brazilian converts to Evangelical Christianity translated the message of the missionaries but also for the manner in which it continues to be translated and transmitted in today's Brazilian cultural context. While this dissertation has a very solid theoretical framework it also has very practical application for contemporary Christian ministry.

Daniel R. Sanchez, DMin, PhD
Distinguished Professor of Missions
Southwestern Baptist Theological Seminary, Fort Worth, Texas, USA

Abstract

Christ Meets Culture: The Influence of Sociocultural Factors on the Translation of the Gospel in Brazil

THIS DISSERTATION ARGUES THAT sociocultural factors play a significant role in the translation of the Gospel in Brazil as expressed among the Brazilian Baptist Convention [BBC]. It also examines sociocultural work to discover whether it facilitates what is known in World Christian Studies [WCS] as biblically sound translation within the BBC as suggested by key leadership writings, practices, and memoirs. In the end, this dissertation assesses the role of the Gospel in transforming Brazilian ethics and culture, especially as it critically considers the bridges and barriers within the cultural and religious milieu of the country. Through literature review and oral history methodology, this dissertation analyzes how Christ meets, engages, changes, challenges, dialogues, interacts with, and bridges cultures.

Chapter 1 introduces the notion of Christ meeting culture. It explains the thesis, the general context of the research, and presents an overview of the dissertation. Chapter 2 presents the notion of Christ engaging culture through the discussion of the WCS' core concepts for this investigation. Chapter 3 discusses Christ changing culture. It summarizes the history of the translation of the Gospel in Brazil from an evangelical perspective. Chapter 4 considers Christ challenging culture. It critiques the major cultural influences on evangelism and discipleship in Brazil, as seen in the Igreja Multiplicadora (Multiplying Church) model the BBC currently promotes. Chapter 5 investigates Christ dialoguing with culture by analyzing the impact of Brazilian culture on the translation of the Gospel within the BBC, based upon the sociological factors portrayed in the personal accounts and memoirs of BBC leaders. Chapter 6 continues the critique of the oral history material in order to probe the interaction of Christ with culture as presented by the interviewees. Their perspective on the impact of Brazilian culture through major sociocultural traits on the translation of the Gospel reveals how they consider the traits as bridges and/or barriers for evangelism and discipleship in Brazil. Finally, Chapter 7 considers how Christ bridges culture. It summarizes the findings of the research and how they contribute to the translation of the Gospel through the BBC churches, pointing to avenues for future research.

Jair Fernandes de Melo Santos, Ph.D.
Advisor: Daniel R. Sanchez, Ph.D., D.Min.
Roy Fish School of Evangelism and Missions
Southwestern Baptist Theological Seminary, 2018

Abbreviations

BaBC	Bahia Baptist Convention
BBC	Brazilian Baptist Convention
BCPC	Baptist Convention of Planalto Central
CBC	Carioca Baptist Convention (Rio de Janeiro city)
FBC	First Baptist Church
FlBC	Fluminense Baptist Convention (Rio de Janeiro state)
IMB	International Mission Board of the Southern Baptist Convention (US)
NBTS	Northern Baptist Theological Seminary (Brazil)
NeBTS	Northeastern Baptist Theological Seminary (Brazil)
NMB	National Mission Board of the BBC
NT	New Testament
OT	Old Testament
US	United States
SBC	Second Baptist Church
SBTS	Southern Baptist Theological Seminary (Brazil)
WCS	World Christian Studies

Figures

1 Major Religious Group in Brazil, 1970–2010
2 Breakdown of Protestants in Brazil, 1991–2010
3 Brazilian Sociocultural Traits Divided by Categories
4 Sérgio Buarque de Hollanda's View on Brazilians
5 Geert Hofstede's Findings on the Brazilian Culture
6 Filtering Systems Based on the Culture or the Scripture
7 Factors that Impacted the growth of Evangelical Christianity in Brazil
8 The Three-Wave Movement of Pentecostalism Around the World
9 Brazilian Church Contemporary Scenario
10 Zaqueu Moreira de Oliveira's Historiography of the BBC
11 Sociocultural Traits as Classified by the Interviewees
12 Cultural Iceberg Metaphor
13 The Levels of Culture Inside a Nation
14 Cordiality as Both Bridge and Barrier
15 Scale of Evangelism Styles
16 Collectivism as Mainly a Barrier with Few Bridges
17 Religiosity: Barrier with Bridges
18 Projection of the Growth of Religions in Latin America
19 Reasons for Latin American Leaving Catholicism

Tables

1. Research on the Translation of the Gospel in Brazil
2. Profiles of the Eight Brazilian Baptist Leaders Interviewed
3. Traits According to Interviewees Defined as Bridge and /or Barrier
4. Ranking of Traits that Appeared in the Interviews
5. Cordiality: Bridges, Barriers, Indigenizing and Pilgrim Principles
6. Collectivism: Bridges, Barriers, Indigenizing and Pilgrim Principles
7. Religiosity: Bridges, Barriers, Indigenizing and Pilgrim Principles
8. Brazilian Way of Coping: Bridge, Barrier, Pilgrim and Indigenizing Principles
9. Religious-Collectivistic Mindset: Barriers Found and Bridges Proposed
- A1. Soares' Suggestions on Reaching out to Indigenous Brazilian Communities
- A2. Antonio's Suggestions on How to Reach Collectivistic Groups
- A3. Religious-Collectivistic Mindset: Barriers Found and Bridges Proposed
- A4. Religiosity: Barriers Found and Bridges Proposed
- A5. The Brazilian Way of Coping: Barriers Turned into Bridges

Preface

By God's grace, this dissertation was written under the guidance of wise and experienced men. My supervisor Dr. Daniel Sanchez was a mentor, encourager, and pastor during the whole journey, challenging and teaching me through the dissertation process. Dr. Keith Eitel, Dr. Matt Queen, Dr. Brent Ray, and Dr. William Goff were invaluable. They coached me during the ups and downs of the race and gave me important help to finish this project. Dr. Queen and Dr. Ray were the first ones to invite me to consider doing the World Christian Studies Ph.D. program. Many other people were involved in this endeavor.

First, I should mention my wife Letícia. I need to thank her forever for such a selfless attitude and lovely support amidst the daily challenges of family and ministry life. She was supportive beyond measure during my times out of the country in the United States in 2015, 2016, and 2017, and Nigeria in 2018. I pray I will remember this season of our lives and be there for her when she needs me. Our son Efraim is a constant source of happiness and encouragement for us. I was absent during three Father's Days—the Brazilian date is on the second Sunday of August, when I was out of the country for the on campus classes in Fort Worth, Texas—and he did not complain. Besides that, Letícia became pregnant with our second child in the last year of this program. This exciting news added even more joy in the final phase of the Ph.D. journey. In the sovereignty of God, the baby died on its ninth week. That was a challenging time, but we thank the Lord for His care and consolation and for our family and friends for being alongside us during those weeks in the first two weeks of August 2018. In January 2020, God blessed us with the birth of our beloved daughter Marília.

My deep gratitude to the people who supported me in prayer, financially, and in wise counsel. First, Southwestern Seminary generously and graciously granted me scholarships. Northeastern Seminary (Brazil) also supported this project with funds for proofreading and other administrative expenses. My parents, Pr. Jair and Zete Santos, tios Daniel and Lindóia Melo, tio Dr. José Pereira, Dr. Elizabeth Mariana, Maria do Rosário (Zau), and Eliete Moraes were faithful and generous sponsors throughout the Ph.D. program. Bart and Pam Nicholson, Dr. Brent and Elaine Ray and their children Jared, Ariel, and Jordan were part of this journey too with their support, friendship, and prayers. My brother Ciro, sister-in-law Fabiana, nephew Daniel, my brother Jeter, sister-in-law Carla, nephews Levi, Max, and Karis were always there for me. My father-in-law Pr. Geovani Sousa, mother-in-law Graça Sousa, and sister-in-law Heloisa were alongside me, Letícia and Efraim while I was out of the country and in many other occasions. Finally, Pr. Geremias Bento da Silva was an advisor, mentor, and friend in many ways.

Many precious people participated in the Nigeria Project, namely Dr. Eliaquim Almeida, Drs. Lucas and Justina Oliveira, Dr. Gabriel Vidal, and Glória Vidal, among other friends. Thank you very much. Dr. Luiz Nascimento was a mentor and encourager during both my master's and doctoral degrees and specially during the final phase of this process. I appreciate also the work of those who proofread and edited my work, in particular Mrs. Ulrike Guthrie and Dr. Brian Roberston, who were invaluable during the final part of this journey. Adam and Sarah Robinson and Eliézer and Jaqueline Perruci were kind hosts during my trips to the United States in 2015 and 2016. My WCS Brazilian doctoral colleague and friend Jefferson Chagas, his wife Nice, and daughter Hannah were like family to me. My classmates in this doctoral program, specially Bruno Molina and Nelson Kalombo Ngoy, were like old friends I just got to know in 2014.

The leaders and flock of Bethel Baptist Church (Pouso Alegre, Minas Gerais state) and First Baptist Church of Serrinha (Bahia state) understood and blessed me with time off for traveling to the United States and Nigeria. They also helped to finance this project, since I conducted my research and writing during work hours. Proclamation Baptist Church (Feira de Santana, Bahia state) was a generous sponsor during my first year of the doctoral program. Pr. Olney and Carminha Lopes, the prayer warriors of Shepherd Ministries (Brazil), and Dr. Mirhelen Abreu prayed and stayed there for me in the most difficult times of this endeavor. Many other prayer partners, family members, friends, and brothers and sisters in Christ are not listed here, but I offer them my deepest gratitude. And to God, our Lord Jesus Christ, and the Holy Spirit be thanksgiving, honor, glory, and praise forever.

1

Christ Meets Culture

The Influence of Sociocultural Factors on the Translation of the Gospel in Brazil

THIS DISSERTATION ARGUES THAT sociocultural factors[1] are significant in the translation of the Gospel in Brazil as expressed among the Brazilian Baptist Convention [BBC]. This research investigates whether the sociocultural traits of cordiality,[2] religiosity,[3] the Brazilian way of coping,[4] and collectivism[5] provide bridges and/or barriers for a biblically sound translation of the Gospel in the country.[6] Studying Brazilian Christianity as a

---

1. These traits had the greater recurrence in the literature review and found more affirmation in the preliminary survey conducted by the author, as detailed on Chapter 1.

2. It means that Brazilians are emotional and warm in their relationships, intimate and affectionate, against formalisms and social conventions. Holanda, *Raízes do Brasil*, 117.

3. As a religious people, Brazilians highly value the "other world" beyond the "street" and the "house," as presented by Matta, *O Que Faz*, 93.

4. The Brazilian way of coping is basically a problem-solving strategy. Brazilians generally resort to a network of friends and acquaintances to find solutions. Vincent, *Culture and Customs*, 90.

5. It means that the people's self-image is defined more regarding "We" rather of "I," and members of the society have a high level of interdependence between themselves. Hofstede and Hofstede, *Cultures and Organizations*.

6. "Biblically sound" means that it reflects the Bible per The Chicago Statement on Biblical Inerrancy. This dissertation adopts Lamin Sanneh's definition of translation as the contextualized preaching of the Gospel.Sanneh, *Translating the Message*, 53. See more on this discussion on Chapter 1. Besides that, this author defines translation of the Gospel as a dual and concomitant process of evangelism and discipleship, similarly to what the

phenomenon of an evangelical explosion in terms of growth and diversity is still an emerging academic trend in World Christian Studies [WCS]. Scholarship concerning contemporary Brazilian and Latin American Christianity does not equate in breadth and depth to the studies of forces such as Chinese, Nigerian, Asian, and African Christianities, even though all are powerful entities in the Global South.[7] It is time to seize the moment and attempt to make a contribution to the field, as this dissertation proposes to do in its own small way.

Wherever and whenever Christ meets culture, the encounter produces a vibrant and complex expression. Perhaps nowhere is this currently truer than in Brazil. Richard Niebuhr proposes, "Christ converts humankind inside their culture and society, and not apart from it."[8] He suggests four aspects of this debate: (1) Christ against culture, (2) Christ as part of the culture, (3) Christ above culture, or (4) Christ and culture in paradox.[9] The central point is that Christ is the transformer and redeemer of culture.[10] D. A. Carson refined Niebuhr's thesis to relate only to cultural freedom in depending on Christ in an orthodox and thoroughly biblical way, with Christ sometimes against culture and transforming culture work simultaneously.[11]

To that end, this introduction presents an overview of the research. It explains the author's interest in the topic, and describes the context of the study. This chapter includes a literature review, a definition of WCS terms and Brazilian sociocultural values. It ends with an historical panorama of Brazilian Evangelicalism and Baptist work in the country.

Justification for the Study

There are four primary reasons for this study. First, as noted by Philip Jenkins, World-Wide Christianity—of which Brazilian Christianity is an influential part—is in a sense, a new phenomenon.[12] Over the last century, Christianity shifted its dominant presence from the Global North to the

---

National Mission Board calls "discipling relationship," as explained on Chapter 4.

7. An overview of the scholarship on Chinese Christianity is observed by Thurston, *Studying Christianity in China*.

8. Niebuhr, *Cristo e Cultura*, 65.

9. These questions are debated in Chapters 2, 3, 4, 5, and 6 of *Cristo e Cultura*.

10. Niebuhr, *Cristo e Cultura*, 288–94.

11. Carson, *Cristo e Cultura: Uma Releitura*, 196–97.

12. Jenkins, *Next Christendom*, 113–15.

Global South. Jenkins considers the growth rates in the southern portion of the globe impressive.[13] In 1900, only 13 percent of the world's Christian population was in Africa and Latin America; presently, both continents comprise 21 percent, and by 2050, it is anticipated to be 29 percent.[14] Timothy C. Tennent describes the same shift in the "center of gravity" of Christianity, although he prefers the term Majority Christianity, as this author also prefers, rather than Global South, since the former seems to place the North as the center of the world.[15]

A second reason to study the translation of the Gospel in Brazil is that this country has the second largest Christian population in the world and is one of the fastest growing evangelical communities in the Global South. Based upon research conducted by the Center for the Study of Global Christianity [CSGC] at Gordon-Conwell Theological Seminary, Brazil has the largest Christian population in Latin America. Brazil has the third highest Protestant population in the world (34 million), behind the United States [US] (56 million) and Nigeria (53 million).[16] The study notes that "Protestants and Independents combined represented 12.9% of the population in 1970 but are expected to grow to 28.8% by 2020."[17]

The national census (2010) indicated that 86.8% of the Brazilian population identify as Christians, of whom 64.6% are Catholic (making Brazil the nation with the largest Catholic population), and 22.2% evangelical. According to the CSGC's report, Brazil has the second largest Protestant denomination in the world—the Assembly of God Church (25 million). In comparison, the Chinese Three-Self Movement has 26 million adherents.[18] The growth of the evangelical church in Brazil is reflected in the fact that, in 1970, 91.8% were Catholics, while evangelicals comprised 5.2%.[19] The graphic below shows the major religious groups in Brazil.

13. Jenkins, *Next Christendom*, 113–15.

14. Jenkins, *Next Christendom*, 102.

15. Tennent, *Theology in the Context*, 8. A discussion about the use of the terms, "World Christianity," "Global Christianity," and others is presented by Daughrity, *To Whom Does Christianity Belong?*, 9–14.

16. Center for the Study of Global Christianity, "500 Years of Protestantism."

17. CSGC, *Christianity in its Global Context*, 52.

18. The Han house churches are considered the largest Protestant/Independent denomination in more recent data, though it is not an organized network. See Center for the Study of Global Christianity, "Global Christianity: A Look at the Status of Christianity in 2018."

19. Jardim, "O IBGE e a Religião—Cristãos são 86,8% do Brasil."

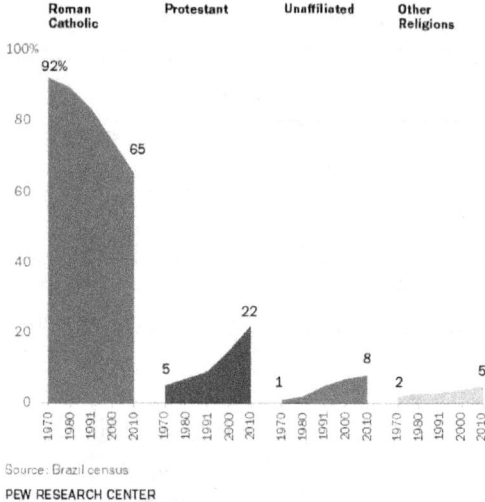

Figure 1: Major Religious Groups in Brazil, 1970–2010[20]

The third justification for this study is its originality and newness regarding Brazilian Baptists. A survey of the translation of the Gospel inside the BBC from a WCS perspective has not yet been done.[21] To the knowledge of the author, there are no other dissertations or books dealing with the influence of Brazilian sociocultural traits in the translation of the Gospel within the country inside the BBC.[22]

20. Pew Research Center, "Brazil's Changing Religious Landscape."

21. Searches done using the keywords "World Christian Studies," "World Christianity," "Global Christianity," "Brazil," and "Translation," both in English and Portuguese, through The American Theological Library Association [ATLA] Religion Database with ATLASerials, ProQuest, JSTOR, and WorldCat show no parallels to this research. Searches were made from February 11–14, 2017.

22. Searches were done on titles in the databases May 31, 2017. There are relevant studies about evangelism and discipleship in Brazil from both etic and emic perspectives, as detailed in Chapter 4. However, studies such as the present one from a WCS perspective dealing with the translation of the Gospel in Brazil were not found. Generally, Brazilian Christianity studies are done from a missiological perspective. One example is the respected journal *Capacitando Para Missões Transculturais* (Training for Transcultural Missions), a missiological journal published by the Association of Professors of Missions in Brazil [APMB], with Brazilian and foreign authors, such as Durvalina Barreto Bezerra and Margaretha Nalina Adiwardana. The journal translates and publishes authors such as Paul G. Hiebert. The publication deals with evangelism and discipleship inside Brazil.

	a) "Translation" and "Gospel" and "Brazil"	b) "Gospel" and "Culture" and "Brazil"	c) "Sociocultural" and "Gospel" and "Brazil"
ProQuest	0	0	0
ATLA	0	2	1
WorldCat	1	21	0

Table 1. Research on the Translation of the Gospel in Brazil

Finally, the author's involvement with evangelism and discipleship, particularly since college and during his professional career as a journalist, prompted an initial curiosity about the relation between Christianity and Brazilian culture. The researcher's life history predisposed him to pursue research from an emic perspective about his people and the translation of the Gospel. The emic perspective refers to a study done from inside the system, whereas, an etic viewpoint studies behavior from outside the system.[23] In this case, the goal is an emic-theological analysis in which the culture is studied by an insider to expound the Gospel in a living, applicable, and comprehensible way in the universe of the people.[24]

The author interacted with diverse cultures while studying for the Master of Divinity degree at Southwestern Baptist Theological Seminary in Fort Worth, Texas. He also served in an American church (Greater Vision Fellowship, Azle, TX) for eight months and as an associate minister at Central Brazilian Baptist Church (Bedford, TX) for two and a half years. He was further involved with the international community on the seminary campus. Besides that, the author traveled to seven states and preached revivals in churches of different nationalities, including a Brazilian one, an American one, and two Hispanic ones in three different states. These

---

Additionally, *Ciências da Religião* (Religion Sciences) is the more proximate academic field to WCS in Brazil. However, a piece of major research such as the present one from a WCS perspective dealing with the translation of the Gospel in Brazil is unknown. To mention, it should be noted that the books written by Lamin Sanneh or Andrew Walls, key authors to this field, are not translated into Portuguese.

23. Pike, *Human Behavior*, 37. For more ideas on evangelism and missions through cultural systems see Hesselgrave, *Communicating Christ Cross-Culturally*. For an explanation of etic and emic from a Brazilian perspective, read Silva, *Fenomenologia da Religião*, 39–40.

24. Lidório, *Comunicação e Cultura*, 57.

experiences provided him a broader awareness of cultural differences and diversity and their impact on the translation of the Gospel.

The practice of personal evangelism explored in the course, "Contemporary Evangelism," taught by David Mills in the Fall of 2011 and in the following years of study under the supervision of Matt Queen strengthened the author's passion for evangelism and prompted questions about how effectively the translation of the Gospel is done in the Brazilian culture. For the last four years, the author has lived in Brazil, and served as pastor at Bethel Baptist Church in Pouso Alegre, Southern Minas Gerais state (2015—2016), and First Baptist Church of Serrinha, Bahia state (2017-present). The author's academic and ministry experiences made him aware that sharing the Christian message intrinsically requires dealing with sociocultural values. To pursue this investigation in more depth, the author entered the World Christian Studies Ph.D. program at Southwestern Seminary in May 2014.

World Christian Studies Literature Review

The purpose of the data collected during the literature review phase is to provide a WCS theoretical framework for how translating the Gospel into local cultures fulfils the Great Commission.[25] Particularly prominent or widespread Brazilian values are the objects of analysis here, in terms of their contribution to the translation of the Gospel.[26] A study to ascertain whether and how sociocultural factors influenced the translation of the Gospel in Brazil can potentially increase expertise in the field of WCS. The agenda of the study is the scientific construction of an informed discussion on the theme. In part, this research analyzes how Sanneh's and Wall's concepts relate to concepts that sociological studies use to describe Brazilian cultural characteristics.

First, this research deals with the translation of the Gospel inside the BBC. The denomination resulted from Southern Baptist missionary efforts toward the end of the nineteenth century. The BBC is considered "conservative" in its doctrine, meaning that Brazilian Baptists hold to a traditional

---

25. Matthew 28:19–20, Mark 16:15–16, Luke 24:44–49, John 20:21, and Acts 1:8.

26. The literature review was initiated in the second semester of 2014 at local reference university libraries (e.g. Federal University of Bahia and State University of Feira de Santana), the public library at State School Yeda Barradas Carneiro, and catalogs of national and international journals on the Internet.

view of the Bible as inerrant and infallible.[27] The convention has been influenced by liberal theologians, such as the ones from the contemporary national movement *Aliança de Batistas* (Alliance of Baptists).

Especially in the 1970's and 1980's, professors in the denomination's seminaries contributed to the BBC's theological hybridism. As a result, the denomination is conservative in its doctrine and moderate in certain practices. A typical example is the acceptance of women as pastors by some churches and groups, while most churches do not accept women pastors as biblical.[28]

Besides that, BBC is one among many other denominations. The following graphic reveals the number of Protestants in Brazil (1991–2010) and may raise questions such as: Why did historical churches grow so little and Pentecostal churches more than double in size?[29] Some answers to this crucial question are suggested throughout this dissertation.

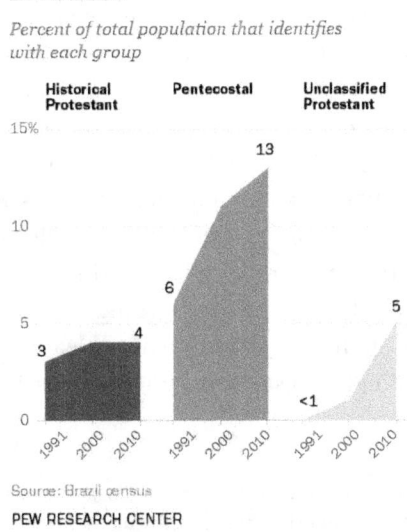

Figure 2: Breakdown of Protestants in Brazil, 1991–2010[30]

27. For a more detailed discussion about the differences between conservatives and liberals, see Benson, "Understanding Liberals and Conservatives," 69–78.

28. In 2016, Pinheiro Baptist Church (city of Maceio, Alagoas state), whose Pr. Wellington and his wife, Pr. Odja Barros, are prominent leaders of *Aliança de Batistas*, was expelled from the BBC because the church voted to accept homosexuals as members. This sparked a review in the doctrinal statement of the BBC currently under study.

29. This debate is indeed a fruitful one for future research endeavors.

30. Pew Research Center, "Brazil's Changing Religious Landscape."

Second, the data provide a significant amount of material concerning the four major Brazilian sociocultural values, and this allows an in-depth study of how these values constitute bridges and/or barriers to preaching the Gospel in Brazil. The data are relevant because they present an accurate review of the literature on the Gospel translation through the traits of the Brazilian people. The vantage point of the researcher, as a Brazilian national, well acquainted with the subject, and with how people live and serve in the place of study, gives him certain familiarity with and therefore, an advantage in finding and interpreting the data.

The author analyzes the data by narrowing the information to four Brazilian values: cordiality, religiosity, the Brazilian way of coping,[31] and collectivism. There are other national sociocultural traits. For example, Geert Hofstede works with features such as high-power distance, masculinity, intermediate pragmatism, and indulgence.[32] While these are characteristics of the Brazilian people, the four selected occurred more frequently in the literature review and were affirmed more often in the preliminary survey conducted by the author and by the BBC leaders interviewed.

Studying all the character traits of Brazilian people was not feasible for this doctoral endeavor. Since doctoral level research implies the use of objective data, methods, and a limited timespan to analyze the translation, the researcher used major sociocultural characteristics as analysis clusters, and focused on the translation concept with its indigenizing and pilgrim principles. The research methodology included studying what the BBC's evangelism and discipleship leaders are teaching to local believers. The oral history methodology applied to denominational leaders furnishes original data for this dissertation and tests the validity of the selected approach.

---

31. The May 6th, 2018 issue of *O Jornal Batista* ("The Baptist Newspaper"), the official newspaper of the BCC, published the *Declaração de Poços de Caldas* (Declaration of Poços de Caldas). The one-page document aimed to express the BCC's "approach to present matters with which Brazilian society is uneasy." It was drafted by a committee comprised of Guilherme Gimenez, João Reinaldo Purin Júnior, Linaldo de Souza Guerra, and Rubens da Costa Monteiro, and approved by the 98th Meeting of the BCC, which took place April 26–29, 2018 in Poços de Caldas, Minas Gerais state. Under the topic "Justice," the BCC "challenges each Brazilian Baptist to act in the most correct way possible, rejecting the famous philosophy of the 'Brazilian way' and embracing the ideal of justice expressed by the Word of God." *O Jornal Batista*, "Declaração de Poços de Caldas.". A provocative book which explains historical origins on this problem is Giannetti, *Vícios Privados, Benefícios Públicos?*.

32. Moreau et al, *Effective Intercultural Communication*.

This study reveals omissions and gaps in the current knowledge about the Gospel translation in Brazil. The research intends to encourage the Brazilian church's continuing reflection on evangelistic strategies and approaches so that it might take advantage of the positive and overcome negative implications of the traits pointed out by the pastors and leaders as being relevant for a Brazilian context. Yet, such strategies are not the objects of study in this doctoral dissertation. Instead, this work indicates possibilities for future academic inquiries based on these strategies and approaches.

The analysis of different traits of a local culture contributes to the expansion of WCS in the Global South. By studying a society's cultural values, one opens a path to understanding emotional, ethical, spiritual, and sociological facets not only of the Brazilian people, but also of other countries in South America, because there are many similarities in their national cultures. It may also be utilized as a methodology to study the translation of the Gospel in other national, regional, and local cultures.

Reasoning Process

The literature review furnished the theoretical scientific basis for constructing the thesis. Three claims compose the core of the thesis. The first claim is that translation is the contextualized preaching of the Gospel in each culture.[33] The claim presents a proposed fact, i.e., translation which relates directly to the argument which is a biblically sound translation in Brazil. The claim provides a compelling reason, i.e., contextualized preaching of the Gospel, to agree with the argument. The claim is supportable since the evidence for the claim is the concept of translation as presented by the WCS field and, its primary authors, and as argued using its categories of thought.

The second claim is that cultural traits may work as bridges and/or barriers for translating the Gospel in Brazil. The bridges and barriers found

---

33. Translation as the main concept provides a conceptual framework for research in WCS. A definition of terms and concepts is a pre-requisite for academic work. The dissemination of the Christian faith in Brazil demands a conceptual framework. Translation and its indigenizing and pilgrim principles are pivotal concepts of this research. The translation framework enables the emic analyst to identify and channel his biases, opinions, feelings, and intuitions towards the comprehension of the process per se, instead of reaffirming personal perceptions and preferences. The focus on the object of study determines the need for an evaluation of the major cultural traits and its bridges and barriers for preaching the Gospel. This evaluation is done according to the leaders interviewed as analyzed by the author of the study.

in the traits relate directly to the argument, which is to have a biblically sound translation in Brazil. The claim provides a compelling reason to translate the Gospel. If there are bridges and barriers, the translation is both possible and necessary. The claim is supported since the evidence gathered about the sociocultural traits gives confidence to the researcher to proceed with the study. Finally, the claim is clearly and precisely presented.

Reviewing, cataloging, tabulating, and critiquing the data from the literature review helped this writer focus on the research, shape a thesis, and make an original contribution to the field. The present step produced an objective literature review and led to the writing of a consistent thesis proposal. First, the literature search and cross-referencing maps clarified the connections between authors and concepts, such as translation, the Brazilian traits (cordiality, Brazilian way of coping, religiosity, and collectivism), and fields of study with which the data intersected such as WCS, sociology, and ecclesiology. They became the building blocks of the author's knowledge of the field. Second, the literature review led this writer to narrow and explain the thesis statement to define the translation of the Gospel. This central and guiding concept of the research was used to interrogate the major traits of the Brazilian culture.

Third, thanks to this reflection, the author chose to approach the translation of the Gospel through BBC churches by both contributing through a critique of evangelical evangelism and discipleship literature in Portuguese, and, more specifically, the *Igreja Multiplicadora* literature; this also includes an analysis of interviews with BBC leaders. This writer used the oral history methodology with pastors and denominational leaders to learn how these selected four Brazilian traits plus their bridges and barriers interfere in evangelism and discipleship. The data from the survey enriched the analysis and conferred uniqueness to the present research.

Qualifying the Evidence

In another area of the literature review, the author organized the evidence by collecting data for a purpose and with an agenda. The purpose of the data collected is to provide a WCS theoretical framework and an analysis of major Brazilian traits. The arrangement of the data is the construction of an informed discussion on how the four Brazilian sociocultural traits affect the translation of the Gospel in the country through BBC churches. In summary, the review was done by filtering the core ideas of main authors, connecting those ideas with one another, and analyzing how the Gospel in Brazil is translated in light of the bridges and barriers found.

The data discovered in the writer's research gives compelling reasons for the pursuit of the present study. As mentioned before, translating the Gospel fulfills the Great Commission. Yet, there are traits of the Brazilian culture that both facilitate and challenge the translation task. The data is credible because it includes research by leading authors in WCS, sociology, and those who research national characteristics. The data is relevant because it is appropriate and true to the context. It is appropriate because it fits the context of the claim. To aid this explanation, the following section describes how translation of the Gospel is understood in urban Brazil. Background information concerning the four major sociocultural traits from the standpoint of a native Brazilian interpreter will be assessed.

The Significance of Translation

The following literature review assesses the theoretical background research of the study, including the relevance of the knowledge about the topic. Furthermore, there is a summary of the review, with an analysis and interpretation of the data and the implications of the present study for the churches and the academic field of research.

The first main claim of this research is the preeminence of the translation concept based on Sannehs' and Walls' definitions, including the indigenizing and pilgrim principles for the analysis of Brazilian sociocultural values. In other words, translation is the guiding concept. Sanneh explains, "Translation is the contextualized preaching of the Gospel."[34] This research takes the concept beyond the idea of contextualization. It deals more profoundly and broadly with the cultural implications of Christianity. Sanneh asserts, "When one translates, it is like pulling the trigger of a loaded gun: the translator cannot recall the hurtling bullet. Translation thus activates a process that might supersede the original intention of the translator."[35] In summary, translation considers the complex interaction between Christianity and cultures.

The interaction between Christianity and culture happens every time the message of the Gospel is proclaimed. How can one comprehend the message without connecting it to one's own reality? How does one compare

34. Sanneh, *Translating the Message*, 53.
35. Sanneh, *Translating the Message*, 53.

the good news to other news one already knows? As Paul Tillich poses, religion "as [an] ultimate concern is the meaning-giving substance of culture, and culture is the totality of forms in which the basic concern of religion expressses itself . . . Religion is the substance of culture and culture is the form of religion."[36] The discernment of what is substance and what is form is imperative.

As Walls asserts, Christianity does not exist in a vacuum. There are cultural expressions and local features that are a part of the life of the believer. God, he says, "does not take us as isolated, self-governing units, because we are not. We are conditioned by a particular time and place, by our family and group and society, by 'culture' in fact."[37] When God became flesh in the person of Jesus, people transmitted this message through language, and in an intelligible way, they translated the Gospel into their different cultures and local, regional, national, and global realities.

Yet, as Walls affirms, such translation is in fact a retranslation of the Gospel.[38] When an individual from one culture translates the Gospel message to another culture, he retranslates the Gospel. In this sense, translation and retranslation are equivalent for Walls. The difference is that the latter begins a second cycle of translation, different in place/culture and time, whether Jesus' time to a century or twenty centuries later, and whether to the neighboring country or a faraway continent.

Such a concept of translation of the Gospel encompasses indigenizing and pilgrim principles, says Walls.[39] What is meant by the indigenizing principle is that an individual can only live as a Christian inside his own culture. In other words, the indigenizing principle is seen when the Gospel feels at home in one culture, and there are no tensions between Christianity and the local features of the culture. For example, the Christian fellowship is easily assimilated and lived out by Brazilians evangelicals in their collectivistic culture. What is meant by the pilgrim principle is that the Gospel is not contained in one culture but transcends and sometimes counteracts the culture. The pilgrim principle is seen when the Christian message counters some local features of the culture. For example, Brazilian ways of coping as lying or being corrupt are at odds with Christian ethical standards.

---

36. Tillich, *Theology of Culture*, 42.
37. Walls, *Missionary Movement*, 7.
38. Walls, *Missionary Movement*, 29.
39. Walls, *Missionary Movement*, 7–9.

The indigenizing and pilgrim principles are both a bifurcation of translation. The indigenizing principle relates to Christian teaching that finds resonance and affirmation in local cultural expressions. In other words, aspects of the Brazilian culture that reinforce the Christian lifestyle and message exemplify the indigenizing principle. In turn, the pilgrim principle points to the transcendent and sometimes contrarian character of the Christian faith in relation to a local culture. The cultural expressions that are not in agreement with the Gospel need to find a new format or content.[40] As Bárbara Burns, Décio de Azevedo, and Paulo Barbero F. de Carminati articulate, "The Holy Spirit and a deep study of God's Word will show what new believers need to reject and what they need to retain and better for the glory of God, in their own culture."[41]

There is also a tension between the indigenizing and pilgrim principles.[42] When should one compromise culture for the sake of the Gospel? How one can deal with this tension?[43] How may one overcome or reconcile such differing ideas? Here, Donald B. McGavran's sociological categories of "bridges" and "barriers" are useful and facilitate the comprehension of the subject to readers outside the scholarly arena.[44] *Bridges* facilitate the translation of the Gospel. For example, the cordiality of the Brazilian people opens doors for reaching out to people for Christ. Bridges relate directly to the indigenizing principle, because they are a path of connection with the local culture. *Barriers* block the communication of the good news. For example, the habits of lying or deceiving in a culture serve as a barrier for Christian ethics. Barriers are related to the pilgrim principle, as they point out aspects of the culture that may seem dissonant with the Gospel.

In terms of ecclesiology, this research deals with how the local church can approach non-believers in a more contextualized manner, share the Gospel, and make disciples. Contextualization is an important concept to both missiology and WCS. Bruce J. Nicholls explains that the Gospel is supra-cultural and evaluates all cultures as might a judge. Contextualization should eliminate what is contrary to the Bible and highlight eternal standards

---

40. Walls, *Missionary Movement*, 8.

41. Burns et al, *Costumes e Culturas*, 43. The book is an adaptation to the Brazilian reality of Nida, *Customs, Cultures and Christianity*.

42. This dynamic tension between the pilgrim and indigenizing principle is "the creative heart of Christianity as a world religion." Eitel, "Notes on the Oral Defense".

43. These issues are explored by some interviewees, while they propose to build bridges over the barriers in the translation of the Gospel in Brazil, as seen in Chapters 5–7.

44. McGavran, *Bridges of God*.

revealed in the Scriptures and local cultural settings.[45] This means that individual contexts and settings can reveal Christian faith in practical forms.[46] It is another way of saying the Gospel is relevant and should be communicated in such a way that it speaks to a particular people in a local context.[47]

According to Paul G. Hiebert in *The Gospel in Human Contexts*, a similar approach to the phenomenon of translation is the Gospel present in human contexts. Hiebert contrasts the concepts of the "Gospel in culture" and "Gospel versus culture."[48] These ideas echo the indigenizing and pilgrim principles. How does this echoing occur? The "Gospel in culture" is the manifestation of the biblically sound news in a specific context; it is the indigenization of the Gospel. When the Gospel collides with some aspects of the values of a people group, the Gospel message must transform these values, which will go away as a pilgrim from that culture.

Brazilian Sociocultural Values

Having analyzed the first claim of the thesis, that translation is the preeminent concept for this research, one should consider Brazilian cultural aspects. The second claim is that sociocultural values of the Brazilian culture may facilitate (bridge) and/or obstruct (barrier) the Gospel's translation in that country. These values provide Christians with various opportunities to connect the Gospel with culture. A careful study of these connections reveals the indigenizing and the pilgrim principles in action, validating the viability of the translation process in the country.

The chief task of this section is to explain and explore the Brazilian sociocultural traits. One should keep these traits or values in mind when considering the translation of the Gospel in Brazil, the history of evangelicalism and Baptists in the country, the Multiplying Church model, and interviews with the BCC leadership. In what follows, the research describes and assesses the impact of the four main values of the Brazilian people, namely cordiality, religiosity, the Brazilian way of coping, and collectivism. Figure 3 relates these values to particular authors who write about them.

---

45. Nicholls, *Contextualization*, 61.
46. Jennings, "Tapestry of Contextualization," 24–31.
47. Calderón, "Ground Level Contextualization," 58.
48. Hiebert, *Gospel in Human Contexts*, 31.

Christ Meets Culture

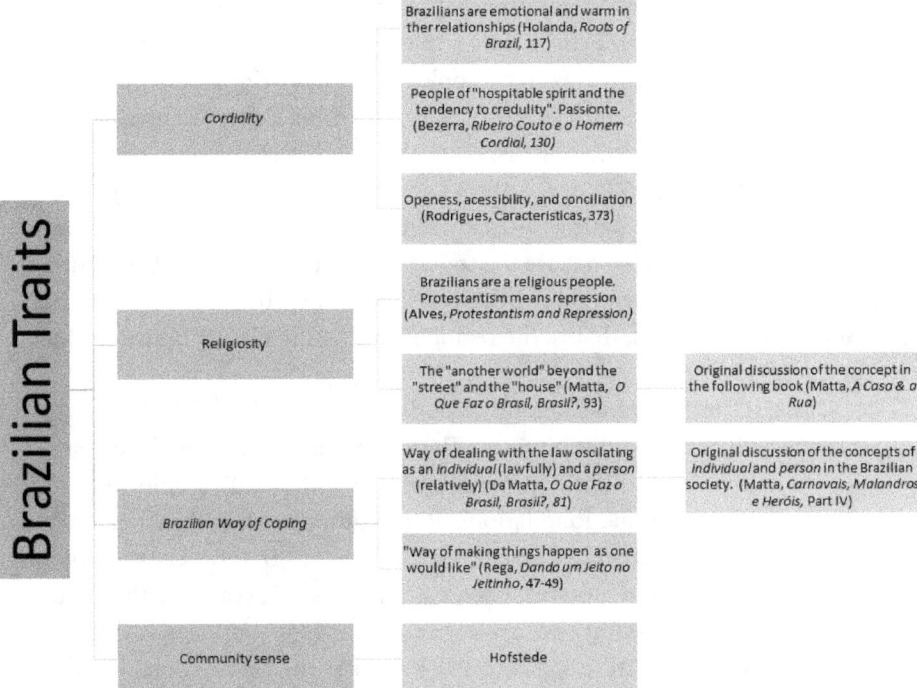

Figure 3. Brazilian Sociocultural Traits Divided by Categories

These four traits were the most recurrent ones in the literature review. The first three originate from Brazilian sociology, while the other (community sense) comes from a comparative study on national characteristics by Geert Hofstede.[49] Each trait either works with or against the Gospel, or both.

An initial and indispensable set of resources for examining the *cultura brasileira* are classic books discussing what it means to be Brazilian and the Brazilian culture in general.[50] Some Brazilian authors who provided

---

49. Hofstede, "Brazil."

50. *Culture and Customs of Brazil* by Vincent can be useful for beginners. Even though the title points toward culture and customs only, the book covers more ground than this, including areas such as history and sociological traits. In Chapter 2, "Race, Ethnicity, and Class," the author comments perceptively on the Brazilian ethos. Indeed, Brazil is formed by three main people groups: Portuguese, African, and, to a lesser degree, Brazilian Indigenous people. European and Asian people started to populate mainly South Brazil in the last century, before and in between the World Wars. Chapter 6 ("Social Customs"), describes concepts such as *parentela* (family ties), *Jeitinho Brasileiro* (the Brazilian way of coping), food and drink, soccer, Carnival, the culture of the beach, and popular festivals, such as *Festas Juninas* (Saint John's festivities in June) and *Bumba-Meu-Boi*.

foundational work for the comprehension of the country are Darcy Ribeiro and Caio Prado Júnior. First, Ribeiro, in *O Povo Brasileiro—A Formação e o Sentido do Brasil* (The Brazilian People—The Formation and Meaning of Brazil), gives an insider's critique of Brazil.[51] In his informed and critical historical analysis, the author discusses the ethnic origins of the country. What are our roots? What was the extent of influence of the indigenous Brazilian people, Portuguese, African, and many other people on the formation of the nation? What are the traits that distinguish Brazil from other countries? Besides assuming these questions, Ribeiro also explores the "Brazils" inside Brazil, that is, the regionalisms and regional cultures inside the country.

The second main author to be considered is Caio Prado Júnior. In *Formação do Brasil Contemporâneo* (The Formation of Contemporary Brazil), the author identifies the main features of the Brazilian culture in its historical and economic foundations. Prado describes Brazil as a colonial by-product which was aimed only for providing "sugar, tobacco, and other items; later, gold and diamonds; later, cotton and, after, coffee, to the European commerce. Nothing else."[52] How can the Gospel infiltrate and transform the culture, considering that the Brazilian people are heirs of such deleterious and imperialistic historical roots and that the nation's primary sociocultural characteristics are deeply affected by its history marked by exploitation and pragmatism?

Two other authors add critical and diverse insight to the matter: Renato Ortiz and Thomas Skidmore. Renato Ortiz in *Cultura Brasileira e Identidade Nacional* (Brazilian Culture and National Identity) introduces the idea of "culture" in modern Brazilian sociological studies. He critiques the concept of the "Brazilian culture" among scholars and in specialized literature by affirming that only saying Brazilians are "different" than the other people of the world is not enough. Instead, he argues, there is a need to show how Brazilians identify themselves as a nation, specifically, how certain social groups promote the reinterpretation of this plural identity.[53] In this sense, the present study supplies answers for Ortiz.

Thomas Skidmore, in *O Brasil Visto de Fora* (Brazil Seen From Outside), summarizes the work of renowned authors, such as Gilberto Freyre and Gilberto Prado. Skidmore is a Brazilianist, i.e., and foreign person who

---

51. Ribeiro, *O Povo Brasileiro*.
52. Prado Júnior, *Formação do Brasil Contemporâneo*, 26.
53. Ortiz, *Cultura Brasileira e Identidade Nacional*.

writes about Brazil. A highlight of the book is part 1, which debates these architects of the Brazilian identity. One of the weaknesses is the that the author does not consider other authors such as Sérgio Buarque de Holanda and Celso Furtado. The interpretation of the work of Freyre lacks contextualization, given that Skidmore values Freyre's racial debate in excess. Skidmore considers Prado's work, even though this author is anti-American, and uses the influence of politics more than culture in the definition of the national identity.[54]

Finally, Gilberto Freyre, in *O Mundo que o Português Criou* (The World that the Portuguese Created), compares Brazil and the other countries born out of Portuguese domination and gives examples of Brazilian identity.[55] In *New World in the Tropics: The Culture of Modern Brazil*, the author defends the idea of one Brazil inside the many Brazils (Portuguese-Brazilian, German-Brazilian, etc.). This claim is similar to the one of Ribeiro, who defends the existence of many Brazils.[56]

Four Selected Traits

This dissertation contributes to the conversation about Brazilian culture through an emic perspective. It introduces contemporary architects of Brazilian identity, namely strategic Brazilian Baptists leadership. These specific sections build a case on the four main features of the Brazilian culture, as follows.

Cordiality

The first value in this analysis is cordiality, which became famous through the writings of historian Sergio Buarque de Holanda in *Raízes do Brasil* (Roots of Brazil), published in 1936. The "cordial man" is described widely in sociological studies of Brazil.[57] As the main proponent of this trait

---

54. According to Ricardo Musse, Freyre's valorization of the racial debate is related to the author's time living in the United States, while Prado's political analysis of the Brazilian nationalism is more "fruitful and intelligent." Musse, "O Brasil de Skidmore."

55. Freyre, *O Mundo que o Português Criou*.

56. Freire, *New World in the Tropics*.

57. Cordiality is the fundamental nucleus of Buarque's reflections and has its roots in the colonial beginnings of Brazil. For more discussion on this topic, see Ramirez, *Sérgio Buarque de Holanda*.

affirms, Brazilians are emotional and warm in their relationships.[58] The "cordial man," as analyzed by Holanda, is intimate and affectionate; in other words, he has an aversion to cold relationships. Cordiality opposes formality and social conventions.[59]

To be cordial is to be friendly. Per Holanda, hospitality, generosity, and candor in dealing with other people are aspects of such cordiality. At the same time, the author proposes that the Brazilian's open heart is expressed internally as much as externally and is both a pathway by which to cope with loneliness and an expression of the communitarian lifestyle of this people, something that will be addressed later as collectivism. Figure 4 (below) depicts Hollanda's main ideas about Brazilian cordiality.

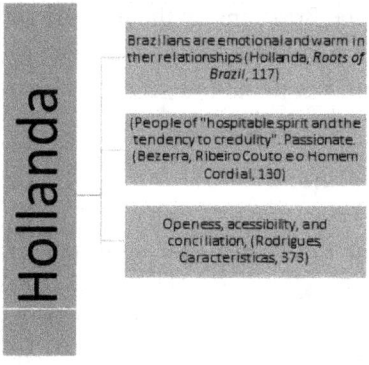

Figure 4. Sérgio Buarque de Holanda's View on Brazilians

Ribeiro Couto was the first to discuss the "cordial man" (1931). He describes the people as passionate, of "hospitable spirit and the tendency to credulity."[60] Cordiality includes openness, accessibility, and conciliation.[61] It involves being "gentle," as proposed by Fernando de Azevedo. While Japanese are known for their perfectionism and the British for their punctuality, Brazilians are depicted as gentle and kind, with a character

---

58. Holanda, *Roots of Brazil*, 117. Though published in 1936, this classic work is still considered one of the primary pieces about Brazil. The concept of the "cordial man" has not been replaced. It can be discussed and examined in future research, since globalization and cultures are not immutable.

59. Schwarcz, "Sérgio Buarque de Holanda."

60. Bezerra, "Ribeiro Couto e o Homem Cordial," 130.

61. Rodrigues, "As Características do Povo Brasileiro," 373.

marked by respect for the human person, tolerance, and hospitality.[62] In this sense, there is a preference for a more family-based approach to social life, again contributing to a sense of collectivism. The boundaries between public and private interests are blurred, highlighting the communitarian features of social life.[63]

Religiosity

The second value of the Brazilian culture addressed in this research is religiosity. Brazilians are a religious people. Demography attests to the religiosity of the people.[64] Per the 2010 census, 64.6% of Brazilians identify as Catholic, while only 8% reported having no religious affiliation. The expansion of the Protestant church in Brazil is even more astonishing. Between 2000 and 2010, Protestants grew 61%. Whereas, in 2000, around 26 million people identified as Protestant, which is 15.4% of the population, by 2010, the number was 42.3 million, which is 22.2% of Brazilians. This is a significant increase not only in those ten years, but also in the previous decades, when the percentage of Brazilian Protestants was only 9% in 1980. In the last decades, as the evangelical tradition has started to grow, some scholars suggest that dialogue and syncretism have diminished.[65] Others see syncretism growing in the evangelical milieu.[66] As presented below and in Chapter 3, Animism (Afro-Brazilian spiritism) is a strong force in the religiosity of the country, which also demands further studies.

This religiosity is mostly the domain of the "other world" beyond the "street" and the "house," as presented by Matta.[67] This spirituality is visible in the original indigenous tribe's beliefs in fortuity, unforeseen events, and bad luck. Alongside this, there is also an African heritage to diffuse terror, hope in protection from unknown forces, and the inclination to evaluate life on the basis of risks and magical possibilities, as Affonso Arinos de Mello Franco discusses in his classic book, *Conceito de Civilização Brasileira*

---

62. Azevedo, *Brazilian Culture*, 11.
63. Nogueira. "A diferença que Aproxima," 25–42.
64. Additional demographic study is done also in Chapters 5–6.
65. Andrade, "A Religiosidade Brasileira," 106–18.
66. BBC leaders denounced syncretism inside Neopentecostal churches, see more in Chapters 5–7.
67. Matta, *O Que Faz*, 93.

(Concept of Brazilian Civilization).⁶⁸ For example, some people ask African deities for protection from the "evil eye" and other forms of appeals for sorcery and witchcraft, especially in the Northeastern and Northern regions but also in other parts of the country.

Catholicism and devotion to saints are pillars of Brazilian society and allow the individual to connect with the spiritual realm in an intimate and familiar way.⁶⁹ For example, the devotion to Saint Ann, the grandmother of Jesus, is official in the city of Serrinha, where the author lives. *Santana* names neighborhoods and even cities such as Feira de Santana. Truck drivers are devotees of Saint Cristopher, their protector. As seen, the Catholic faith inherited from Portugal, together with the indigenous and African religious traditions, plays a major role in the religiosity of the Brazilian people, as it is also the case in Mexico, another country with a large Catholic and indigenous heritage.⁷⁰

The Brazilian Way of Coping

A third national feature studied in this dissertation is the Brazilian way of coping. In a country that still struggles economically and structurally, there is a particular need for creativity and mutual support to foster development. The Brazilian way of coping is basically a problem-solving strategy, in which Brazilians resort to a network of friends and acquaintances and other sources to find solutions. For example, instead of looking up at the GPS for directions, a driver may stop his car to ask for help. Or the same driver can also take as many shortcuts as possible instead of following a conventional route. Thus, social skills and healthy relationships are part of the Brazilian ethos, especially in a society marked by bureaucracy and a slow justice system and government. This trait is akin to Holanda's comprehension of cordiality, given that its generosity and hospitality are relational and imply being open to help other people in times of need.⁷¹

As a comparative example, just as there is a so-called "American way of life," there is also a "Brazilian way of coping." While Americans focus on succeeding and achieving comfort and security in life ("the American Dream"), Brazilians "favor cooperation, interdependence, and

---

68. Franco, *Conceito de Civilização Brasileira*, 157–58.
69. Tavares, "A Religião Vivida," 35–47.
70. *World Atlas*, "Which Countries Have The Most Christians."
71. Maciel et al, "Representações Sociais," 149.

connectedness," as Margo Milleret explains. For her, the Brazilian way of coping is "an adaptation for coping with society."[72] The Brazilian way of coping comes into play when something becomes a barrier to a given goal. Then, the one with the power to solve the conflict may reinterpret the context of the situation and prioritize the uniqueness of the individual case despite a law or rule. Under this principle, the personal aspect is more important than the universal, and sometimes the universal must cede (or be ignored) in favor of the individual.[73]

The Brazilian way of coping is symbolized by a case when an expressed "no" means "maybe" or even "yes" depending on one's ability to dialogue, negotiate, and find a solution to something apparently unnegotiable.[74] Matta, for example, distinguishes how people deal with the law oscillating between individual (lawful) acts and personal (relative) behavior.[75] Matta discusses this issue in *Carnavais, Malandros e Heróis* (Carnivals, Rogues, and Heroes).[76] Lourenço Stelio Rega, Director of the Baptist College of São Paulo, offers an evangelical approach in *Dando um Jeito no Jeitinho* (Coping with the Coping Way). In this thorough work, Rega defines the Brazilian way of coping as a "way of making things happen as one would like" and treats the issue from a biblical perspective. The main critique of Rega concerns the unlawful and corrupted forms of the Brazilian way, when it means lying, breaking the law, or paying bribes to make something happen.[77]

Collectivism

The fourth and final trait of the Brazilian people considered in this research is collectivism. Two authors furnish data for this analysis, namely Geert Hofstede and Harry C. Triandis. Hofstede does an extensive world survey, counting 76 countries, of the cultural effects on the workplace.[78] Hofstede's main book is *Cultures and Organizations: Software of the Mind*.[79] Brazil-

---

72. Vincent, *Culture and Customs of Brazil*, 90.
73. Motta and Alcadipani, "Jeitinho Brasileiro, Controle Social e Competição," 9.
74. Barlachl, "O Jeitinho Brasileiro," 230.
75. Matta, *O Que Faz*, 81.
76. Matta., *Carnavais, Malandros e Heróis*. Part IV discusses the concepts of the individual and person in Brazilian society.
77. Rega, *Dando um Jeito no Jeitinho*, 47–49.
78. Hofstede, "Cultural Dimensions."
79. Hofstede and Hofstede, *Cultures and Organizations*.

ians score 43 out of 100 on a scale of Individualism.[80] People's self-image is defined more by the collective "we" than the individual "I," and members of the society have a high level of interdependence between them, explains Hofstede. In individualist societies, people's core concern is themselves and their direct family. The concept of collectivism highlights this peculiar Brazilian trait. Hofstede claims, "In collectivist societies people belong to 'in groups' that take care of them in exchange for loyalty" and are included in "strong, cohesive groups (especially represented by the extended family; including uncles, aunts, grandparents and cousins) which continue protecting its members in exchange for loyalty."[81] Figure 5 (below) presents the author's overview about the Brazilian culture in this regard.

Figure 5. Geert Hofstede's Findings on Core Traits of the Brazilian Culture

Triandis corroborates Hofstede's sociological conceptualization. Triandis uses the expressions "idiocentrism" and "alocentrism," whose Latin

---

80. Hofstede, "Brazil."
81. Hofstede, "Brazil."

roots point to individualism and collectivism respectively.[82] His most relevant idea for this study is that,

> People in collectivist cultures, compared to people in individualist cultures, are likely to define themselves as aspects of groups, to give priority to ingroup goals, to focus on context more than the content, in making attributions and in communicating, to pay less attention to internal than to external processes as determinants of social behavior, to define most relationships with ingroup members as communal, [and] to make more situational attributions.[83]

Following Triandis' studies, Valdiney V. Gouveia and Miguel Clemente analyzed Brazilian culture in comparison with Spanish culture. Both cultures are more collectivist, emphasizing communal well-being and harmony above individual interests. As the authors says, "all individuals are conceived as united by network of interrelations, fit and situated in roles and particular statuses . . . each one is encouraged to put the interests of the *endogrupo* before one's own."[84] Gouveia and Clement also noted the higher the religiosity of the group, the higher the collectivism rate.[85]

In a final comparative study done among Brazilians and North Americans, Affonso Henriques de Azevedo Nogueira, Eda Castro Lucas de Souza, and Cláudio Vaz Torres perceive that Brazilians, while still more collectivist in nature than many other nationalities, are becoming more biased towards equality between the members of the society.[86] This may be a sign that as time passes, culture changes, and such change might indicate the need for more scholarship on the topic. Brazilian sociocultural traits were presented in the present section. In the next one, contemporary Brazilian Evangelicalism is analyzed panoramically.

Brazilian Evangelicalism

The richness of contemporary Brazilian and foreign authors' work on the state of Christianity in the country attests that there is active Brazilian

---

82. Triandis, "Individualism-Collectivism and Personality," 907–24.

83. Triandis, "Individualism-Collectivism and Personality," 907.

84. *Endogrup* refers to a particular group to which one belongs. Gouveia and Clemente, "O Individualismo-Coletivismo."

85. As seen in the other sociocultural traits, they affect each other. This particular interaction between collectivism and religiosity are analyzed on Chapters 4–7.

86. Nogueira et al, "Dimensões de Culturas Nacionais e Padrões Culturais."

scholarship concerning this topic.⁸⁷ These studies also suggests works in Portuguese are relevant to the field of WCS and warrant broader inclusion in the wider academic community. The material presented below is a sample of the breadth of Brazilian scholars' interests. That breadth suggests dialogue between these and other scholars around the globe would be fruitful. These books are useful for one interested in an introduction to Protestantism and Evangelicalism in Brazil.

First, José Oscar Beozzo and Luiz Carlos Susin's book, *Brazil: People and Church(es)*, presents a portrait of the church in the country.⁸⁸ The authors divide the book into three parts: a profile of Brazil, the activities of the church today, and the "future demands and challenges of being the church in Brazil." In the first and second parts, the chapters that are perhaps particularly relevant for this discussion are "The Formation of the Brazilian People," "Pastoral Strategy in the Brazilian Mega-Cities," and "Shifts in Theology; Socio-Ecclesiastical Changes: Recent Developments in Theology in Brazil." "The Contribution of Brazilian Ecclesiology to the Universal Church" is another critical chapter. Finally, in the third part of the book, the chapter, "The Globalization of Continental Challenges: A Call from Brazil on Understanding the Christian Faith" adds value to the present research given the global character of the analysis. Emile G. Leonard's, *O Protestantismo Brasileiro* (Brazilian Protestantism), depicts the Brazilian church from a historical perspective.⁸⁹ It is a classic work, ideal for those interested in an introduction to the matter. Chapters 9 and 10 provide insight into understanding the challenges churches faced in translating the Gospel in

---

87. As previously mentioned, the field of *Ciências da Religião* is a growing field of studies in Brazil. The primary programs in the country compose the Association of Graduate Studies and Research in Theology and Religion Sciences [ANPTECRE]. According to the Coordination of Faculty Improvement of Graduate Studies [CAPES], there were (from 2013–2016), in the field of Religions Science and Theology, 21 programs (12 in Religion Sciences and 9 in Theology), consisting of 3 professional degrees and 18 academic degrees, with 388 faculty members and 3238 students. CAPES, *Relatório*. According to the Sucupira Platform, the official data source for the Brazilian Ministry of Education on graduate studies, there are 21 programs on Theology and Religion Sciences which offer six master degrees, three professional master degrees, and 12 master's and doctoral degrees. The same source asserts there are 33 courses consisting of 18 master's, 12 doctoral, and three professional master level degrees. See Plataforma Sucupira, "Cursos Avaliados e Reconhecidos."

88. Beozzo and Susin, *Brazil: People and Church(es)*.

89. Leonard, *O Protestantismo Brasileiro*.

the middle of the twentieth century and reveal what the future could bring for Brazilian Protestants.

Raimundo César Barreto Jr.'s, *Evangélicos e Pobreza No Brasil—Pistas Para Uma Ética Social Evangélica Brasileira* (Evangelicals and Poverty in Brazil—Ideas for a Brazilian Evangelical Social Ethics), describes the Brazilian identity as fundamentally relational and hybrid.[90] The primary source of Barreto Jr.'s research is Gilberto Freyre.[91] Barreto Jr. discusses a crucial theme for the Brazilian reality, which is social action. However, the author proposes a model which blends evangelical, Pentecostal, and liberal (or ecumenical as he prefers) approaches. In the end, this is essentially Ecumenism.

Rubem Alves' book, *Protestantism and Repression—A Brazilian Case Study*, is a controversial and critical study of Protestant churches and Evangelicalism in Brazil.[92] It is a development of his Ph.D. dissertation at Princeton Theological Seminary. In summary, the book is an attack to what he calls the Right-Doctrine Protestantism [RDP]. Alves builds upon Max Weber's approach to criticize the conservative doctrine of Brazilian Evangelicalism, as expressed by the *Igreja Presbiteriana do Brasil* (Presbyterian Church of Brazil), which expelled him as a minister for doctrinal issues.[93] Alves also discusses some of the barriers to the expansion of the Christian faith among high culture, educated people, and skeptics. The richness of this work is the dialogue with other fields of studies, particularly sociology. The downside is the bitterness of the author towards Evangelicalism, which he despises and treats as a repressive system.

Rivanildo Segundo Guedes, in *Uma Igreja com a Nossa Cara* (A Church With our Face), reflects on the Brazilian evangelical church in a country that

---

90. The book is a development of his doctoral dissertation. Barreto Jr., *Evangélicos e Pobreza no Brasil*. Barreto Jr. is also the author of other books, such as Barreto Jr. et al, *World Christianity as Public Religion*, which was published in Portuguese as *Cristianismo Mundial como Religião Pública*.

91. Barreto Jr. is one of the Brazilian voices in the WCS in the US. The author served as director of the Freedom and Justice Division of the Baptist World Alliance [BWA] and now serves as Assistant Professor of World Christianity at Princeton Theological Seminary and regularly travels to Brazil to teach classes and participate in academic events. According to his profile page, Barreto Jr. is "an ordained Baptist minister. He holds a Ph.D. from Princeton Theological Seminary, and degrees from the Northern Baptist Theological Seminary in Brazil and McAfee School of Theology/Mercer University. Before joining the PTS faculty, Barreto Jr. taught at the Northeastern Baptist Seminary and at Brazilian Baptist College in his home country." Princeton Theological Seminary, "Raimundo César Barreto Jr.."

92. Alves, *Protestantism and Repression*.

93. Campos, "O Discurso Acadêmico de Rubem Alves," 102.

has traditionally been overwhelmingly Catholic.[94] Guedes explores the possibilities for a transformative Brazilian theology with a community-based ecclesiology. His study contrasts presentations on the church of Brazil found in the classic literature mentioned above. Guedes' contribution is explored in more breadth in Chapter 3 and affirmed by the *Igreja Multiplicadora* model and by the interviewees, as seen in Chapters 6–7.

Manoel Arturo Vásquez, in *The Brazilian Popular Church and the Crisis of Modernity*, deals with the political and economic influences on the Catholic church and assesses how Pentecostals played a role in this religious shift currently in progress.[95] Christopher Duraisingh edited *Called to One Hope– The Gospel in Diverse Cultures*, a work about the conference "Called to One Hope," which happened in 1996 in the city of Salvador, Bahia state.[96] The book is the result of these days of discussion around World Christianity. It has an ecumenical tone and encompasses a keen debate on the Gospel influence on cultures, including the Brazilian perspective.

Although these books are an introduction to the study of Brazilian Christianity from an emic perspective, the texts do not deal directly with the influence of sociocultural traits on the translation of the Gospel in Brazil. Instead, they contextualize research on Brazilian Christianity as an established and active research field open to new endeavors and approaches. Though the present work focuses on Brazilian Baptists, it also compares them with other denominations and evangelical groups such as Pentecostal Christianity, the largest branch of the religion in the country. In the following section, there is an overview of Brazilian Baptist history.

Baptist History

To consider how the Gospel has been translated inside the BCC, one should have an overview of the history of Brazilian Baptist translation. While Chapter 3 presents critical factors that contributed to the growth of Evangelicalism in Brazil, this section introduces the work of world-class scholar and Brazilian Baptist historian Zaqueu Moreira Oliveira, whose contributions to the contemporary writings on Baptist history is particularly critical.[97] In *Perseguidos, Mas Não Desamparados* (Persecuted, But Not

---

94. Guedes, *Uma Igreja com a Nossa Cara*.
95. Vásquez, *Brazilian Popular Church*.
96. Duraisingh, *Called to One Hope*.
97. Oliveira holds a Th.M and a Ph.D. from Southwestern Baptist Theological

Helpless), he presents an overview of the years of religious persecution of Brazilian Baptists from 1880–970.[98] The chapters about the outcome of the persecution are the most useful for the purpose of this research.

In *Desafios e Conquistas Missionárias* (Missionary Challenges and Conquests), Oliveira peruses the century-long work of the National Mission Board [NMB] of the BBC.[99] He includes fifteen biographies, forty-one experiences and four interviews that give clues to the success of Baptist missionary work in this country. In *Um Povo Chamado Batista: História e Princípios* (A People Called Baptists: History and Principles), the author surveys the history of the denomination.[100] He includes in his book images of original documents and a history of the origin of Baptists in England, the US, and Brazil, with principles and an analysis of the Doctrinal Declaration of the BBC. His study of Baptist identity, especially the Brazilian segment, adds insight to the study of the translation of the Gospel in Brazil, namely to its North American and English Baptists roots and background. Finally, *Princípios e Práticas Batistas: Uma Abordagem Histórica* (Baptist Principles and Practices: A Historical Approach), is a perspective on the Baptist principles and practices in the church in Brazil.[101]

Additionally, two books are a must-read for those interested in the study of Brazilian Baptists given their definition of terms and global perspective. First, David W. Bebbington, in *Baptists Through the Centuries*, identifies Baptist distinctives.[102] He presents an overview of Baptist history and introduces the reader to the men who shaped Baptist thought and life. The starting point is the Reformation. Next, he discusses the Anabaptist movement and Particular and General Baptists in the 17th century. Bebbington examines the journey of Baptists around the world in chapters such as "Baptists and Foreign Mission," "The Global Spread of the Baptists," and "Baptist Identity." He also gives some hints about the interaction between a denomination and cultures. Considering the Baptist origins and its varied colors aids one in seeing the specificities of the Brazilian Baptist case.

Seminary. He has taught in BCC seminaries and in the secular academia in Brazil. Oliveira's work is chosen given his vast prolific service in writing the history of the BCC, as a successor of Brazilian Baptist historians such as José dos Reis Pereira's, a classic book on Baptist heritage in BCC seminaries. See Pereira, *Breve História dos Batistas*.

98. Oliveira, *Perseguidos, Mas Não Desamparados*.

99. Oliveira, *Desafios e Conquistas Missionárias*.

100. Oliveira, *Um Povo Chamado Batista: História e Princípios*.

101. Oliveira, *Princípios e Práticas Batistas: Uma Abordagem Histórica*.

102. Bebbington, *Baptists Through the Centuries*.

Finally, Wilbert R. Shenk's book, *Enlarging the Story—Perspectives on Writing World Christian History*, brings one of the most important chapters for the present research goal, "The Ongoing Task—Agenda for a Work in Progress."[103] As one volunteers to study how Brazil fits into global Christianity, this particular chapter is relevant, particularly in the perspective of refining the accomplishment of the Great Commission through the Baptist church in this particular culture in the Majority World. Mark Hutchinson, Pablo Deiros, Klaus Korschorke, Donald Lewis, and Melba Maggay suggest four ways of doing Christian historiography: (1) diverse ways of knowing Christian history, (2) trying a research methodology of historiographical enterprise, (3) pursuing new definitions, and (4) proposing an agenda for accomplishing tasks, as this dissertation proposes to do considering Brazilian Baptists. The following section introduces the Brazilian Pentecostal and Neopentecostal movements.

Pentecostalism and Neopentecostalism in Brazil

It is enriching to study how to evangelize and make disciples in Brazil while paying attention to the literature concerning Pentecostals and Neopentecostals.[104] These are the largest Brazilian evangelical groups. Given the weight and impact of Pentecostalism upon Evangelicalism in Brazil, books that provide an overview of the status of recognized authors of contemporary Brazilian Evangelicalism that give clues to the translation of the Gospel in Brazil, particularly the influence of sociocultural traits on translation, require further examination.

A classic work about Brazilian Pentecostals written by Richard Shaull and Waldo Cesar is *Pentecostalism and the Future of the Christian Churches*. It is a study of the promises, limitations, and challenges for the Christian

---

103. Shenk, *Enlarging the Story*.

104. For more on the issue (e.g. Neopentecostalism), see Coelho Filho, *Neopentecostalismo: Uma Avaliação Pastoral*. Former Director of the Baptist College of Campinas, in São Paulo state, Coelho Filho was one of the most respected and prolific Brazilian Baptist authors, marked by world-class scholarship and breadth of reading and critical analysis. Another important book on the issue of contemporary Brazilian Charismatic Evangelicalism is Romeiro, *Evangélicos em Crise*. At the time of the publishing of the book, Romeiro was the Director of the *Instituto Cristão de Pesquisas* (Christian Research Institute), a respected center for the studies of Brazilian Evangelicalism and religiosity. He is a journalist and holds a Master of Divinity from Gordon-Conwell Theological Seminary.

church in Brazil.[105] Together, Shaull, an American scholar, and Cesar, a Brazilian sociologist, furnish original ideas about the relationship between the economic situation of the country and the growth of the Pentecostal movement in Brazil. They affirm that historical Protestant churches have not been able to address the poor in their needs and context. For them, Pentecostals are growing given their ability to deal with poverty in a challenging and liberating pace.

Another author who makes a positive contribution is Brazilian theologian Leonildo Silveira Campos. In *Teatro, Templo e Mercado: Organização e Marketing de um Empreendimento Neopentecostal* (Theather, Temple, and Market: Organization and Marketing of a Neopentecostal Enterprise), the author describes the phenomenon of the largest Charismatic church in Brazil, the *Igreja Universal do Reino de Deus* (Universal Church of the Kingdom of God or UCKG).[106] Campos explains the growth of the church by its media power and its business approach to the religious activity. Indeed, in a society where the media is in the center of the cultural process, it is essential to discuss the role of the media in preaching the Gospel and making disciples.

André Corten, in *Between Babel and Pentecost: Transnational Pentecostalism in Africa and Latin America*, also concentrates on the history and expansion of the UCKG in the chapter, "Brazilian Pentecostalism Crosses National Borders."[107] The church is not an example of a healthy church, but it contains, at least, the elements of the national *ethos* and *pathos*. In addition to the church's formula on reaching out to the people of the largest country in Latin America through its influential media empire, Corten points out the church focus on the attack on the African-Brazilian religion.

Finally, Mike Berg and Paul Pretiz, in *Spontaneous Combustion—Grass-Roots Christianity, Latin American Style*, give a panorama on the indigenous churches in Latin America.[108] The authors present a fair description of the primary "grassroots" churches in Latin America. "Grassroots" is the concept they chose for the national churches that did not originate from the missionary work from other countries. These could be churches that split from other churches too. The merit of this book is the list of national

---

105. Shaull and Cesar, *Pentecostalism and the Future of the Christian Churches*.
106. Campos, *Teatro, Templo e Mercado*.
107. Corten, *Between Babel and Pentecost*.
108. Berg and Pretiz, *Spontaneous Combustion*.

churches that are useful for the sake of understanding the features of a Brazilian church per se.

Ph.D. Dissertations

It is essential to scrutinize several Ph.D. dissertations related to missions and church growth within the Brazilian context. These are written mostly from Presbyterian, Pentecostal, and Reformed perspectives. Some of these dissertations deal with the Brazilian culture but do not weigh the influence of the sociocultural traits on the translation of the Gospel. Additionally, as shown below, there is no study dealing with the influence of sociocultural traits on the translation of the Gospel inside the BBC that can be useful in a global scholarly scale for dialogue with international scholars.

In "Discipling Brazilian cities: Incarnational Ministries of Historical Protestantism in Greater Metropolitan Vitoria, Espirito Santo," Valdeci da Silva Santos proposes a threefold approach of "incarnational ministry" to urban evangelism: (1) the Great Commission, (2) relational evangelism, and (3) compassion for man as a whole.[109] Paul Brown Long, in "Disciple the Nations: Training Brazilians for Inter-Cultural Mission," provides examples of the use of methodologies such as interviews, questionnaires, and case studies.[110] Sirgisberto Queiroga da Costa, in "Church Multiplication: A Grounded Theory Study of the Missiological Paradigm of Multiplying Presbyterian Churches in the Synod of Brasilia," addresses the works of Gilberto Freyre, Darcy Ribeiro, and Camara Cascudo on Brazilian cultural group systems and Fernando Motta and Miguel Caldas on Brazilian group systems.[111]

Esdras Borges Costa, in "Protestantism, Modernization and Cultural Change in Brazil," builds an overview of the Baptist church movement between 1860 and 1960, regarding doctrine (until 1930), modernization (1945), ideology and politics (until 1960).[112] Arthur W. Duck, in "Attraction and Retention Factors in Three Pentecostal Churches in Curitiba, Brazil," analyzes interviews with converts from Pentecostal churches in the city in Southern Brazil. The author uses a modified version of Lofland and Stark theory of conversion (1965).[113] Sergio O. Pereira, in "Society-Individual and

---

109. Santos, "Discipling Brazilian cities."
110. Long, "Disciple the Nations."
111. Costa, "Church Multiplication."
112. Costa, "Protestantism."
113. Duc, "Attraction and Retention Factors."

Postmodern Condition: Understanding the Explosion of Pentecostalism in Brazil," brings a participant observation method of analysis, pointing out some features of the evangelical growth through Neopentecostal churches.[114]

Conclusion

This dissertation argues that sociocultural factors play a significant role in the translation of the Gospel in Brazil as discovered and expressed among the BBC. This research aims to promote an original investigation in WCS on Brazil, one of the main forces of Christianity in the Majority World. Sanneh's concept of translation and Walls' indigenizing and pilgrim principles are at the conceptual heart of this study. The assessment of sociocultural values as bridges and/or barriers by Brazilian Baptists for translating the Gospel should lead to the comprehension of the impact of culture in Gospel translation in the country and to the discovery and development of contextualized evangelistic and discipleship strategies. Such theoretical demarcation narrows the investigation to an objective category of historiography. This chapter presented Christ meeting culture in Brazil. Chapter 2 will propose that the power of Gospel translation from the WCS standpoint is that Christ not only meets, but He actively engages culture.

---

114. Pereira, "Society-Individual and Postmodern Condition."

2

Christ Engages Culture

Biblical, Theological, and World Christian Studies Terms Defined and Applied

CHAPTER 1 PRESENTED AN overview of how Christ meets culture in Brazil. Chapter 2 discusses how Christ engages culture and argues that sociocultural factors play a significant role in the translation of the Gospel in Brazil as discovered and expressed among the BBC. This chapter begins with definitions and applications of biblical, theological, and WCS concepts and terms to this discussion. First, it demonstrates the relationship between the Bible, theology, and culture, specifically Brazilian culture. Second, it tailors the concepts of translation and indigenizing and pilgrim principles to the Brazilian culture. Third, the chapter presents the ideas of bridges and barriers for evangelism and discipleship as analytical tools in applying the indigenizing and pilgrim principles in the translation process in Brazil.

Bible and Culture

To communicate the Gospel and biblical truth, biblical writers spoke from their specific cultural perspectives. They emphasized that one cannot adequately communicate the Gospel of divine truth without speaking to a given culture. This section begins by considering that Jesus is an example of such communication.

Christ Engages Culture

World, Salt, and Light

Jesus connected the Gospel and the Hebrew culture many times and in diverse ways in His earthly ministry. In John 17, He prayed for His followers, asking not only for their unity, but also for their state, which He described as being immersed in the "world." Considering ongoing spiritual warfare, the Lord's desire was for His church's safety and deliverance from the evil one (v. 15). He knew that Satan would affect His followers' lives. Rather than asking God to take the church out of the local culture, Jesus shows He is aware that His church must remain in the "world" to change it. Christianity always exists within a local culture and is affected by that culture and the spiritual forces around it.

Thomas L. Brodie highlights not only that the believers are certainly "in the world" (v. 11 and 15), but also that they are not "of" (ἐκ) it (v. 16). For this reason, "they do not draw their ultimate identity and strength from it."[1] Pointing to the Johannine perspective, Andreas J. Köstenberger instead sees "obedience, dependence, and faithfulness" as a model Jesus' followers should imitate there and now.[2] C. S. Lewis notes that, in John 15, the Lord spoke about His disciples as His property. With that in mind, "It is wholly foreign to all later groups who a heavenly people are, by divine exaltation and transformation, wholly different from all peoples that have been or ever will be on the earth."[3] Thus, they should interact within the culture. Culture and the kingdom of God affect one another, as seen in the pilgrim and indigenizing principles.

In Matthew 5:13–14, Jesus reminds His followers that their role is to be "salt of the earth . . . light of the world," transforming the "world" (culture) through the power of the Gospel. Interpreting this text, R. T. France avers that, as salt gives flavor and prevents corruption, the disciples should work to make this world "a purer and a more palatable place" by their godly character.[4] Furthermore, as light affects the environment by giving its form and distinctiveness, so too Christians should be visibly and positively distinct from others.[5] Don Garlington classifies the disciples as "proof

---

1. Brodie, *Quest*, 515.
2. Köstenberger, "Challenge," 454.
3. Chafer, "Teachings of Christ Incarnate [3]," 389–413.
4. France, *Matthew: An Introduction and Commentary*, 117–18.
5. France, *Matthew: An Introduction and Commentary*, 117–18.

positive that the kingdom is a reality in the world."[6] Further, as seen in many passages of the Old Testament [OT] referenced by Garlington, since salt is a symbol of permanence and fidelity, table fellowship and purity, the disciples of Christ should experience the same realities in their lives.[7] David L. Tuner adds that salt implied what the Christ's followers would be in their local contexts: "Salt is thus a metaphor for one's exercising a beneficial influence on the world, in a manner analogous to the way light is beneficial in illumining darkness."[8]

Rural Examples

During His three years of earthly ministry, Jesus regularly included elements from the rural culture in His teaching. Not only salt (Cf. Matt 5:13; Mark 9:50; Luke 14:34), but also weeds (Matt 13:24–43), and soil (Matt 13:1–23; Mark 4:1–20, 26–32; Luke 8:4–15 John 12:24) were common items that spoke to the hearts of His disciples. Similar metaphors were part of His proclamation of the Gospel and teaching.[9] Under those circumstances, Jesus translated in both linguistic and cultural forms. This study discusses the cultural translation approach, and leaves for another project discussion about the literal translation of the scriptures into Portuguese. However, since language is part of culture, there will be areas of intersection between language and culture in this study.[10]

Living Sacrifice

The Apostle Paul wrote a symbolic passage in Romans 12:1–2 as he paints a picture of Christians transforming the culture. Douglas J. Moo calls this

---

6. Garlington, "'Salt of the Earth,'" 730.
7. Garlington, "Salt of the Earth," 716–23.
8. Turner, *Matthew*, 154–55.
9. Flemming, "Paul the Contextualizer."
10. Jon S. Vincent, in the third chapter on "Language" of *Culture and Customs of Brazil*, points out that Brazilians build their identity around their language. Since Brazil is the only Portuguese-speaking country in South and Central America, Brazilians have a unique and distinct sense of identity. They have an advantage since they understand more Spanish than the people from other Latin American countries can understand Portuguese. This facilitates Brazilian missionary and commercial activities.

section a "basic call."[11] To offer "our bodies" as a living sacrifice means to present "the whole person in relationship to the world [which we do] . . . by avoiding the pattern of thinking and behaving that is characteristic of this world and by instead aligning ourselves with the values of the world to come."[12] Translation, in this sense, means that what is against the good news should become a pilgrim and leave the Christian life. For example, if in a particular culture, lying is the norm, the believer should banish it from his life as soon he comes to know Christ and recognizes that Satan is the father of lies (John 8:44).

The same biblical passage serves as a dialectical paradigm of living, first, in the perspective of dialogue with the OT and, second, interacting with the world, according to Nobuyoshi Kiuchi.[13] The author connects Romans 12:1b, especially the "living sacrifice" concept, with the Azazel-goat (Scapegoat) of Leviticus 16:10 and 22. Kiuchi asserts that the Apostle Paul was encouraging his readers, like an Azazel-goat, to suffer on behalf of others by the power of the Holy Spirit. The Azazel-goat was the prescribed means by which the whole people of Israel could atone for their sins. In the same sense, Christians, by living in the "wild nature" (sinful nature) of the world, are living sacrifices for the Lord. Believers should be an example pointing to Christ, the supreme atoning sacrifice.

How does being a "living sacrifice" apply in practical terms, in people's daily lives? Robert A. Bryant explains that a Christian's perspective about such matters as divorce, knowledge, power, denominational fights, and wealth, will be different from that of the world or non-Christians. Bryant argues "to be alive in Jesus, . . . means to live under the ever-transforming power of God's grace, a power that enables Jesus' followers to remain faithful and to be instruments of God's transforming love."[14]

In the Brazilian culture, for example, to be a living sacrifice means to present the physical body as something pleasing to God, by which are meant certain standards of modesty and purity. Brazilians are known as exhibitionists who promote strong sexual appeal through the carnival, beachgoing, TV, and movies. In this environment, believers live out the

---

11. Moo, *Encountering the Book of Romans*, 162.

12. Moo, *Encountering the Book of Romans*, 163.

13. Kiuchi, "Living like the Azazel-goat," 251. Kiuchi is an OT scholar at Tokyo Christian University and author of the volume on Leviticus in the Apollos Old Testament Commentary Series.

14. Bryant, "Romans 12:1–8," 288.

Gospel by understanding that their bodies are not to be used anymore in sinful ways.[15] They should make a "spiritual impact on the world," as D. Edmond Hiebert posits.[16]

Paul in the Areopagus

In another episode, the Apostle Paul had a balanced approach when interacting with the local culture in the Areopagus in Athens. Paul denounced idolatry yet viewed God's purpose as being accomplished in culture according to Acts 17:10–34. The Apostle communicated with his audience in a culturally contextualized manner. Darrell L. Bock describes this episode as a complete example of Paul's interaction with an audience composed only of Gentiles, in which he was attempting to build a bridge to the culture to present the Gospel effectively.[17] Rodney Matthew Woo develops this bridge metaphor and suggests that in building a bridge Paul becomes an Athenian to the Athenians. Woo notes that since Paul was speaking to a Gentile audience, he shared an idea comprehensible to them to "bridge the gap between the Gospel organically rooted in the history and the faith of Israel and religious axioms of the Gentile context."[18]

Joshua W. Jipp notes that Paul uses Hellenistic philosophical concepts in his critique of idolatry from a Jewish point of view.[19] Paul, says Jipp, not only argues that Christianity is not superstition (which Stoics and Epicureans would challenge), but demonstrates it is a superior kind of philosophical knowledge of God.[20] Robert E. Dunham calls this Pauline speech a model for proclamation because Paul employs reason and a cordial tone rather than reproach, common in the Hellenistic philosophy.[21]

---

15. Bryant, "Romans 12:1–8," 316.
16. Hiebert, "Presentation and Transformation," 315.
17. Bock, *Acts*, 558–59.
18. Woo, "Paul's Contextual Approach."
19. Jipp, "Paul's Areopagus Speech," 567.
20. Jipp, "Paul's Areopagus Speech ," 588.
21. Dunham, "Acts 17:16–34," 202–3.

Theology and Culture

The biblical basis for this research was expounded on the first part of this chapter. In this second portion, it is essential to define theology and culture. Millard J. Erickson sees the two as inseparable or interactive. He notes that theology "strives to give a coherent statement of the doctrines of the Christian faith, based primarily upon the Scriptures, placed in the context of culture in general, worded in contemporary idiom, and related to issues of life."[22] Schubert M. Ogden proposes a more philosophical definition, but also keeps a strong emphasis on cultural placement. "Theology, in the sense explicitly conveyed by the words 'Christian theology,' is the fully reflective understanding of the Christian witness of faith as decisive for human existence."[23] In this sense, "Christian witness" exists only inside a given culture and for the sake of people.

In turn, culture, according to Richard Niebuhr, is man's superimposition of meaning on what is natural. Hence, for him, culture is the "artificial, secondary environment."[24] The author includes in the definition cultural instances such as inherited ideas, language, values, technical processes, habits, customs, social organization, and beliefs. Still, per Niebuhr, culture is about human achievement, values, the well-being of humankind, and pluralism.[25] For him, humankind is always producing culture, since culture is the embodiment and translation of life in material and immaterial senses. Thus, Christianity has meaning as it succeeds in connecting with culture.[26]

Paul Tillich finds theology's place only in the daily life of people, in other words, in culture.[27] "Religion opens up the depth of man's spiritual life which is usually covered by the dust of our daily life and the noise of our secular work."[28] In his opinion, there is a natural imbrication between theology and culture. Tillich conceives of religion as the basis of human existence, given its ultimate meaning. He understands preaching the Gospel as interacting specifically with local culture as Paul did at the Areopagus

---

22. Erickson, *Christian Theology*, 23.
23. Ogden, "What Is Theology?," 22.
24. Niebuhr, *Christ and Culture*, 32.
25. Niebuhr, *Christ and Culture*, 32–39.
26. Niebuhr, *Christ and Culture*, 32–39.
27. Tillich, *Teologia da Cultura*, 259.
28. Tillich and Kimball, *Theology of Culture*, 8–9.

Hill.[29] In this sense, Jorge Pinheiro dos Santos summarizes there is a cultural community outside the church, in which the decisions of an individual are rooted in a contemporary global culture.[30] As Paul Matheny notes, "All theology is local and contextual with global reach and contact."[31] For Tillich, this will always encourage people in making a decision for or against the Gospel.[32] The goal is to remove all cultural "stumbling blocks" so that the Gospel may remain the stumbling block.[33]

Church Fathers

The Early Church fathers also wrote theology communicating with and embedded in culture. Prominent figures such as Tertullian, Augustine, and Clement of Alexandria, presented their faith persuasively to their contemporaries, with culturally familiar images and language, so that the audience could interpret and understand Christianity more easily.[34] It is not the goal of this dissertation to address the contextual theology done by the Early Church fathers, but a brief survey of the matter enriches the discussion.[35] Tertullian, for example, discusses some cultural practices by considering what the Bible says is forbidden and permitted. Tertullian takes a very narrow and literal perspective by asserting instead of saying "whatever is not forbidden is, without question, allowed," one should assume, "Whatever is not specifically permitted is forbidden."[36]

In one of his letters, Augustine recommends his readers maintain their good works as prescribed in Philippians 1:27 and set their thoughts on eternal life when they encounter crises and probleRms related to this world such as "the sack and siege of Rome by the Alaric and the Goths in 410."[37]

---

29. Tillich and Kimball, *Theology of Culture*, 203.

30. Santos writes the introduction to the Portuguese edition of Tillich, *Teologia da Cultura*, 15.

31. Matheny, *Contextual Theology*, 81.

32. Tillich, *Teologia da Cultura*, 259–60.

33. Tillich, *Teologia da Cultura*, 272.

34. Other Early Church fathers, such as Justin Martyr, Origen, and Cyprian, are mentioned by Bosley, "Theology and Social Experience," 376.

35. Another venue one could pursue to consider the impact of the Gospel in culture is archaeological study. A valuable example is found in Harland, *Dynamics of Identity*.

36. Sider, *Christian and Pagan in the Roman Empire*, 120.

37. Augustine, *Letters*, 334.

Clement of Alexandria compares God with Zeus, for the sake of explaining the concept of "godly childlikeness" to his readers. He writes: "Heraclitus tells us that his Zeus, too, indulges in such a pastime. Indeed, what occupation is more becoming a wise and perfect man than to play and rejoice at the celebration of a solemn religious festival, with submissive reception and the performance of what is holy?"[38] This section presented the relationship between theology and culture, and summarized the basic definitions of terms and the Church Fathers' perspective on the issue. Finally, contextual theology's approach is presented in the following section.

Contextual Theology and Politics

Contextual theology sees theology from a local standpoint. In a certain sense, this approach may make theology subservient to local traditions, practices, and worldviews, which is dangerous given the changing nature of culture and the unchanging nature of the Word of God. Michael Grimshaw, for example, proposes a consideration made "on the margins of academia and orthodoxy, institutionalized Christianity and theology," far from the "white and imperialistic" perspective.[39] Grimshaw's approach affirms contextual theology while denouncing its perils. By the same token, another mistake to be avoided is the one made by liberal theologians. Per William D. Dean, liberals try to accommodate to modern culture, embracing relative conclusions about God, and this can lead to culture dominating theology and a portrait of a God who is not working locally—a non-historical being.[40]

One final and likewise more contemporary example of the critical relationship between culture and theology is seen in the intersection between politics and religion in the US. The North American fusion of Christianity and democracy is very particular in history, specifically its influence over the congregational church government. Dean suggests that Puritans were the main source for American democracy.[41] One may ask, "Why should democracy be considered in Baptist churches instead of theocracy"? Jared Hickman likewise notes in regard to Evangelicalism, that Calvinism was the context where pragmatism, a North-American treasure, was born.[42]

38. Alexandria, *Christ the Educator*, 22.
39. Grimshaw, "'Redneck Religion and Shitkickin' Saviours?," 93.
40. Dean, "Can Liberal Theology Recover?," 201.
41. Dean, "Can Liberal Theology Recover?," 201.
42. Hickman, "Theology of Democracy," 205.

As can be seen from such examples, while culture influences theology, theology also has a considerable impact over culture. There is no theology without culture, and vice versa. Translation is an ongoing and unending process in whatever place Christianity is rooted.

Leslie Newbigin observes the Gospel is always presented in a specific language, the "primary vehicle of a culture," and through the church, it becomes an aspect of the culture.[43] Thus, Portuguese is the vehicle of the Gospel, and the church is the channel of translation of the Gospel to the local Brazilian culture.

Religious Culture

This chapter has discussed the connections between Scripture, theology, and culture. The previous section defined and discussed theology and culture, their imbrication and mutual interposition, with brief references to the North American context. So how do such connections between theology and culture happen in Brazil? The cultural aspect to be sought is the religious culture. From this standpoint, there is an assumption that evangelical Christianity in Brazil may be considered a sub product of a Catholic culture, as will be developed further in the next chapter.

Catholic Predominance

Sergio Buarque de Hollanda's work, *História Geral da Civilização Brasileira*, is considered a milestone in the study of Brazilian culture.[44] Part of the book describes the development of Roman Catholicism in Brazil. Holanda highlights the work and investment of religious orders from Europe that transformed Brazil into the largest Catholic country in the world. He explains that even after the separation of church and state, in the middle of the 19th century, people maintained their idolatry, pilgrimages to holy temples, and civil dependence on the church for registering children and weddings. Currently, religious (meaning Catholic) holidays are still observed, an example of the ongoing Catholic influence in Brazil.

---

43. Newbigin, *Gospel in a Pluralist Society*, 188.

44. Holanda, *História Geral da Civilização Brasileira*, 280–81. The information in this paragraph comes from this source.

Conversely, Charles Wagley suggests that most Catholics in Brazil follow religion by tradition, rather by faith, given that most were baptized when infants and did not have a choice.[45] The Presbyterian and Lutheran faiths, while sacramental regarding the ordinances as the Catholic faith and infant baptism, did not grow as they could have in a country such as Catholic Brazil. The similarities between those Christianities could have helped people move from Catholicism to Protestantism. For this reason, in some contexts, it is a challenge to instruct believers about Christianity as a real faith commitment, instead of a tradition or family inheritance.[46]

In data collected by Philip Raine in the early 1970s, the church itself estimated that only about 15 percent of nearly 100 million Brazilians were faithful Catholics. At that time, the Catholic Church was already diminishing, as the Pentecostal movement and other evangelical churches grew. Raine's studies help also to describe the power of the priests over the laity. Catholicism stresses a separation between priests and lay people, while Pentecostals and Neopentecostals encourage their members to be active Christians and even become *obreiros* (lay workers), presbyters, and pastors. Raine also suggests that the political conscience and a much-intellectualized activity among the Catholic flock favored development of Liberation Theology.[47] On the other hand, the Pentecostal church relies heavily on a lay workforce and a pragmatic political conscience, which makes it very successful in a Third World country.[48] There are many connections between religion and economics in Brazil, as it will be discussed in more depth in the next section.

Towards a Balanced Approach

In this sense, there is a strong influence of Liberation Theology upon Latin America, especially through the Catholic Church. An important concept in this movement is the one of "solidarity with the poor."[49] Liberation Theology's ecclesiology describes a church that is involved in transforming the

---

45. Wagley, *Introduction to Brazil*, 213.

46. A broader treatment of the topic of Catholicism and its relationship with other religions is presented in Chapters 3, 5, 6, and 7.

47. Raine, "Catholic Church in Brazil," 280.

48. Pentecostalism works as a pluralistic force as explained by Furtado, *Criatividade e Dependência na Civilização Industrial*, 119–20.

49. Bucher, "Toward a Liberation Theology for the 'Oppressor,'" 534.

social, economic, and political realities of its context. In this sense, the Gospel is not only a personal matter, but a "material and historic process of solidarity with the poor."[50] In other words, in societies where poverty is rampant, disciples of Christ should engage in social causes as one of the main tasks of the church.[51] For years, Liberation Theology had a considerable impact over evangelical churches. Leonardo Boff, a Brazilian Catholic theologian and defender of the Liberation Theology movement, is respected and read in some evangelical circles.

As seen, religion and economy are interwoven, particularly in a country such as Brazil, where there is a real need for social change given poverty and other problems such as drug addiction and low educational levels. Economic and social transformation are expected to be a byproduct of Christian outreach and service to the community. A healthy example in evangelical circles is Manfred Grellert's, *Os Compromissos da Missão* (The Compromisse of the Mission). Here, Grellert defines the Gospel in solidly evangelical terms including social action and a balanced approach to life.[52]

In summary, the author defends the proclamation of the good news giving priorioty to the poor in Brazil, which is a strong and divisive claim, but keeping with the conservative evangelical stance of sharing the Gospel through words and personal testimony. For him, "Evangelistic growth does not happen without organic growth, in fellowship, in the worship service, in the edification, and in the service/social action."[53] Grellert defends a holistic mission with solid biblical foundations.

Finally, Brazilian missiological scholarship considers culture mainly in a transcultural context. For example, Burns, Azevedo, and Carminati affirm, "If we want to communicate the Gospel to a people whose way of life is different of ours, we need to be in such a condition to analyze the reasons for their way of thinking, acting, and living."[54] A question that needs to be

50. Herndl and Bauer, "Speaking Matters," 564–65.

51. Herndl and Bauer, "Speaking Matters," 564–65.

52. Grellert, *Os Compromissos da Missão*, 57. Former vice-president of World Vision for Latin America, Grellert is a Brazilian with German roots who holds a Ph.D. from the Southern Baptist Theological Seminary in Louisville, Kentucky. The author served as pastor at Capunga Baptist Church in Recife, Pernambuco state and was a Professor at Northern Baptist Seminary [NBTS] in the same city before becoming president of Brazil's World Vision arm and then moving to the US and leading the organization in Latin America.

53. Grellert, *Os Compromissos da Missão*, 73.

54. Burns et al., *Costumes e Culturas*, 9.

raised is: "Why are cultural studies not imperative also to the translation of the Gospel inside one's own culture"? There are many cultural variations inside the same country. However, Burns, Azevedo, and Carminati missed the opportunity to affirm the need for the study of the Brazilian culture as diverse and transcultural. Many examples given regarding customs, food habits, or language are applicable inside a neighborhood. While most Brazilians will generally speak Portuguese and eat "beans and rice" at lunch, there are different regions and vocabularies around the nation, types of beans, and ways of cooking rice inside Brazil. Brazilian culture per se is a vibrant and challenging source for this type of analysis still to be explored. Thus, translation and its indigenizing and pilgrim principles require further exploration.

Translation: A Dialogue between Gospel and Culture

This dissertation chooses to interpret the dialogue between theology and culture by utilizing the concept of translation. As Vincent J. Donovan argues, the Gospel is supra-cultural, while, at the same time, meant to reach every culture: "It comes from outside our cultures and yet is designed for all of them—a supra-cultural, unchanging message of good news."[55] In a general sense, the Gospel becomes intelligible and tangible to the local people through re-appropriation and adaptation, according to Sanneh. It means that the transmission of the faith by missionaries was not a mere repetition of the translation process experienced by them but an expansion and deepening of Christianity's cultural frontier into new forms.[56] In becoming local and appropriated by the new people, the Gospel shifts from being an outsider's worldview to acquiring the insiders' flavor and colors. It starts with linguistic translation and morphs into cultural appropriation.

Why is translation necessary? As Sanneh notes, translation is necessary because the Gospel does not make sense outside of its cultural milieu. "The pure Gospel, stripped of all cultural entanglements, would evaporate in a vague abstraction, although if the Gospel were without its intrinsic power it would be nothing more than cultural ideology."[57] In other words, the Gospel is visible only if embodied in cultures, such as Brazilian, Nigerian, or South Korean, among others. At the same time, there will be a discrepancy if, for

55. Donovan, *Christianity Rediscovered*, 47–48.
56. Sanneh, *African Transformation of Christianity*, 33.
57. Sanneh, *African Transformation of Christianiy*, 117.

example, a foreign missionary tries to impose his combination of Gospel and culture, and in so doing, suppresses indigenous expressions.[58]

Sanneh's concept of translation reverberates in the work of other authors such as Spike. This author understands the Christian message to be above culture. At the same time, he acknowledges that for the Gospel to be considered, it must be communicated in words local people can understand.[59] How does a Brazilian understand the message of the cross when the preacher uses the word *pecado* (sin), for example? *Pecado* is a concept present in this culture given the Catholic origins of the country, but because of that, it is also a word that connotes a works-based salvation mentality and the intercession of Catholic saints. Thus, when proclaiming the good news in Brazil, evangelicals need to use words and concepts that resonate with the worldview of the hearer, given that some words may "provoke impressions in the mind of the hearer different than the ones produced in the mind of the messenger," as Nicholls argues.[60] Or, as Burns, Azevedo, and Carminati propose, the Gospel needs to be comprehended in terms known to people in their ways of thinking and living.[61] Cultural translation encompasses language and even idiomatic expressions.[62]

Indigenizing and Pilgrim Principles

The indigenizing and pilgrim principles are some of Walls's main contributions on translation adopted in this dissertation. These principles are akin to Sanneh's proposals to "relativize" and "destigmatize" the Gospel in a given culture. To "relativize" means to leave the doctrine's original cultural roots (in this case, Jewish roots) as one embraces Christianity.[63] "Destigmatize" means to incorporate the new religion into the culture, indigenizing the Gospel but not divorcing culture and religion. [64] On the other hand, the

58. Sanneh, *African Transformation of Christiniaty*, 120.

59. Spike, "Evangelism and Culture," 777.

60. Nicholls, *Contextualização*, 8. This is the Portuguese translation of Nicholl's classic work.

61. Burns et al., *Costumes e Culturas*, 16.

62. In his book *Walk Through the Bible*, Newbigin proposes a "trialogue" between the Gospel, the church and culture, which is the proposal of this dissertation.

63. In other words, "the concepts of the word of God are not changed, but demonstrated and applied in a logical and natural way to a given culture." Burns et al., *Costumes e Culturas*, 61.

64. Sanneh, *Translating the Message*, 1.

pilgrim principle applies when the Gospel "relativizes" aspects of the culture that are contrary to the teachings of Jesus Christ.

The Gospel is supreme, and culture cannot determine it, as Eitel affirms.[65] To explain what he means by this, he diagrams a way to identify worldviews. This picture, coupled with Eitel's five Pauline "principles for filtering culture through the grid of Scripture" is valuable in identifying the indigenizing and pilgrim principles in action. The following chart expresses this thought.

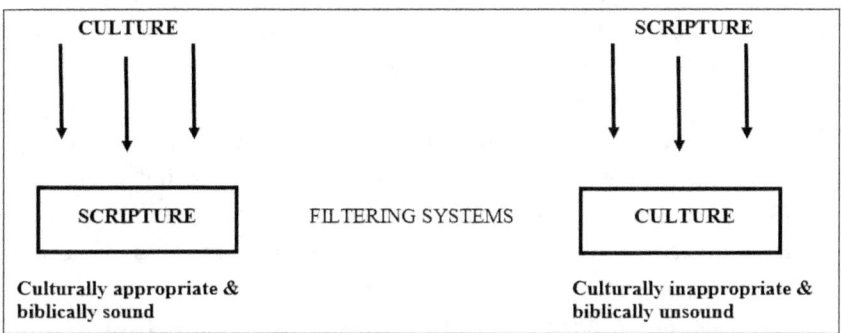

Figure 6. Filtering Systems Based on the Culture or the Scripture

1. Does it contradict any clear teaching of Scripture (2 Tim 3:16–17)?

2. Does it violate or do harm to my body (mentally, physically, or spiritually) as the temple of the Holy Spirit (1 Cor 16:19–20)? Or, will it enhance the Holy Spirit's development and expression of Christ's holiness in and through my life (1 Thess 4:1–8)?.

3. Does it cause my weaker brother (or non-believer by implication) to stumble in coming closer to Christ (1 Cor 8–10)?

4. Does it violate the express will of my spiritual head (Eph 5:22—6:9; Rom 13:1–7)?

5. Does it glorify God (1 Cor 10:31)? Or, Can I ask God to bless it with a clear conscience (Rom 14:19–23)?[66]

If the answer to questions 1 to 4 is "no," and the answer to question 5 is "yes," then the indigenizing pilgrim is at work. However, if one answers "yes"

---

65. Eitel, "Scriptura or Cultura," 74–75.
66. Eitel, "Scriptura or Culture," 74–75.

to questions 1 to 4 and "no" to question 5, the pilgrim principle needs to be applied and transformation happens. In other words, the believer needs to confront the culture with the Gospel and its ethical changing power.

Cultural Bridges and Barriers

The idea of bridges and barriers in preaching the Gospel and in discipleship comes together with the application of the indigenizing and pilgrim principles in the translation of the Gospel. The consequence is that after realizing what principle is at work, one will need to give an answer to questions such as: How does the perception of the indigenizing principle lead an evangelist or discipler to share the Gospel or to show how Jesus' teachings abide with the culture? How does the knowledge of the pilgrim principle encourage one to raise a prophetic voice and denounce sin or ethical incongruences? This section aims to discuss the connections between the pilgrim and indigenizing principles and the concept of bridges and barriers in evangelism and discipleship.

Translation of the Gospel implies the transformation of cultures and peoples. In this sense, the Gospel is to be the source of the judgment of the society. Newbigin affirms that this evaluation of cultures ought to come from the Gospel itself and not "from the cultural presuppositions of the person who makes the judgment."[67] Interacting with culture is a balanced approach. It may mean that the Gospel will transform culture and people even if that means confronting governing authorities.[68] One example is the issue of gay marriage, as seen in the Western church. Churches should stand up and not accept gay weddings in their buildings. The pilgrim principle means that the church will confront politicians and proclaim the biblical message about it. Practical action may include Christians voting for candidates who are in conformity with the biblical view of marriage. Pastors and denominations are to preach and express their concerns to politicians regarding the biblical model of the family.

Another example of conflict between culture and theology may be seen in the relationship between church and culture in the Three-Self Movement [TSPM], the official Protestant church in China. Christians who are on the side of the Communist party and, in some cases, do not hold a

---

67. Newbigin, *Gospel in a Pluralist Society*, 186.
68. Newbigin, *Foolishness to the Greeks*, 129.

real faith commitment may compose this group.[69] How does the TSPM work in relation to the indigenizing and pilgrim processes? The church neither supports any political party, nor endorses governing blocks. It could appear to be an indigenization of the Christian faith, but that is not the case because the Communist party in China persecutes all denominations but the TSPM. It is a similar to what happened in Rome after Constantine declared Catholicism the official religion of the Roman Empire. In such a model, other religions typically become victims of persecution. Instead of transforming the culture, official churches become part of the establishment. There is no impartiality or autonomy. The political power becomes the spiritual head of the church.

A native Brazilian example attests that culture needs to studied from a theological standpoint. Brazilian people use homeopathy for daily health issues. This practice goes back to the beliefs and customs of the indigenous people of Latin America and those from an African heritage. People trust in the power of plants as a reflection of their confidence that a local deity can heal them. Certainly, the Bible affirms the healing power of nature/plants in passages such as Ezekiel 47:12 and Revelation 22:2. In the OT text, God declares He is the author of healing and of all good, as Carl L. Beckwith emphasizes.[70] Other commentators see the tree and its leaves as an analogy to the healing power of the Word of God, which is also true.[71] Revelation 22:2 resembles the Ezekiel passage, expanding the healing from the leaves of the tree to all the nations, not only the chosen people of the OT.[72] Christians in Brazil may tend to draw upon natural health treatments, highlighting God's power to heal, instead of adopting an animistic worldview.

These biblical examples attest that preaching the Gospel always involves dialoguing with particular cultural forms of thinking. In post-Western Christianity, there will be a pattern of cultural adjustment and translation, as Walls affirms.[73] Syncretism or other kinds of mixes are not mandatory practices. Yet, theology should influence and transform the culture, not the opposite. As William Goff argues, "Translation of the Gospel in a culture is

---

69. Newbigin, *Foolishness to the Greeks*, 90.

70. Beckwith. *Ezekiel, Daniel*, 227.

71. Stevenson et al., *Ezekiel, Daniel*, 147. A fruitful piece of additional research on this text is found in Luo, "Ezekiel in Revelation."

72. Fee, *Revelation*, 304. The same approach is taken by Blount, *Revelation: A Commentary*, 398.

73. Walls, *Missionary Movement*, 29.

the modus of interpretation and clarity of proclamation so that it connects with the culture and is transformative within that culture."[74]

Conclusion

This chapter discussed how Christ engages culture. It explains how biblical, theological, and WCS concepts are applied to the translation of the Gospel in Brazil. In summary, the local culture is the laboratory of theology. Given the discussion proposed in this chapter, translation is proximate to contextualization, but it is not the same phenomena. Contextualization may imply syncretism or indigenization of costumes that are against the core values of Christianity. As Eitel proposes, Scripture is the supreme judge of all cultures and not the opposite.[75] It is Christ who should change the culture, as discussed in Chapter 3, not the message that should be accommodated to fit the culture.

---

74. This quotation comes from a comment made by William Goff in his marked copy as second reader of the dissertation draft.

75. Eitel, "Scriptura or Cultura," 74.

3

Christ Changes Culture

A Critique of the Quantitative and Qualitative Growth of Evangelical Christianity in Brazil

As the previous chapters showed, Christ meets and engages culture. When it happens, He changes it. This chapter considers those changes more closely and critiques the quantitative and qualitative growth of evangelical Christianity in Brazil. If sociocultural factors play a significant role in the translation of the Gospel in Brazil, what are the reasons for the exponential growth of the Brazilian evangelical population from the Portuguese colonization around 1500 AD to the present?[1] Along with classic books and articles in Christian history, evangelism, missions, sociology, and religion, the author's emic perspective informs this exploration, which points out a complicated diffusion of the Christian message in Brazil.[2]

Four primary factors contributed to the expansion of Christianity in Brazil as indicated in the chart below and explained hereafter. The first factor is the Catholic beginning of the country. How did Roman Catholics contribute to the introduction of the Christian message in Brazil starting in the sixteenth century? The introduction of the Protestant faith in the

---

1. In 1500, when the Portuguese colonization began, the evangelical population in Brazil was practically nil. In 1950, it was 3.4 percent, according to the national census, and fifty years later in 2000, it was 15.6 percent. This fifty-years period saw the fastest ever growth of the evangelical population in the country.

2. Barfield, *Dictionary of Anthropology*, 148.

nineteenth century is the second factor that shaped the contemporary face of Christianity in Brazil. Protestant missions planted the seeds for the growth of evangelical Christianity in Brazil.

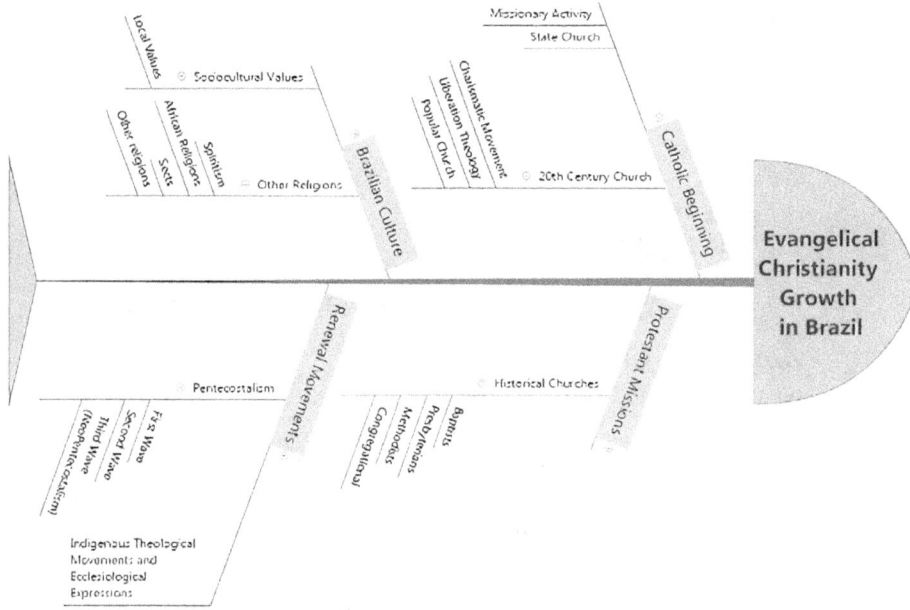

Figure 7. Factors that Impacted the growth of Evangelical Christianity in Brazil

The third and, probably, most impactful factor in the expansion of the evangelical faith (*Evangélico* or *crente*, in Portuguese) was the twentieth-century renewal movements in Brazil.³ Indigenous churches and indigenous leaders were responsible for establishing a Brazilian way of being the church; this was pivotal for an explosion of the faith in the nation. Finally, the Brazilian culture, with its national and local particularities, and religiosities contributed to evangelical growth. Before entering an historical discussion, one should examine the religious background of the indigenous people of Brazil (Animism) and then, some particularities of the evangelical faith in Brazil.⁴

3. *Crente* is the Portuguese word for believers. *Evangélico* is equivalent to evangelical. That use of renewal (rather than revival) nomenclature follows Mark Shaw's definition: "Global revivals are charismatic people movements that transform their world by translating Christian truth and transferring power." Shaw, *Global Awakening*, 17.

4. In Chapter 4 ("History") of *Culture and Customs of Brazil*, Jon S. Vincent explains

Animism: Indigenous Background

The Gospel journey in Brazil, before the Catholic endeavor, started with the encounter with an Animistic worldview.[5] The indigenous people of the new land were Animistic. Animism is a belief system in which invisible spiritual forces are the cause of every single activity in the visible world. This means that the movement of the leaves in the forest or the growth of a tree are visible effects of invisible forces.[6] Burns, Azevedo, and Carminati assert that Animism is a broad term, but it encompasses at least five features. First, humankind is part of nature. Second, humankind is composed of more than one reality (body and soul or body, soul, and spirit). Third, there are supernatural powers. Fourth, supernatural powers are, at least, controllable. Finally, there is not, necessarily, a relationship between morality and religion.[7]

In Animistic societies, sea, sky, fire, mountains, lakes, rivers, and other natural elements are led by spiritual beings. The spirits of the dead are "spiritual forces" which manifest themselves through natural forces and phantasms. All these spiritual beings are evoked in witchcraft. Given that there is not a relationship between morality and religion, people can call out for these powers to work for good and evil.[8]

The appeal to spiritual forces to act in the life issues such as revenge, love, and health is vital to the Animistic worldview in Brazil. These practices are still alive in Brazil and became much stronger after the arrival of

---

the Portuguese exploitation. The author mentions that it left deep wounds in the Brazilian economy and society. On the one hand, there is a wide gap between the poor and rich in Brazil. Socially, the existence of workers who clean the house, cook for the families, and wash the clothes, even in low-medium class families, is a vestige of slavery. In the US, slavery fabricated an inheritance of exploitation. The existence of a kingdom system at the beginning of Brazil, after receiving its independence from Portugal in 1822, collaborated with the understanding of the patriarchal government style still prevalent in many parts of the country. Populism was high in the mid-1900 with President Getúlio Vargas. At present, Populism is still seen in the neighbor countries of Venezuela and Colombia and even in Brazil with the former president Luís Inácio Lula da Silva. In the past, Argentina and Chile went through patriarchal governments, with the president seen as the savior of the country who provides, leads, and enhances the countries development and growth. A strong component of military power and force was part of this equation.

5. Azevedo, *Cruzadas Inacabadas*, 44. Belo highlights that Latin America was a house for a blended group of polytheist and Animistic beliefs.

6. Grenz et al., *Pocket Dictionary of Theological Terms*, 10.

7. Burns et al., *Costumes e Culturas*, 70–71.

8. Burns et al., *Costumes e Culturas*, 72.

Catholicism and African religiosity, which is also Animistic.[9] Typical Brazilian syncretism blends indigenous Animistic practices with Catholic saints, African deities, and Kardecist Spiritualism.[10] Its main representative is the *Umbanda* religion.[11] It is also generally called *Macumba* around Brazil and is called *Candomblé* in Bahia state, and Quimbanda in other states.[12] This syncretic religion worships African deities such as the *preto velhos* (*Black Old Men*) and Indigenous deities such as the *caboclos*.[13] The Animistic roots of Brazil play a substantial role in the religious scenario of the nation, as it will be developed further. Before analyzing the reasons for evangelical growth, it is relevant to define some terms regarding Brazilian Evangelicalism.

Brazilian Evangelicals

Brazilian Evangelicalism has some particularities. In the common sense, Evangelicalism in Brazil refers to uniting denominations such as Baptists, Presbyterians, Pentecostals, Charismatics, and other churches that have some basic Christian doctrines in common.[14] Brazilian evangelicals include traditional evangelical traits as described by Bebbington's quadrilateral, meaning conversionism, biblicism, crucicentrism, and activism, even

---

9. Barreto, *Mitologia Dupla*, 14. This classic book was published originally in 1899, only 17 years after the First Baptist Church of Brazil was inaugurated. Barreto exposed the relationship between the Catholic saints and the Greek mythology. She also addresses Animistic, African, and indigenous influences.

10. As Nicholls defines, syncretism is "an attempt to conciliate diverse or conflicting beliefs and religious practices in a unified system." Nicholls, *Contetualização*, 38. In Brazil, syncretism involves the use of amulets such as crosses and pictures of saints or Indigenous or African deities hanging on the wall believed to have power in themselves. Burns et al., *Costumes e Culturas*, 70.

11. *Umbanda* is a Spiritualist religion with African, Catholic, and Indigenous roots. Camargo, *Católicos, Protestantes, Espíritas*, 32.

12. Bezerra, *Orixás, Cablocos e Guias*, 15. Bezerra, known in Brazil as *Bispo* Macedo (Bishop Macedo), is the leader of the Universal Church of the Kingdom of God [UCKG], the NeoPentecostal church which grew between 1980 and 1990. The book details the basis of the UCKG's practices for exorcism and war against demons and the syncretic religions in Brazil.

13. Lima, *Analisando Crenças Espíritas e Umbandistas*, 30.

14. A critical study of the phenomenon is found in Berg and Preitz, *Spontaneous Combustion*, 114–15 and Garrard-Burnett and Stoll, *Rethinking Protestantism in Latin America*, 3.

Christ Changes Culture

though churches with liberal theology are called evangelicals in the country.[15] Catholics and sects are not part of the evangelical group in Brazil.

Second, the concept of translation—meaning, in Sanneh's definition, to proclaim the Gospel in a contextualized way—enables one to capture more accurately the dynamics of the Christian movement in history.[16] Sanneh argues that the Christian message needs to address the local culture because Christianity and culture are in "problematic relation."[17] Andrew Walls, for his part, sees in translation a double movement, that he calls the indigenizing and pilgrim principles.

If the population of believers in Jesus Christ increased quickly in Brazil over the last century, that would indicate that the growing churches understand how to translate the Gospel adequately for the Brazilian people. However, some of these churches may not be preaching the Gospel of Jesus Christ, but another Gospel.[18] In other words, churches that are successful in indigenizing the faith may be contributing to the rapid spread of the Gospel message across the country more rapidly. Twentieth century renewal movements in Brazil are an example of this reality.

Other concepts from WCS that are helpful for our purposes and inherent in evangelism and missions are transmission and appropriation. Transmission is the spread of the Christian message.[19] It is what Catholic and Protestant missionaries did in Brazil between the sixteenth and twentieth centuries. Each time a Congregational or Presbyterian minister taught about God, the cross, sin, heaven, hell, and the devil, they were transmitting the ancient faith. In turn, appropriation is the way one assimilates the faith into one's mind and living.

Sanneh states, "Converts were not cultural orphans or undiscriminating neophytes; rather, by virtue of the choice they have made, converts

---

15. For more information on the definition of "Evangelical," see Beggington, *Evangelicalism in Modern Britain*, 2–17.

16. Sanneh, *Translating the Message*, 53.

17. Sanneh, *Translating the Message*, 53.

18. The historical nature of this chapter does not allow for a further development of the matters of church growth and ecclesiology. More information on these topics can be found in Chapter 4. A crucial question to be asked at this point is: Is growth a reliable indicator of good translation? How is Brazilian society being transformed considering the supposed growth of the evangelical church in the country?

19. Walls, *Cross-Cultural Process in Christian History*. Transmisstion is also a rudimentary mechanism of any other religion, such as Islam and Buddism, Latourette, *History of Expansion of Christianity*, 3.

were involved in judgment and discernment at the same time that they were involved in appropriation and assimilation."[20] Once converted to the Christian faith, the neophytes had to assimilate their new spirituality into their old system of values, beliefs, and personal experiences. They had to ask questions that related their cultural and spiritual background with the new faith: What does the death of Christ have to do with the sacrifices from the ancient African religion? How sufficient is the work of Christ on the cross in comparison to the Catholic doctrine of good works? The answers depend on how a new convert appropriates the faith. As argued in the previous chapter and as one can see in these examples, WCWS concepts can help one to understand the reasons for the development and growth of the evangelical faith in Brazil, as detailed in the next section.

Factors That Contributed to Evangelical Growth

How did Brazil become one of the leading nations of Christianity in the Majority World and the whole world? Why is the evangelical population growing so fast in this country? First, the country had a Catholic beginning, a byproduct of its Portuguese colonization. Second, Protestant missions conceived and gave birth to the evangelical wing within the nation. Third, the renewal movements that happened in the twentieth century precipitated the growth. Finally, Brazilian culture and its evangelical variations are the most relevant background factor for the explosion of the Christian faith in Brazil.

The Catholic Beginning

When Portuguese colonizers arrived in Brazil in 1500, they brought with them the Catholic faith. Sherron K. George, a former Presbyterian missionary in Brazil asserts, "Catholic symbols and influence, imported from the Iberian Peninsula, have become an integral part of Brazilian culture and public space."[21] She describes the significant impact of Catholicism on the local culture.[22] Crosses, along with saints' statues, became commonplace inside houses, in the main square of the city, and on jewelry around

---

20. Sanneh, *Disciples of All Nations*, 12.
21. George, "Brazil: An 'Evangelized' Giant," 104.
22. George, "Brazil: An 'Evangelized' Giant," 104–9.

women's necks. Statues of Jesus Christ with open arms are seen not only in Rio de Janeiro, but also in smaller cities of Southern Minas Gerais states, such as Pouso Alegre and Poços de Caldas.[23] Even though there is no official religion in Brazil, the average Brazilian is likely to identify himself as either Catholic or Protestant.

Another example of the Catholic impact on Brazilian culture is the predominance of those churches in most cities. Whereas, in the southern region of the US, it is common to see a Southern Baptist or United Methodist church building in the downtown area of a city, and in Muslim countries, a mosque is the religious center of the city, in Brazil, Catholic churches are ubiquitous in town centers. However, evangelical churches are becoming more and more visible and present around the country, accompanying the religious demographic shift.[24]

Brazilian historians explain this Catholic predominance by describing the religious character of the Portuguese colonization. Brazilian Baptist historian, Israel Belo de Azevedo dedicates one section of *Cruzadas Inacabadas* to "The Church in the Colonial Period (1492–1810)" and another to "The Church and the National States (1810 to the Present)." Azevedo states that Catholic missionaries arrived in Brazil and found a native population with its own religiosity. The transmission of the Catholic faith in the country therefore witnessed several battles between colonizers and the original people of the Americas. Catholic translation took place in some brutal ways.

Azevedo affirms that the battles between the native population and the colonizers negatively shaped how local communities reacted to the imposition of Catholicism, especially given the violence used by the colonizers and the consequent destruction. The author concludes that all these lies, the treason, and the war that left deep emotional and behavioral scars among the indigenous people and "provoked . . . a justified anger for everything related to the invaders."[25]

The results were disastrous for the cause of Christianity. There was a clear rupture between the Christian message of love and care proclaimed by the missionaries and the horrendous destruction and death of many people

---

23. The author lived in the city of Pouso Alegre and visited Poços de Caldas. Southern Minas Gerais has a strong Catholic influence.

24. In cities such as Feira de Santana, Bahia state, where the author lived in the 1990's and early 2000's, there are as many evangelical temples as Catholic ones, even though Catholicism is still the predominant religion there.

25. Azevedo, *Cruzadas Inacabadas*, 49.

caused by their compatriot colonizers. Consequently, negative feelings in the hearts of the tribal nations became a barrier to the evangelization of the people, Azevedo points out. In Brazil, these previous conflicts among Catholic missionaries and the indigenous people still have negative impacts today for missionary work done by both foreigners and nationals.[26] For this reason, authorities responsible for overseeing the indigenous people tend to be restrictive of evangelical missionary work in Brazil.[27]

The decline of Catholicism began modestly with the arrival of evangelical missionaries in Brazil in the nineteenth century. The Protestant missionary incursion was the "turning point," for the evangelical revolution to come, as church historian Mark Noll states.[28] In this sense, since the arrival of the Protestant missionaries in the nineteenth century, conversionism, part of Bebbington's quadrilateral on Evangelicalism, has been a key practice for the transmission, appropriation, and translation of the Gospel in Brazil.[29]

The reason for the conflict between the established Catholic Church and the new evangelical expression was clear. Anti-Catholicism had long been one of the components to Protestant missionaries' transmission of the faith.[30] Yet in a similar dynamic, Southern Baptist missionary pioneers, also suffered opposition and persecution from the Catholic Church.[31] One of the founders of the First Baptist Church of Brazil, in the state of Bahia, was a priest who became a pastor.[32] The converts from Catholicism had

26. Fonteles, "Insertion of Protestantism in Brazil," 174–88.

27. Survival International describes the National Indian Foundation (Funai) as "the Brazilian government body that establishes and carries out policies relating to indigenous peoples," and "includes opposition" to the evangelical missionary enterprise. See more in http://www.survivalinternational.org/ about/funai.

28. According to Mark Noll, "turning points" in church history are "events, actions, or incidents . . . [that] may have marked an important fork in the road or signaled a new stage in the outworking of Christian history." Noll, *Turning Points*, 12.

29. Bebbington, *Evangelicalism in Modern Britain*, 2–17.

30. For this dissertation, anti-Catholicism is an important concept, given the Brazilian context of the research. In translating the Gospel into the Brazilian culture, especially in very Catholic cities, how is the soul-winner able to present the Gospel to a Catholic friend or neighbor? For comparative historical data on this topic, see the chapter "Anti-Catholicism and Evangelical Identity in Britain and the United States, 1830–860" in Mark Noll, David Bebbington, and Rawlyk, *Evangelicalism: Comparative Studies*. A similar study would be intriguing in Brazil and other Portuguese-speaking countries.

31. Oliveira and André, *Panorama Batista em Pernambuco*, 13–17.

32. Oliveira, *Centelha Em Restolho Seco*, 359. She is one of the main defenders of the idea that the church in Bahia is not the first one in the country. The author argues that there were other two Baptist churches founded by immigrants from the US.

to deal with their background, since religious experience is colored by the past. The coming of evangelical Christianity in Brazil meant people had to deal with the country's Catholic past.

Protestant Missions

The second reason for the growth of the evangelical people in Brazil is the Protestant missions that worked there, mainly from the eighteenth to the twentieth centuries.[33] That work officially began with the Scottish Presbyterian pioneer Robert Reid Kalley, who baptized the first Brazilian—Pedro Nolasco de Andrade—on July 11, 1858. This is considered the date when the Protestant work began in Brazil.[34] The following year, the North-American Presbyterian missionary Ashbel Green Simonton disembarked in Brazil.[35] The First Baptist church in Brazil was founded October 15, 1882, as a result of the work of the Southern Baptist missionaries William Buck and Ana Luther Bagby, from Texas, and another couple, Zachary Clay and Kate Crawford Taylor.[36]

Despite this evangelical beginning, in 2010, the Protestant population was 60 percent Pentecostal, 18.5 percent of groups originated from missionary work called historical churches, and 21.8 percent from other groups.[37] Pentecostalism became the major force in the country. David Stool, in the introduction of *Rethinking Protestantism in Latin America*, recalls that, despite the missionary "waves" from immigrant churches and

---

33. The first evangelical service in Brazil was officially held March 10, 1557, by French Calvinists. It was done inside a French colony called Antartic France. French colonization in Brazil was not successful. For more on the issue, read Mariz and Provençal, *Os Franceses na Guanabara*.

34. Léonard, *O Protestantismo Brasileiro*, 50.

35. Léonard, *O Protestantismo Brasileiro*, 54.

36. Oliveira, *Perseguidos, Mas Não Desamparados*, 51. It is relevant to add some works invaluable to studying Baptist work in Brazil. Two of them were written by Southern Baptist missionaries and another by a 20th-century Brazilian Baptist historian, Solomon Ginsburg. *A Wandering Jew in Brazil* is an autobiography of a Congregationalist missionary who became Baptist while in Brazil and was a leading figure in early stages of the denomination in the country given his evangelistic and musical skills, translating dozen of hymns into Portuguese. Second, A. R. Crabtree wrote *Historia dos Baptistas do Brasil*, the first volume of the historical summary until 1906. Also see Mesquita, *Historia dos Batistas do Brasil*. B books are rich in reliable details of the first churches, state conventions, and mission boards, containing pictures, dates, and other data.

37. IBGE, "Censo 2010."

mainline denominations in the US, Pentecostals became the main Christian power in Latin America.[38]

As George recounts, Protestant denominations planted the seeds for the evangelical expansion in the following century by focusing on "the centrality of the Bible, evangelistic preaching, and planting new churches."[39] Factors such as the centrality of the Bible in Protestant preaching, preaching in Portuguese, and the distribution of Bibles were all crucial for opening people's hearts to the Gospel, particularly because Catholic masses were in Latin—a colossal barrier for communicating with the people.[40]

To handle and interact with the Bible in one's own language—linguistic translation—is one example of Walls' indigenizing principle. A convert who is a Christian and yet, a member of his own people, identifying as the community of speakers of a language, has the power to show that Christianity and local culture can be compatible.[41] The translation of the Bible to the vernacular is an example of cultural translation. The diffusion of the Bible into Portuguese through Protestant missionaries is another turning point for evangelical growth that is still taking place in contemporary Brazil.

Mortimer Arias' overview of the Christian faith in Latin America reinforces this narrative of the indigenization of the Gospel through the translation of the Scriptures.[42] In "The Protestant Transplant: Missionary Evangelization," he depicts the Protestant work as taking place particularly through methods such as distribution of the Bible, tracts, and Christian literature. In 1959, another author made a similar statement. In presenting the state of evangelism among Brazilian evangelicals, Antônio de Campos Gonçalves mentions the increasing number of copies of the Bible available to the people, along with other evangelical literature and media such as radio and TV, which, he notes, contributed to the growth of evangelical Christianity in Brazil.[43]

Both Gonçalves and Arias note that Gospel indigenization occurred through cultural means. The former, a Presbyterian minister and scholar, highlights the positive impact of evangelicals occupying social and political

---

38. Garrard-Burnett and Stoll, *Rethinking Protestantism in Latin America*, 3.
39. George, "Brazil," 105.
40. Schwaller, *History of the Catholic Church*.
41. Walls, *Missionary Movement*, 7.
42. Arias, "Contextual Evangelization in Latin America," 19–28.
43. Gonçalves, "Evangelism in Brazil Today," 302–8.

positions of influence in Brazil.⁴⁴ Arias, a Uruguayan Methodist bishop, praises the presence of educational institutions in the Portuguese-speaking country. João Camilo de Oliveira Torres mentions this same type of indigenizing practice. The evangelical schools made new converts "thanks to a type of religion more participative, to the reading of the Bible, to a more moralized and conscious education."⁴⁵ Christian schools became a form of "indirect evangelization."⁴⁶

Even though Catholic missionaries and their churches continued to be hegemonic, another kind of Christianity was subtly coming into play. Brazilian Evangelicalism was born with the arrival of Protestant missionaries at the end of the nineteenth century and the Pentecostal start in Brazil in the twentieth century accelerated its growth. A shift in the leadership of the new Brazilian Christian church was decisive for the establishment of evangelical in the country as detailed in the next section. At the same time, renewal movements were birthed in Protestant and in Pentecostal churches. The evangelical boom had started in the largest country in South America.

Renewal Movements

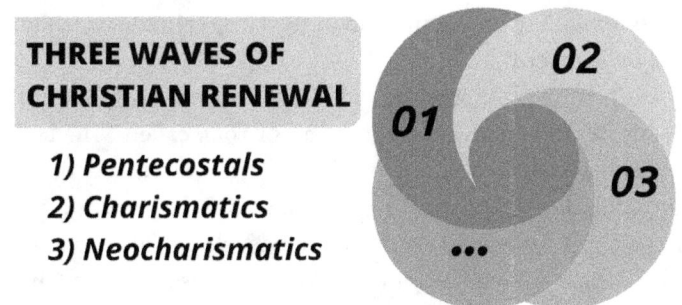

Figure 8. The Three-Wave Movement of Pentecostalism Around the World

When the Pentecostal movement arrived in Brazil at the beginning of the twentieth century, Protestant churches were undergoing diverse changes.⁴⁷ Foreign missionaries provided the initial leadership and then

---

44. Gonçalves, "Evangelism in Brazil Today," 306–7.
45. Torres, *História das Ideias Religiosas no Brasil*, 280.
46. Léonard, *O Protestantismo Brasileiro*, 315.
47. Pew Research Center, "Spirit and Power."

relinquished that role to nationals. The Protestant missionary movement in Brazil went through a series of "waves" or phases, as detailed in the chart above.[48] These phases represent how Evangelicalism grew in Brazil in the twentieth century. In the first wave, the missionaries came from overseas and planted churches. In the second one, nationals became the leaders of local churches and denominations. In the third wave, new churches and denominations were birthed out of the preceding ones. Garrard-Burnett and Stoll consider Pentecostalism a fourth wave of the Protestant movement.[49] Other authors use the same three-wave's model to describe the Pentecostal movement in Brazil, such as Mark Shaw in *Global Awakening*.[50] Pentecostalism is a major player in the explosion of Christianity not only in Brazil but in the Majority World.[51]

The second and third waves, i.e., the birth and explosive growth of indigenous churches, point out the indigenous principle of translation. Part of the reasons for this success is that Pentecostalism offers its followers an open door for meeting needs and fulfilling aspirations in a fast-paced changing socio-cultural reality over the last decades.[52] The offering of healing, emotionally exciting experiences, and community-based life, with a network of support and accountability, makes Pentecostal churches attractive to people from different socio-economic strata. In a general sense, this is an expression of the indigenization of the Gospel in the Brazilian culture promoted by Pentecostals.[53]

To study this phenomenon, Historical Protestants, Catholics, and Pentecostals held a symposium in the Fall of 1965 called "The Holy Ghost and the Pentecostal Movement," at which they discussed the Brazilian Christian landscape. Their observations and debate present a portrait of the church at that time and specifically the development of Evangelicalism in Brazil. Leaders such as Manoel de Melo, represented the Charismatic wing in the symposium. Melo was the head of *O Brasil para Cristo* (Brazil for Christ), a second wave Pentecostal church and one of the fast-growing

---

48. Garrard-Burnett and Stoll, *Rethinking Protestantism in Latin America*, 3.
49. Garrard-Burnett and Stoll, *Rethinking Protestantism in Latin America*, 3.
50. Shaw, *Global Awakening*, 138–46.
51. George, "Brazil, an Evangelized Giant," 105 and Johnson et at., *Atlas of Global Christianity 1910–2010*.
52. Camargo, *Católicos, Protestantes, Espíritas*, 147–48.
53. The Brazilian Baptist approach is dealt with in Chapters 4–7. The communitarian feature is shared by all Brazilian evangelicals.

denominations in the 1960's. During the meeting, Melo affirmed that Pentecostals are faithful to the poor, both in soul saving and the practical side of daily life. "The Brazilian situation provides the topics for Pentecostal evangelism" and finds resonance with the basic needs of the Third World, summed up Walter J. Hollenweger, Secretary for Evangelism in the Division of World Mission and Evangelism of the World Council of Churches, writing about the symposium.[54]

Renewal (Charismatic) movements also sprouted inside evangelical churches, causing splits in the Baptist, Presbyterian, Methodist, and other denominations. The new churches were also responsible for the explosive growth in the overall evangelical Brazilian movement. With the new groups, the Evangelical church gained prominence in the country while interacting and morphing with the local culture, as discussed in the following chapters.

Brazilian Culture and Evangelical Morphing

The Catholic beginning, Protestant missions, and renewal movements, with the explosion of Pentecostalism, were the three factors that contributed to the evangelical growth in the country. Finally, the Brazilian culture welcomed the Protestant faith to the country. The social and political crises, especially during the 1960s and 1970s, stimulated new forms of transmission, appropriation, and translation of the Gospel.

To study the history of the church in Brazil and other Latin America countries, one must take into consideration how cultural, social, economic, and political factors interacted with the Christian proclamation. Some authors highlight and even emphasize these factors, especially scholars who represent a Liberation Theology perspective. Arias, for example, discusses how the political revolution affected the church in Brazil.[55] This discussion clearly expresses the pilgrim principle in action. For example, torture, corruption, and other evil realities present in oppressive regimes in Brazil from the 1960s to 1980s were against human life and freedom. For this reason, Christians ought to pray for the political situation of the country and its politicians, and in some cases, engage actively in the public arena. Arias insists that the church "cannot compromise with any force that oppresses or dehumanizes man."[56]

---

54. Hollenweger, "Evangelism and Brazilian Pentecostalism," 163–70.
55. Arias, *Contextual Evangelization in Latin America*, 24–26.
56. Arias, *Contextual Evangelization in Latin America*, 26.

David Martin observes, "It was during this period of population growth, of movement and of intermittent populism that Pentecostalism expanded most rapidly. Pentecostalism was fully indigenous and able to provide an all-encompassing world-view for marginalized people, especially in the vast urban agglomerations in the Southeast and São Paulo."[57] Martin is a foreign scholar who become curious about the role of Pentecostals in the religious scene in Brazil.[58] As he points out, several factors worked towards the leadership of the Pentecostals in the steady growth of evangelicals in the last sixty years.[59]

In this sense, the sociocultural forces operating in Brazil in the twentieth century shaped the evangelical church. The Prosperity Gospel, Liberation Theology, and Conservative Theology offer a different approach to the same reality. The first one focuses on financial success. Liberation Theology, a Latin American version of the Social Gospel from the US, Europe, and Africa, prioritizes meeting the needs of the poor. Gonçalves portrays this debate and traces the influence of theologians such as Richard Shaull, from Princeton University, over a generation of Brazilian scholars towards Liberation Theology.[60] Meanwhile, Conservatives continued to defend the primacy of the proclamation of the Gospel and the teachings of the Bible over all else, including poverty and political issues.

Modern Protestant movements in Brazil in the 80's and 90's went beyond Liberation, Conservative, Pentecostal, or Neopentecostals (Prosperity Gospel) theologies to an alternative and indigenous kind of renewal movements, such as Salt of the Earth church. Mark Shaw studied this group and narrated that, for this church, contextualization went beyond local church planting. They explored *glocalization* while doing missions in England.[61] The church also had "a strong commitment to the poor."[62] This demon-

---

57. Martin, *Tongues of Fire*, 65.

58. Paul Freston is another example. He is one of the lead contemporary Christian scholars in Brazil, with teaching positions at both international and Brazilian schools. His main interests are the intersection between politics and evangelicals in Brazil and the Neopentecostal movement. For a glimpse of his work, see his chapter (the ninth) of Lewis, *Christianity Reborn*.

59. A comprehensive study of diverse facts (geographical, demographical, missionary, among others) is done by Read and Ineson, *Brazil 1980*.

60. Gonçalves, "De Uma Teologia Canned," 65. Shaull's influence is studied also by Barreto Jr.

61. Shaw, *Global Awakening*, 149.

62. Shaw, *Global Awakening*, 150.

strated that churches can offer contextualized answers to their cultures, which go beyond traditional labels or formats.

Culture invites contextual transmission, appropriation, and translation of the Gospel. This is particularly true in a hybrid culture such as Brazil. It is formed first by its Indigenous people (the *Índios*), then, since colonization by the Portuguese and Africans, it has been further mixed thanks to immigrants from Europe, Asia, and other continents. Thus, the Brazilian evangelical church gained breadth and width, and its new leadership found a Brazilian way to promote growth, though not always in terms of evangelical theology. Yet, it was God who provided the solution for sin, a supranational reality.

The art of touching the hearts of the local people and offering solutions to their practical problems has become a challenge to some churches, especially the Historical ones. Pentecostals and particularly the renewal movements have been more efficient in dialoguing with the national realities, though sometimes they did not affirm the basic tenets of the Christian faith. This issue is discussed in the following section.

Pentecostal Growth

Scholars have observed several reasons for this discrete growth of churches that originated from foreign missions. Take, for example, Torres and his 1968 book *História das Idéias Religiosas no Brasil* (History of the Religious Ideas in Brazil). His evaluation of the Protestant churches is brief since he deals with the breadth of religious groups and ideas in the country, but he notes two main reasons for the relatively small presence of groups such as the Presbyterians, Methodists, and Baptists, on Brazilian soil.[63] First, the minority presence of Reformed churches inspired prudence and lack of involvement in public matters. One can imagine that this hidden style in the public arena did not give the necessary visibility and consequent exposition and openness to Historical evangelicals. Second, the author classifies the international groups, such as the Lutherans with the German people, for example, as a barrier to cultural engagement.[64]

Concerning Protestants in Brazil, Torres presented two more facts which were both bridges and barriers for the expansion of the traditional

---

63. Torres, *História das Ideias Religiosas no Brasil*, 279–80.

64. This issue is discussed further in Chapter 5, where there are interviews and analyses about immigrant churches.

churches. First, he reinforces that these churches started the so-called *Colégios Americanos* (North American schools). As previously noted, these institutions proselytized and became competition to the Catholic schools. In so doing, they increased the educational level of people in the country. One can also contend that the elitism of those schools was a barrier to the spread of historical churches. Torres praised groups that emphasized biblical teaching among the popular social strata. The interest of such groups in translating the Gospel for the poor promoted transformation, for they modeled a type of religion that was more participatory, encouraged the reading of the Bible, was more moralized, and provided a conscious education.[65]

Both Catholics and Pentecostals made a clear option for the poor in Brazil in the twentieth century. Catholics chose Liberation Theology in the 1960s, but in so doing, they forgot to teach the message of the cross. Pentecostals tried to translate the Gospel for the poor, providing room for social and financial improvement. Martins and Pádua aptly remarked, the Catholic church made an option for the poor with Liberation Theology, but paradoxically, the poor chose the Pentecostal church.[66]

The working class and poor strata of the population are attracted to those kinds of churches, and this fact favors the emergence of a religious market.[67] Martins and Pádua highlight the promotion of self-esteem as a triumph of the Pentecostal church, together with the moral strictness that keeps families united and provides support for good times and bad. This support system is very necessary in major cities, where Pentecostal growth is particularly visible.[68]

As Rudolf von Sinner notes, in the largest Catholic and Pentecostal nation of the world a strong escapist discourse contrasts with the consciousness of bearing the Holy Spirit, which empowers people to overcome hardships and sufferings in life. Besides that, the political representation of Pentecostal churches, which has increased so greatly in the last twenty years, has strengthened the broader perception of their prestige and relevance.[69]

Another author points to some features of Brazilian religiosity to explain the Pentecostal growth in Brazil. Adilson Schultz suggests that Brazilians see God as the supreme being powerful enough to overcome the devil,

---

65. Torres, *História das Ideias Religiosas no Brasil*, 280.
66. Martins and Pádua, "Option for the Poor," 154.
67. Martins and Pádua, "Option for the Poor," 147.
68. Martins and Pádua, "Option for the Poor," 154.
69. Sinner, "Pentecostalism and Citizenship in Brazil," 112–13.

who causes unhappiness, death, pain, demonic possession, unemployment, illness, and corruption, among other things. As Schultz puts it, "The irreducibility of the evil demands an irreducible God, who is always beside the believer to deliver him from evil."[70] With a clear theology of spiritual warfare, the Pentecostal church became attractive to people in a country with a background of Animism and African religions and where economic growth benefits only a small part of society. Many of the aforementioned evils are still prevalent and addressed in the preaching of Pentecostal and Charismatic churches.

The literature on the Pentecostal church in Latin America is vast. One of these relevant works is *Born Again in Brazil—The Pentecostal Boom and the Pathogens of Poverty*, by R. Andrew Chestnut. The book is an analysis of the Pentecostal expansion among the poor, occupying the space left void by the Catholic Church and other evangelical ones. The author notes that the Pentecostal movement infiltrated the historic churches too.[71] In the 1960's, the BBC split because of differences over the doctrine of the Holy Spirit. The churches of the new group, called the National Baptist Convention, have more visibility than the ones from the BBC.[72]

Another classic work on the topic is the *Pentecostalism and the Future of the Christian Churches*, by Shaull and Cesar. One of the dynamics they note regarding the reasons for the growth of the Pentecostal communities in Brazil is the frequency of their church attendance. By contrast, they suggest that only a minority of Catholics attend mass regularly, and that some members of historical churches attend only for Christmas, Easter, and special services, such as baptisms, marriages, and funerals. In some churches, there are essentially two "congregations": one group goes to the morning service and the other to the evening service.[73] This reality may point out to a spiritual coldness in historical evangelical churches. Thus, there are

---

70. Schultz, "Estrutura Religiosa do Imaginário Religioso Brasileiro," 60.

71. Chesnut. *Born Again in Brazil*, 3.

72. One example is the Lagoinha Baptist Church, in Belo Horizonte, the capital of Minas Gerais state. Lagoinha is one of the larges churches in Brazil, well-known because of its music ministry called *Diante do Trono*, TV network, and fashion brands, beside other products and celebrities.

73. This observation comes from the author's experience as a local church pastor. Some churches, such as Metropolitan Baptist Church, in Salvador, Bahia state, have chosen to have the same service twice in the morning and once in the evening to adapt to this reality. Brazilian Baptists face a challenging time. The *Igreja Multiplicadora* movement is a response to the plateaued state of the BBC.

as many nominal Baptists or Presbyterians as nominal Catholics in Brazil. Meanwhile, many Pentecostals go to church daily or almost daily.[74] Having analyzed the factors for evangelical growth and the Pentecostal boom, the following sections present ways for mutual learning and other factors shaping contemporary Evangelicalism in Brazil.

Mutual Learning

Historical denominations can learn much from their Pentecostal brethren, particularly from their strong focus on prayer, fasting, righteousness (or holiness), and church discipline. In the conclusion of *Pentecostalism and the Future of the Christian Churches*, Shaull and Cesar advise both groups: "to work together in order to draw fully on the resources of the Spirit at work in community to empower such efforts and develop new forms of theological reflection on society."[75] Brazilian Baptists can learn to pray more and recover church discipline with their brothers and sisters from the Assembly of God of Brazil.[76] At the same time, the latter have learned from their evangelical brethren how to translate the Gospel for their context, even in simple matters such as modest clothing, a negative example of translation of the Gospel in the Pentecostal churches. The typical clothing of Pentecostals can be inappropriate and uncomfortable in the hot Brazilian climate. Evangelical women have been able to dress more appropriately for the weather while continuing to be modest.

As David W. Bebbington concludes in *Baptists Through the Centuries*, "Baptists have conscientiously attempted, with varying degrees of success, to embody the Gospel in their cultures."[77] It is an ongoing challenge for the Brazilian Baptist church. The growth of the various types of Pentecostal churches, including those that espouse the Prosperity Gospel, Neopentecostalism, and newer movements known by their charismatic emphasis on signs and wonders, likewise affects Baptist churches.[78] Martins and Pádua analyze the phenomenon and list some of the features of Pentecostalism

---

74. Shaull and Cesar, *Pentecostalism and the Future*, 87.

75. Shaull and Cesar, *Pentecostalism and the Future*, 231.

76. Church discipline, in this case, should be done for biblical reasons. Issues like clothing or customs and habits may still be a prevalent cause for church discipline in the Assembly of God in Brazil.

77. Bebbington, *Baptists Through the Centuries*, 285.

78. Erickson, *Christian Theology*, 872–73.

in Brazil, its marked missionary style, aesthetics, emotional appeal during the services, baptism in the Holy Spirit, healing, speaking in tongues, expulsion of demons and liberation from evil, and prosperity preaching. The Pentecostal style has a strong appeal to the local culture and sociocultural Brazilian realities, even though some of these features are not legitimate translations of the Gospel.[79]

The cultural and religious heritage that impacts Baptist churches include the growth of the Prosperity Gospel movement in the last decades. In one sense, Prosperity Gospel churches are similar to Pentecostal churches, because of their individualistic response to the collectivistic Liberation Theology of the 1960s and 1970s. Under such circumstances, mainline churches felt obliged to combat heresies, argue, and preach the pure Gospel, while being aware of the confusion in the minds of the public among whom they share the transforming message of Christ.[80] As Erickson posits, the Gospel is at the heart of the church, being implicit in all the functions of the church. For him, the character of the church is its willingness to serve and its adaptability.[81]

Music, TV, and Media

Other influences of the Pentecostal and Neopentecostal movement over the Baptist churches are notable. First, one can mention the musical influence. Songs in this tradition tend to emphasize the Holy Spirit and angelic activity "in the middle of the congregation" and life of the believers, the nullification of curses, and other topics related to spiritual warfare. In the last decade, when the Prosperity Gospel and Faith Movement became very popular, the lyrics of the songs started to mirror this interest in prosperity and healing. Some BBC congregations sing compositions whose texts were against the main doctrines of the denomination. The mix of doctrines sparked problems and divisions, while attracting the attention of believers with Pentecostal tendencies.

In the opposite direction, Baptists also influenced, or at least, inspired and modeled Pentecostal, Neopentecostal, and Charismatic churches in

79. Some Pentecostal traits bring about syncretism, as will be discussed in Chapters 5–7.

80. See the memoirs of BBC leaders in their critical analysis of NeoPentecostalism and Prosperity Gospel in Chapters 5–7.

81. Erickson, *Christian Theology*, 1060–61

Brazil regarding the use of mass media. Baptists were present on radio and TV in the middle of the last century. Nilson do Amaral Fanini, former president of both the BBC and Baptist World Alliance, maintained a program for decades in a public TV station. David Gomes, former executive of the NMB, aired a radio broadcasting at stations around the country. At present, the Prosperity Gospel, Pentecostal, and Neopentecostal pastors are the ones who occupy hours and hours of TV time. Where the Baptist leader Fanini was a Conservative champion in the 1970s and 1980s, the Pentecostal leader Silas Malafaia is a notable voice of Brazilian evangelicals today.[82]

Candomblé: African-Brazilian Religion

Finally, the situation in the state of Bahia, challenges the Baptist church in how to reach out to the members of that group, namely the Afro-Brazilian religion known as Candomblé.[83] This introductory case study is an example of the religious diversity that evangelicals face in the country which will be discussed more in the following chapter. In Candomblé, West African deities are worshiped. For the sake of acceptance in the time of slavery, those gods were paired with God, Jesus, Mary, and the saints of the Catholic Church. In a religion where the gods act on behalf of the people for healing, prosperity, and resolution to emotional problems, people look for much the same benefits in evangelical churches. Neopentecostal and Prosperity Gospel churches already offer such benefits. Will historical churches be silent about the healing power of God or try to offer a balanced approach to the matter?

Another feature of *Candomblé* that affects evangelical churches is the use of percussive musical instruments. Both churches in Salvador the capital of the state, and around the country uses the same drums of the African-Brazilian tradition. In *Candomblé*, women also lead the services and ritual activities, functioning as priestesses and mediums. What is the impact of this concept on Baptist churches in a culture in which women are active and have a voice in the house and in the market place? It is one question that Baptist churches are already dealing with, specifically in their ongoing discussion about women's pastoral ordination. One should not assume peremptorily that *Candomblé* directly influences this practice of women

---

82. More about Malafaia's influence is described in the next chapter.

83. In Rio de Janeiro and Rio Grande do Sul states, its correspondent is *Umbanda*. The influence of spiritualists religions in Brazil is addressed in Chapters 5, 6, and 7.

in the pastorate, but the acceptance of the practice by some groups may be connected with their cultural heritage.[84]

The existence of a local religion motivates the establishment of new indigenous churches, with practices that are a counterpart or even a repetition of the local tradition, even more in a place that tended to naturalize the connection between *Candomblé* and blackness.[85] The quick growth of third wave Brazilian churches with small direct influence from foreign denominations focused attention on the indigenous religiosity. Baptist pastors, leaders, and members may consider that phenomenon and rethink their own structures and practices, not forgetting the Baptist distinctives. As Willian Lane Craig notes, "The Gospel is never heard in isolation. It is always heard against the background of the cultural milieu in which one lives."[86]

Conclusion

This chapter discussed the factors that contributed most to the growth of the evangelical population in Brazil. First, the Catholic beginnings of the country since 1500 became both a bridge and a barrier for Protestant missions starting in the nineteenth century. Then, indigenous Evangelicalism opened doors for renewal movements in the twentieth century in Brazil. Finally, the Brazilian culture, coupled with new religious expressions, favored the evangelical growth seen in Brazil as seen today. A summary of the Brazilian evangelical church is pictured below.

---

84. Landes, "Fetish Worship in Brazil," 261.
85. Selka, "Ethnoreligious Identity Politics in Bahia," 92–94.
86. Craig, *Reasonable Faith*.

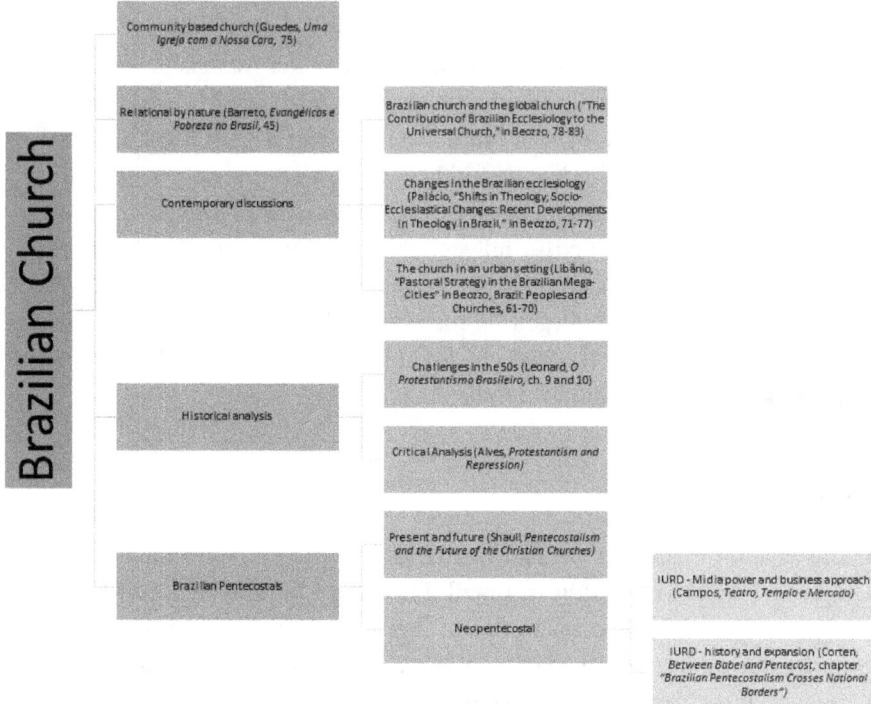

Figure 9. Brazilian Church Contemporary Scenario

How Brazilian Baptists embody the Gospel in their culture is a study worth pursuing. After all, though the Gospel remains the same, cultures are always changing. For this reason, studies on World Christianity are an ongoing task. Given the diversity of evangelicals today, it is hard to foresee what might happen in the future. Campos anticipated four scenarios: (1) Pentecostalized Protestantism; (2) Protestantized Pentecostalism; (3) Decline of the Pentecostal movement; and (4) Decomposition of the present religious field.[87] To maintain their evangelical roots, Brazilian evangelicals should embrace a Conservative theology and a contextualized ecclesiology, for instance, a community-based one, as Guedes suggests. The NMB is attempting to implement this model, as discussed in the next chapter, which also contemplates Brazilian literature on evangelism and discipleship in the second part of the twentieth century. Christ meets, engages, changes and challenges culture.

87. Campos, "Why Historic Churches are Declining." More on these trending topics in Chapters 6 and 7.

4

Christ Challenges Culture

*Towards a Brazilian Baptist Theology
of Evangelism and Discipleship*

THIS DISSERTATION ARGUES THAT sociocultural factors play a significant role in the translation of the Gospel in Brazil, specifically in the BBC. The shorthand for this process of encounter is "Christ meets culture." Whereas, the previous chapters presented the encounter, engagement, and changes promoted by this encounter, this chapter explores how Christ challenges culture in the BBC context as expressed through contemporary theology and practices.

The previous chapter noted that the denomination began in Brazil because of the activity of Southern Baptist missionaries and efforts of Baptist churches in the global North over the last two centuries. This missionary endeavor may be interpreted as an outcome of the marriage between Baptist identity and local cultures, particularly in England and the US, where Baptists assimilated biblical truth and local culture into their ecclesiology, which connects Christianity with particular tenets of democracy. The US, as a product of British colonization, adapted Baptist distinctives to its local reality and gave birth to the Southern Baptist Convention [SBC], the largest Baptist denomination in the world. Southern Baptists kept the core features of British Baptists, but in dealing with local issues, such as slavery, they took different approaches.[1] This diffusion of the Christian faith

---

1. Immigration, ethnicity, and gender identity are the focus of some of the present cultural wars affecting Christians in the US, Brazil, and the globalized world.

around the globe, seen in the growth and strengthening of the church in the global South in countries such as Brazil, warrants an emic study about the proclamation of the Gospel in local contexts.

How are the doctrines of evangelism and discipleship from a conservative evangelical perspective expressed in the contemporary Brazilian Baptist movement? What biblical, historical, and doctrinal influences have affected the development of the present contextual theology of Brazilian Baptists? More specifically, how does culture affect evangelism and discipleship among Baptists in Brazil? Before addressing these questions, one should define self-theologizing. This chapter evaluates the National Mission Board's [NMB] evangelism and discipleship model called *Igreja Multiplicadora* (Multiplying Church), finding it to be an example of self-theologizing, one that is directly influenced by the collectivist traits of the indigenous church models prevalent in Brazil.

Self-Theologizing: Concept and Examples

Walls, in the foreword to *Theology in the Context of World Christianity*, argues that whenever the Gospel crosses cultural frontiers, it meets other faiths and religions in a specific local context. These encounters require "Christians to make a Christian choice and to formulate the reasons for that choice."[2] Consequently, self-theologizing is natural and imperative. First, it is natural because a person naturally "makes" theology as he considers faith issues or the implications of faith for life, reason, contemporary problems, and eternity. The issue in this research concerns analyzing the self-theologizing work of professional theologians and denominational leaders as it reflects the official position of the BBC regarding translating the Gospel to the nation.

Second, self-theologizing is imperative. Peter admonishes Christians "always [to] be prepared to give an answer to everyone who asks you to give the reason for the hope that you have" (1 Pet 3:15).[3] Lewis R. Donelson interprets this passage as encouragement to be ready to give questioners theological explanations and present the Gospel to them.[4] Reinhard Feldmeier argues that the defense of the faith is not realized "in a sectarian separation

---

2. Tennent, *Theology in the Context of World Christianity*, 190.

3. The New International Version [NIV] is used in this chapter unless otherwise noted.

4. Donelson, *I & II Peter and Jude*, 105.

from the surrounding world but in readiness for dialogue."[5] In essence, contextualization is dialogue between the Christian message and local cultures where one intentionally speaks the truth in love so that people can fully understand the Gospel message and make a decision for Christ.

Several biblical texts indicate the transforming power of God's Word and the Gospel. As John Goldingay points out, Isaiah 55:10–11 reveals that Yahweh always succeeds in fulfilling His plans, and that His success can occur through actions of human authorities such as Cyrus.[6] In the same way, Ivan Friesen asserts that just as the Word of the Lord transformed Israel's culture and daily circumstances, God's people in any nation are able to experience this transformation.[7] God is intricately involved in human history, (Cf. Isa 40–55). His words are effective against oppressive nations and cultural systems such as Babylon.[8] Today, God's Word spoken aloud still affects the world and its cultures (Cf. Rom 10:17).

Paul's hymn in 1 Timothy 3:14–16, especially the portion that envisions God as preached among the nations and believed in the world, describes the penetrating effect of truth. As I. Howard Marshall concludes, Gentiles throughout the whole world have a pivotal place in the fulfillment of God's plan of salvation.[9] For this reason, Bill Kynes affirms the church is called to witness to the good news, serving as "the pillar and protector of the truth."[10] The Gentiles, in its broader meaning of "nations," are involved in God's eternal salvific plan.[11] Thus, self-theologizing takes place as believers become heralds of the Gospel, as the next section debates.

Self-Theologizing: World, Latin America, Brazil

This section presents some examples of self-theologizing or contextual theology to show it is a global and ongoing process. It gives a sense of the different ways the subject is approached. First, *Interpreting Contemporary Christianity*, edited by Ogbu U. Kalu, portrays contextual theologies that

5. Feldmeier, *First Letter of Peter*, 195. For an eschatological approach, see Blaising, "Day of the Lord Will Come," 387–401.
6. Goldingay, *Isaiah*, 314.
7. Friesen, *Isaiah*, 347.
8. Lessing, "Yahweh versus Marduk," 240.
9. Marshall, *Pastoral Epistles*, 527–28.
10. Kynes, "Church: A Hidden Glory," 34.
11. Gloer, *1 & 2 Timothy-Titus*, 164.

are diverse and historically relevant for contemporary global Christianity.[12] For example, in Chapter 2, entitled, "Globalization, Religion, and Evangelical Christianity: A Sociological Meditation from the Third World," Freston presents not only a Third World perspective, but also Brazilian particularities, such as the growth of the national Assemblies of God.[13] Other authors, such as Dana L. Robert, Joel Carpenter, and Afe Adogame speak to issues of local and world Christianity. Similar in its transcultural approaches, authors, overview of contextual theology, and description of local beliefs is the book, *Called to One Hope: The People in Diverse Cultures*, edited by Christopher Duraisingh.[14]

Two specific examples of self-theologizing in the Majority World are *Musing with Confucius and Paul: Toward a Chinese Christian Theology*, by K. K. Yeo, and *Biblical Christianity from an African Perspective*, by Wilbur O'Donovan Jr.[15] These authors address Christian truths from a national or continental standpoint. O'Donovan is a North American scholar who taught in Ethiopia while writing this book. He shows how certain aspects of the continent's worldview, such as attitudes and beliefs about ancestors, spiritual warfare, and polygamy, affect believers, pastors, and churches. He comments on what the Bible says about these topics. The authors deal with these topics to interpret and apply biblical truth to local issues so that believers can live out their faith in a contextually relevant and courageous way, as is the ultimate purpose of self-theologizing.

Another book, *Global Theology in Evangelical Perspective*, presents thoughtful considerations on the relationship between theology and culture in diverse settings of World Christianity.[16] This exploration covers a wide range of contexts and expressions of Christianity. Jeffrey P. Greenman and Gene L. Green note, "While all the authors of this volume embrace a high view of the authority of Scripture, they also recognize how God speaks to them where they live and addresses the needs and concerns raised among their communities."[17] In essence, the authors explore how Christianity expresses itself in diverse cultures, times, and places. Andrew Walls' discusses contextual theologies in the NT and Early Church. The other authors

---

12. Kalu, *Interpreting Contemporary Christianity*.
13. Kalu, *Interpreting Contemporary Christianity*, 355–710.
14. Duraisingh, *Called to One Hope*.
15. Yeo, *Musing with Confucius and Paul*.
16. Greenman and Green, *Global Theology in Evangelical Perspective*.
17. Greenman and Green, *Global Theology in Evangelical Perspective*, 64.

address more contemporary issues in Non-Western and North-American contexts; they examine several reasons for the birth and survival of some local realities. The last part of the book proposes some implications for the church, mission, and theological education around the globe.

In Chapter 7, Ken Gnanakan presents the contextualizing dynamic of the Christian message in its journey, noting, "The Gospel that came into a Jewish setting has continued to adapt itself wherever it is making inroads."[18] He asserts that whatever the context or culture, the Gospel kept morphing into new expressions and flavors. As Sanneh argues, sometimes, the Gospel mixes with culture, and the pilgrim principle is identified. Whereas, in other cases, the Gospel challenges believers and churches to proclaim and enable change.

Some of the book's contributors explore Latin American theologies. For example, in her chapter, "Songs of Hope Out of a Crying Land," Ruth Padilla DeBorst questions why Central and South America were receptive to Liberation Theology or *Missão Integral* (Integral Mission) in the second half of twentieth century. Prompted by Padilla's discussions, the reader also considered other implications of dictatorships and imperialistic regimes in those countries at those times. For example: How would one react to being tortured? Is it biblically correct to oppose authorities and governments? What were the feelings and thoughts of North American missionaries serving in Latin American countries at that particular time of political, economic, and social struggles?

Sanneh, in *Global Theology in Evangelical Perspective*, affirms that translation, both linguistic and cultural, is conducive to church renewal and theological reflection. For him, "Religion must adopt the cultural forms of its environment. It is only in the 'feedback' of cultural response that we know when and how the message has struck home."[19] For example, Vincent Bacote challenges the duality of race and theology present in African American theology, with all passion involved in these particular theologies. When making a connection to Brazilian culture, one should determine biblical and evangelical ways for making disciples in the context of local problems, such as poverty and violence. Another provocative and engaging book in the field is *Theology without Borders: An Introduction to Global Conversations*, by William A. Dyrness and Oscar Garcia-Johnson.[20] The fact that

---

18. Greenman and Green, *Global Theology in Evangelical Perspective*, 1159–60.
19. Greenman and Green, *Global Theology in Evangelical Perspective*, 395–96.
20. Dyrness and Garcia-Johnson, *Theology without Borders*.

they are writing from two different perspectives (i.e., White/American and Latino) attests that it is possible to have "global conversations."

Given God's commandment for humanity to love Him above anything (Matt 22:37), and the fact that creation is inferior to the Creator, practicing an ongoing personal relationship with God is an appropriate expression of loving Him. Humankind is essential to God and has its place and value, but to know and love Him is an incomparable task. Thus, Dyrness and Garcia-Johnson propose a theology that considers different people and cultures around the globe by addressing the supernatural and magical realities of Africa in its theological reflection.[21] For example, from an emic perspective, a Brazilian theology might consider healing in the context of the poverty in which so many Brazilian people live. Poor people cannot pay the high costs of health insurance. Public health is in chaotic situation. Thus, healing is one of the emphases of Pentecostalism. In other words, there are always practical reasons for local expressions of faith. For the average church member and pastor of indigenous churches (Assembly of God of Brazil or Christian Congregation of Brazil), a crisis concerning the truthfulness and reliability of the Bible is not part of their daily lives. Given that suffering and the way of the cross are not forgotten in this country, there are more important matters to deal with.[22]

In the end, Dyrness and Garcia-Johnson propose that theology be developed by "dealing with the real subjects affecting the communion-making process in the body of Christ (racialization, colonialism, classism, sexism, militarism, globalism, exploitation, to mention a few."[23] One may ask, "Is engaged theology or socio-political theology, in which practical issues are put first, theology? Is Black Theology real theology"? The goal of theology is to affect real life, since God entered the world through His Son so that it could be saved. Yet, never will those who have been saved and their concerns have priority over the Savior and their Creator, but He cares so deeply about mankind that He enter in those humans realms too.

M. Daniel Carrol R. proposed that authors from Latin America think *latinamente* (a Latino perspective) to promote theological engagement and life impact.[24] However, as cautioned in Chapter 2, one should be careful when approaching theology wearing cultural glasses. For example, Oscar

---

21. Dyrness and Garcia-Johnson, *Theology Without Borders*, 2051.
22. Dyrness and Garcia-Johnson, *Theology Without Borders*, 1323–1325.
23. Dyrness and Garcia-Johnson, *Theology Without Borders*, 3011–3012.
24. Carroll R., "Reading the Bible through Other Lenses," 371.

Garcia-Johnson indicates: "The idea is to build theology at the service of the global population rather than use the population at the service of theology."[25] This statement may sound like a clever wordplay, but several questions remain: "Is there competition between theology and people? Are people and culture above God's agenda and purpose"? The answer to both questions is no. Contextual theology is made by the people and for the benefit of people. There are times when theological thinking may result in oppressing people. For example, legalism or any other case of incoherent or abusive theology is harmful. Theologians, pastors, and leaders would do well to advance a case for a balanced biblical theology based on a human's value in God's eyes. Here, Garcia-Johnson's implication that people and belief exist for mutual benefit may help one think about the connections between theology and local contexts.

Culture and theology are not in competition, though they may at times engage in conflict. When such conflict occurs, Sanneh suggests the indigenizing and pilgrim principles should govern their relationship inside the translation (and transformation) processes.[26] For example, if a culture conflicts with the Gospel, such cultural aspects should abandon their place and become a pilgrim so that the newness of the biblical principles can take root, grow, flourish, and bear fruit. If there is no conflict, the Gospel accommodates itself in the context. It becomes indigenous and adjusts to harmless cultural aspects for the sake of Christ and the glory of God. There is always tension between these principles.

Another book on contextual theology is *Global Voices: Reading the Bible in the Majority World*, by Craig Keener and M. Daniel Carroll R.[27] One of the primary values of this book is the dialogue between the two editors. From their White and Latino perspectives respectively, Keener and Carroll call other authors to produce and analyze contextual theology in the twentieth first century. Initially, the editors are very open and indeed personal about their experiences and origins as they introduce chapters by diverse authors. This helps the reader understand where they are coming from and their goal in producing this volume.[28]

---

25. Dyrness and Garcia-Johnson, *Theology without Borders*, 479.
26. As is discussed throughout this dissertation.
27. Keener and Carroll R., *Global Voices*.
28. The book is a result of a colloquium between authors, who answer one another in a scholarly manner during the annual Society for Biblical Literature conference, promoted by the Institute for Biblical Studies and held in San Francisco (2011).

Next, the editors lay out the mandate for the volume:

> First, worldwide demographic changes demand that other ethnic perspectives, both abroad and at home, be given an attentive hearing. The theology and biblical work of this growing global presence cannot be ignored. The numbers will not allow it. Second, the presence of diaspora communities in this country is part of larger world realities that are having and will continue to have a significant effect on national and church life.[29]

Exemplifying their intention is Chapter 9, "The Bible as Specimen, Talisman, and Dragoman in Africa: A Look at Some African Uses of the Psalms and 1 Corinthians 12– 14," by Grant LeMarquand. It is an interesting example that demonstrates the vibrant and challenging experience when analyzing one own's culture. LeMarquand asks questions such as, "How do people look at the Holy Book with their cultural lenses or glasses? And how do people appropriate not only the ideas, but also the item in its material expression as a book with cover, pages, and letters"?

If only the culture shapes theology, there is a definite risk of theology becoming nothing more than sociology or anthropology. However, when theologians and Christians understand that one can, for example, read the book of Daniel (such as Barbara M. Leung Lai proposes) as a handbook for surviving in the midst of culture wars, then culture and theology come together to help one another.[30] J. Ayodeji Adewuya invites one to read Ephesians 6:10–18 in light of African Pentecostal spirituality.[31] This chapter is an excellent example that self-theologizing has to be accomplished not only with integrity, but also with courage, examining how knowing God can become a powerful and robust tool for facing, engaging, and at times, changing culture. As K. K. Yeo points out, "The biblical imperative of doing a cross-cultural reading is not simply to read the Bible culturally, but more significantly, to read the culture biblically."[32]

In *Globalizing Theology: Belief and Practice in an Era of World Christianity*, Craig Ott and Harold A. Netland include essays that advocate for and model comprehending the globalization phenomena for theology from diverse standpoints.[33] Diversity is a key word in books related to

29. Keener and Carroll R., *Global Voices*, 311.
30. Keener and Carroll R., *Global Voices*, 1449–1450.
31. Keener and Carroll R., *Global Voices*, 1788–1790.
32. Keener and Carroll R., *Global Voices*, 859–60.
33. Ott and Netland, *Globalizing Theology*.

the theme. As the authors state, "To engage in 'globalizing theology' today means that we must guard the commitment to the particular and the local while taking account of the fact that we live with an intensified awareness of the global."[34]

The idea of a polycentric Christianity means that the Christian faith has different "cultural homes."[35] In this regard, in Chapter three, "Globalization and the Study of Christian History," Andrew F. Walls argues, "Christian life and thought, taking as its norm the incarnation of the divine Word, requires incarnation, embodiment in the cultural specifics of a particular time and place."[36] Walls does this by following Ott's and Netland's proposal of producing a contextualized theology.[37] Walls reinforces the reality of the faith ("belief") as something to be lived out by normal people in their culture ("practice"). In this sense, the authors of the chapters remain mostly in the realm of the connections between theology, local cultures, missiology, globalization, and the economy. Intellectual activity and the connection between different areas of knowledge are indispensable for producing contextual theology.

Robert J. Priest in Chapter 8, "'Experience-Near Theologizing' in Diverse Human Contexts," addresses a crucial point. Priest affirms that the word "sin" is a theological construction of two millennia of church history. It can be traced back to the Garden of Eden (Gen 3:1–7) when the first man Adam produced the first piece of self-theologizing while considering the divine commandment. Priest notes, "by creating special religious speech and a vocabulary discontinuous from usage in normal life," theologians become more and more distant from experience.

Therefore, one might ask: "How would a Brazilian describe sin? Besides Catholic and Protestant backgrounds, how could one relate sin to the daily experience of the people? Or again, how will one think about God issues without connecting supernatural and natural, heaven and earth, faith and works"? James 2:14 (ASV) states, "What doth it profit, my brethren if a man says he hath faith but have not works? Can that faith save him?" In other

---

34. Ott and Netland, *Globalizing Theology*, 120–22.
35. Ott and Netland, *Globalizing Theology*, 615.
36. Ott and Netland, *Globalizing Theology*, 1399.

37. Theological education is crucial for the contextualization of the Gospel. See Nicholls, *Contextualização*, 91. This is a Portuguese translation of his classic work. Nicholls combats the mere transference of teaching models and asserts that it may become a stumbling block to the proclamation of the Gospel and edification of churches, which are biblically faithful and relevant culturally.

words, love for God is seen in loving people (Cf. Matt 22:38–39). While love for God and love for people are what God commands, how will Christians and non-Christians understand love for God or one another if there are no real-life situations to place this divine commandment into action? Jesus gave up His life for mankind. If, as Vinoth Ramachandra proposes, "Mission begins in our own backyard," the question in the context is, "How one will catch what it means to love God if there are no real examples"?[38] The same principle applies to other cultures in this globalized world.

Tennent adds value to the discussion about self-theologizing in *Theology in the Context of World Christianity: How the Global Church is Influencing the Way We Think About and Discuss Theology*.[39] The author is theologically rooted in his particularity and uses current rather than old concepts. He prefers terms such as Majority Christianity rather than Global South since the former places the North as the center of the world. Tenent uses the descriptive term "post-Western to refer to Christians and theological developments that are 'beyond' the West."[40] However, it is still a biased term because it once again makes the "West" the center. Each people or civilization of the world can consider themselves the center of the world because it is there that people live their daily lives and self-theologize. The challenge is to change this egocentric mindset.

One critical question to be asked in each case is, "What is the Bible for the authors"? Gene L. Green, in the book's introduction, posits that, "While all the authors of this volume embrace a high view of the authority of Scripture, they also recognize how God speaks to them where they live and addresses the needs and concerns raised among their communities."[41] What precisely does it mean to have a high view of the authority of Scripture? How high is it? Does it mean that the Bible is inerrant? Those questions are fundamental to the discussion.

Walls asserts,

> The true matrix of theology is not the study or the library. Theology arises from situations—social situations, intellectual situations—where one must make Christian choices, and previous Christian experience offers no clear precedent. Christian theology

---

38. Ott and Netland, *Globalizing Theology*, 4475.
39. Tennent, *Theology in the Context of World Christianity*.
40. Tennent, *Theology in the Context of World Christianity* 215.
41. Tennent, *Theology in the Context of World Christianity*, 63–64.

is the attempt to think in a Christian way; it is about making the right choice intellectually.[42]

Brazilian theologians such as Leonardo Boff, Ariovaldo Ramos, Ed Rene Kivitz, Rivanildo Guedes, and Julio Zabatiero, among others, grapple with the same questions. Some of them, such as the Catholic Boff and the Baptist Ramos, are particularly influenced by Liberation Theology, and themselves, influence other Latino and Brazilian theologians. All of them, however, are the products of their own culture and realities.

One such author, who is the product of his own culture and reality, is Ken Gnanakan from India. He maintains that the task of the church is to address how Christianity deals with local cultural religions and traditions.[43] Both linguistic and cultural translation come into play as the Gospel meets culture. For example, Jesus, as Lord, has a cultural and theological meaning for the Greeks. What does it mean for a Brazilian? Does it have anything to do with slavery? Does this idea have biblical resonance? The Early Church father Origen proposed that the church should use heathen concepts and practices and adapt them to worship and serve the Lord.[44] Should a Brazilian play rock and roll, Samba, Forró, or Axé music in their worship services using the appropriate instruments and regional words and concepts? How syncretic is their worship practices? Answers to these questions should be *glocal*.

Brazilian self-theologizing is present in books such as *Brazil: People and Church (es)*, edited by Jose Carlos Beozzo and Luiz Carlos Susin.[45] It contains a portrait of the church in Brazil and is written by Brazilian ministers and scholars. The editors divide the book into three sections: an introduction to the Brazilian church, activities of the contemporary church, and future demands and challenges. The diversity of chapters in the book reflect the broad landscape that any discussion on contextualized theologizing needs to consider.[46] These areas add value to the present research given

---

42. Ott and Netland, *Globalizing Theology*, 127.
43. Ott and Netland, *Globalizing Theology*, 81–82.
44. Ott and Netland, *Globalizing Theology*, 199.
45. Beozzo and Susin, *Brazil: People and Church(es)*.
46. "Formation of the Brazilian People," "Pastoral Strategy in the Brazilian Mega-Cities," "Shifts in Theology, Socio-Ecclesiastical Changes: Recent Developments in Theology in Brazil," "Contribution of Brazilian Ecclesiology to the Universal Church" and "Globalization of Continental Challenges: A Call from Brazil on Understanding the Christian Faith."

the global character of the analysis.⁴⁷ In general, the theological debate in Brazil vacillates between the Liberation Theology influences and conservative discourse.⁴⁸

Conservative Evangelical Heralds on TV

The previous section introduced the concept of self-theologizing and presented world-class examples. A comparison between a straightforward Western case and the discourse of a Brazilian televangelist may help one understand how locals do contextual theology. In the US, whose society is quickly becoming post-Christian, the Conservative/Liberal divide marks the evangelical scenario. Silas Malafaia, leader of the Pentecostal Church Assembly of God Victory in Christ, typically does not refer to the liberal or conservative divide in his TV program. However, he is consciously part of this dispute and addresses it on air.⁴⁹ For example, Malafaia discusses on his TV show, common issues in Western Christianity such as the role of man and woman in marriage.

Concerns regarding low morality in society and its effects on children are likewise debated during the broadcast. While conservative and liberal theologies are both at stake, Malafaia fervently advocates for the conservative evangelical. For example, he has warned his church members about the "gay agenda." Malafaia informs Christians from different denominations about the discussions he has had with members of Congress concerning gender identity policies being implemented in schools.⁵⁰ He (among many other leaders) articulates for common church people the divisions in theological perspectives.

---

47. For more on Brazilian self-theologizing, see Julio Paulo Tavares Zabatiero's work. He advocates a contextual theological reflection on practical theology, ethics, and ecclesiology. His books include titles such as *Na Força do Espírito. Os Pentecostais na América Latina: Um Desafio às Igrejas Históricas* (In the Force of the Spirit. Pentecostals in Latin America: A Challenge to Historical Churches) and *Estágios da Fé* (Faith Stages).

48. A glance of this reality can be found in Dyrness and Garcia-Johnson, *Theology Without Borders*, 2485.

49. Presently, Malafaia's TV program, "Victory in Christ," a one hour weekly edition, is broadcast nationwide on three TV stations, 19 local TV stations in Brazil, and the US and Canada. See "Victory in Christ."

50. This discussion aired August 20, 2016. See Vitória em Cristo, "Programa Vitória em Cristo."

Self-theologizing occurs beyond Malafaia's programs and church. Brazilian Baptists are fighting against corruption and taking their stand in the face of the political chaos within the country. Pastors and churches signed their support for congressional measures to end corruption and prevent corrupt politicians from continuing in power.[51] Self-theologizing is essential across denominations for the Brazilian church to be able to exercise influence and existence. Hiebert calls the church to examine human cultures for the sake of sharing the Gospel "in ways that transform them in the light of God's truth, beauty, and righteousness."[52] In the end, self-theologizing interacts with culture so that the transformative power of the Word of God and the Gospel might become known among its people, including the Brazilian one. This phenomenon will continue to be studied in the remaining portion of this chapter, as it considers the BBC self-theologizing effort, including a historical overview of the evangelism and discipleship Evangelical literature over the last decades.

Influences on a Brazilian Theology of Evangelism and Discipleship

Translation led to transformation whenever the Gospel encountered culture in Brazil; from the beginning of the Baptist work, through the labors of the missionaries, to the present day.[53] For example, the establishment of Baptist schools in the cities of Jaguaquara (Bahia state), Belo Horizonte (Minas Gerais), Recife (Pernambuco), Rio de Janeiro, and São Paulo improved education in these places. Since its inception, the Baptist work in Brazil has demonstrated an active evangelistic zeal as the foreign, national, and state mission boards are thriving and keeping aflame the life of the denomination.

Third Generation Baptists

To study the expression of a Christian church inside a culture is to deal with some concepts pertinent to the field of WCS. Walls affirms that the Christian faith does not exist in a vacuum, but there are cultural expressions and

---

51. During the Brazilian Baptist Convention main meeting of 2016, in Santos, São Paulo, the Pastor's Conference signed the *Manifesto of Santos* (Santos Manifest), supporting the fight against corruption. Pastor's Conference, *Manifesto de Santos*.

52. Ott and Netland, *Globalizing Theology*, 306.

53. For more information from a historical perspective, see Chapter 3.

local features that are part of the life of the believer. When the "indigenizing" principle is in play, translation happens. Given that God became human flesh in the person of Jesus, people transmit the message of the Gospel through human language and in an intelligible way, promoting the translation of the message into different cultures and realities, such as Brazilian.[54]

How have Brazilian Baptists translated the Gospel into their culture? What are the main features of this country that contribute to the contextualized preaching of the Gospel (translation) and making disciples (transformation) on Brazilian soil?[55] Answering these questions means one should consider Brazilian Baptists as a "third generation denomination," for the Baptist movement went from Europe to the US, and from there, Brazil. As it moved from country to country, the Baptist church became acculturated, with all the attendant problems.[56]

Brazilian Baptists face the daunting challenge of leaving behind attempts to translate the Gospel into "formal language" and transitioning to the "local idiom."[57] Using a linguistic metaphor, Sanneh proposes a paradigm shift. For him, Christianity functions better in an informal language, the one spoken by most people. Under such circumstances, the message can reach a larger audience and bear more fruit. One of the presuppositions here is that Brazilian Baptists need to make a distinction between the "formal language" (linguistic and cultural) used by past foreign missionaries and the "local idiom." Brazilian Baptists should perceive, embrace, and continually re-work their identity and the language that describes it starting with their approaches to local evangelism and discipleship, as the following sections propose.

Historical Beginnings

Lester Carl Bell notes that the result of the doctrinal zeal of men such as W. B. Bagby, Z. C. Taylor, and W. E. Entzminger, was "the establishment in

---

54. Ott and Netland, *Globalizing Theology*, 29. This transmission of the faith into a particular culture through Christians may be considered a *re*translation of the Gospel, according to Walls. In the final analysis, it seems that, in one sense, translation and *re*translation are equivalent for Walls. The difference is that one happens after the other. The first translation needs to happen before the second one takes place.

55. The transformation of individuals and of the culture does not happen without discipleship.

56. Elkins. "Conversion or Acculturation?," 170–71.

57. Sanneh, "Renewed and Empowered," 8.

Brazil of a vigorous Baptist doctrine which carried no apology in its defense and offered no compromise in its propagation."[58] The consequent firm preaching tone was also related to the persecution suffered by the religious group in its beginnings.

Reflecting on these afflictions, foreign missionaries and authors such as Bell produced contextual theology from an etic perspective, while nationals, such as Oliveira, did it from a Brazilian and emic perspective. He wrote his Ph.D. dissertation on the topic of persecution as an impulse for the growth of the Brazilian Baptist church. The author concludes that the church grew in numbers but also as a denomination as a byproduct of the perils and trials from Catholic persecution, something the author saw as a missionary kid in Northeastern Brazil.[59] A summary of Oliveira's historical overview of Brazilian Baptists is displayed in the following figure.

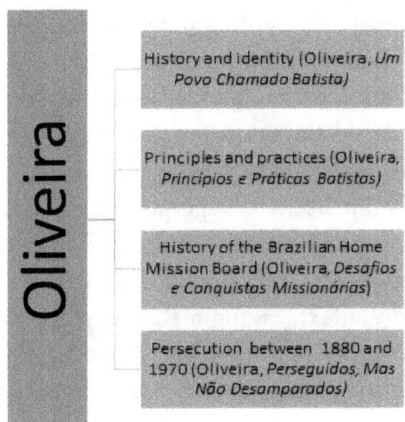

Figure 10. Zaqueu Moreira de Oliveira's Historiography of the BBC

As seen, self-theologizing also happens amid trials and leads to transformation. This same dynamic occurred when the Gospel encountered the culture of Caesarea, as found in Acts 10–11. The struggle among the disciples from Jewish and Gentile backgrounds increased after Peter entered Cornelius' household. The effect of the indigenizing principle is visible. Peter affirmed to Cornelius, and later to the church in Jerusalem, that God accepts and welcomes every nation (Acts 10:34). The Apostle had visions which strengthened his claim as a messenger from God, someone with

---

58. Bell, "Factors," 48.

59. Oliveira, "Persecution of Brazilian Baptists," 202.

divine authority giving directions to the church to be open to every culture and nation.[60]

Self-theologizing is a far-reaching task. Paul's missionary journeys demonstrate that persecution led to missionary activity, growth, more abuse, perils of death, and finally death. This cycle continues up to the present day, especially in the missionary field where there is a small evangelical presence. The Council of Jerusalem (Acts 15), a primer on self-theologizing in the NT, was thus, part of this larger transformative trail of blood, death, and life initiated by Jesus on the cross. It was a divide regarding Gentile circumcision and points to the validity of Christ's sacrifice. As true of the Jerusalem Council, the Holy Spirit (Acts 15:28) leads the decisions of the Christian community through the centuries.[61]

Another NT example of conflict between culture and theology resulting in translation is found in Acts 14:8–20. After Paul healed a disabled person in Lystra during his first missionary journey, the people acclaimed Paul as Hermes and Barnabas as Zeus, both deities of the Greek Pantheon. Even a priest from the local temple dedicated to Zeus brought sacrifices to honor them. Paul and Barnabas rebuked the idolatry and syncretism. Tearing their clothes and explaining the good news provoked a pilgrim effect (v. 15). Dean Philip Bechard suggests that here, Paul is the role of a self-disclosing sage, one who is very genuine and interacts with a provincial audience.[62] In other words, God's herald must deal with people according to the occasion and context, taking a stand for the Gospel. This is what some authors have tried to do while writing on evangelism and discipleship in the past and up to the present day, as detailed next.

Literature on Evangelism and Discipleship

Clearly, foreign missionaries, local pastors, and leaders carried out the translation task of producing contextual theology under diverse influences. The following part of this chapter addresses how the local colors of the theology of evangelism and discipleship in Brazilian Baptist circles are seen in the literature that has been published or translated over the last five decades. The theological reflection made public in books sponsored by evangelical and denominational publishers reinforced the expansionist

---

60. Strelan, *Strange Acts*, 164.
61. Keener, *IVP Bible Background Commentary*.
62. Bechard, "Paul Among the Rustics," 86.

DNA and zeal of Southern Baptist missionaries. Modern church growth models and indigenous awakenings have impacted Brazilian Baptists for over five decades, prompting self-theologizing, and promoting a peculiar and local theology of evangelism and discipleship. The *Igreja Multiplicadora* model, based on the collectivistic traits of the national culture, will be also analyzed in the following sections.

North American and Brazilian Literature

The history of the theology of evangelism and discipleship in Brazil is evident in translation of books such as *Evangelism: The Church on Fire*, by Robert L. Sumner (Regular Baptist Press: 1960). Titles about evangelism and missions published in Portuguese by Russel Shedd are also popular.[63] In the last two decades, translated books with titles such as *One Thing You Cannot Do in Heaven*, by Mark Cahill, and the calvinistic view of Mark Dever in *Nine Marks of a Healthy Church*, *The Gospel and Personal Evangelism*, and *The Deliberate Church*, influenced pastors and leaders, as did popular works by Rick Warren and Bill Hybels. Robert Coleman's, *The Master Plan of Evangelism* (Christian Outreach, 1963), continue to influence Brazilian Baptists to this day, as it will be explained later.

In what ways did these works influence BBC leaders? These books address the communication of the Gospel through strategies and methods without dealing directly with local cultural aspects and particularities of the communities in which that outreach occurs. In recent decades, national publishing houses have released transcultural missiological works such as *Communicating Christ Cross Culturally* by David Hesselgrave and *The Gospel in Diverse Cultures* by Paul Gilbert. However, these books deal with transcultural matters. There has not been an effort to investigate the Brazilian culture for translation purposes.[64] The birth of the academic field *Ciências da Religião* (Religion Sciences) in the 1970s brought greater breadth and depth to such studies, but it still lacks an emic approach to the influence of sociocultural factors on the translation.[65]

---

63. Shedd, *Adoração Bíblica; Lei, Graça e Santificação;* and *Bíblia de Estudo Shedd.*

64. Silva, *Fenomenologia da Religião*, 16.

65. Silva, *Fenomenologia da Religião*, 21. Most of the Brazilian books published during the present decade which are mentioned in this dissertation are a result of the scholarship of the religion sciences graduate programs around the country.

The NMB, which is presently under the leadership of Executive Director Fernando Brandão, is publishing a series of books about evangelism, discipleship, and missions under the umbrella of the *Igreja Multiplicadora* (Multiplying Church) model. The books are the BBC's contemporary self-theologizing effort. In summary, the *Igreja Multiplicadora* church model is the assimilation of small groups to the traditional church model of the BBC, which includes Sunday school, Royal Ambassadors, *Mensageiras do Rei* (equivalent to Girls in Action), and other departments. It is also a development of previous similar models of the NMB, mainly the *Núcleos de Estudos Bíblicos* (NEBs, Small Groups of Bible Studies), that were very popular in the 1980s.[66]

Brandão is the author of *Igreja Multiplicadora*.[67] It affirms that principles matter more than models or strategies. This approach was influenced by Coleman's affirmation that *The Master Plan* "does not seek to interpret specific methods of Jesus in personal or mass evangelism. Rather, this is a study of principles underlying his ministry—principles which determined his methods," such as selection, association, consecration, impartation, demonstration, delegation, supervision, and reproduction.[68]

Some other books by Brazilian and foreign authors paved the way for the *Igreja Multiplicadora* movement. The book *Evangelismo Total* (Total Evangelism) by Damy Ferreira, published by the denominational publishing house in 1990 and translated into Spanish, is a practical manual for evangelists, pastors, leaders, and seminary students and contains a robust biblical theology of evangelism.[69] Ferreira speaks to the theology of evangelism, the theory of communication, the Holy Spirit, soteriology, personal evangelism, and specific evangelism techniques. Edison Queiroz wrote

---

66. Brandão, *Igreja Multiplicadora*, 16. The International Mission Board [IMB] of the SBC continues to impact the translation of the Gospel in Brazil. The NEBs were part of the *Plano Nacional de Evangelização* (National Plan of Evangelism), a strategic plan developed by the NMB in the 1980s with strategic and financial support of the SBC. Discipleship curricula, such as *Experiencing God* and *Masterlife*, and books such as *The Mind of Christ*, were previously published by the NMB and now, Lifeway Brasil.

67. Brandão, *Igreja Multiplicadora*, 16.

68. Coleman, *Master Plan of Evangelism*, 13–20. Coleman's influence is seen across denominations. He writes the foreword to Eims, *A Arte Perdida de Fazer Discípulos*. Atos is a Charismatic publishing house in Brazil.

69. Ferreira graduated with a master's degree from American Baptist Seminary of the West (Berkeley, CA) and served in multiple capacities in the denomination in the US and Brazil. Ferreira, *Evangelismo Total*, 2nd ed. (Rio de Janeiro: Juerp, 1990).

several books on missiology from a pastoral point of view which have influenced evangelicals in Brazil.

Another classic in the modern church growth movement is Christian A. Schwarz's, *Natural Church Development*. It addresses the indigenous Brazilian self-theologizing of evangelism, discipleship, and missions and is found among the recommendations of the textbook *Igreja Multiplicadora* on page vii, by Josue Salgado, former pastor of Baptist Memorial Church in Brasilia, D. C. Schwarz categorically affirms, "If we were to identify any one principle as the 'most important' . . . then without a doubt it would be the multiplication of small groups."[70] The *Pequenos Grupos Multiplicadores* [PGM], or multiplying smalls groups, are the heart of the *Igreja Multiplicadora* model for making disciples through *relacionamentos discipuladores* (discipling relationships). Discipling relationships are a strategy for intentional evangelism and discipleship. Both occur concurrently as will be explained below.

Contemporary Approach: *Igreja Multiplicadora*

As in other Latin America and Asian countries where community is predominant, the small group strategy has increased exponentially. Guedes mentions Brazilians' strong sense of relationality and interpersonal warmth to argue for the use of small groups and circles of relationships in reaching out to the people of Brazil.[71] For him, to preach and live out the Gospel is to dialogue with and transform the local culture. To maintain their roots,

---

70. The *pequenos grupos* (small groups) or *grupos familiares* (family groups) nomenclature began in Brazil in the 1990s for the missionary agency Sepal, initially called *Serviço para a Evangelização da América Latina* (Service for the Evangelization of Latin America). It is presently *Servindo Pastores e Líderes* (Serving Pastors and Leaders). David Kornfield's series *Grupos de Discipulado* (Discipleship Groups) and *Grupos Familiares* (Family Groups) were essential in this work. Also see, Lyman Coleman, *Serendipity Training Manual for Groups* (Littleton, CO: Serendipity House, 1989). The title in Portuguese is *Manual de Treinamento para Grupos Pequenos Serendipity*, with the addition of the word "small" before "groups." It was the textbook for the 23rd Sepal Conference for Pastors and Leaders in Águas de Lindoia (1996). The book presents biblical foundation, theory, methods of small groups, and a summary of its history in the US from 1950–1980. The book also contains a substantial contribution to the different models of small groups and a plan to start small groups in the church. Sepal is affiliated with the *Associação de Missões Transculturais Brasileiras* ([AMTB], Brazilian Transcultural Missions Association) and the Aliança Cristã Evangélica Brasileira ([ACEB], Brazilian Evangelical Christian Alliance). ACEB is the most representative evangelical coalition in Brazil, except for Neopentecostals.

71. Guedes, *Uma Igreja com a Nossa Cara*, 80.

argues the author, the *Evangélico* people of Brazil should embrace a conservative theology and contextualized ecclesiology—a community-based theology. This collectivistic emphasis is the primary face of the contemporary theology of evangelism and discipleship among Brazilian Baptists, which also shows the influence of other sociocultural traits, as detailed in the following sections of this chapter. *Igreja Multiplicadora* starts from the standpoint that evangelism is more effective when done in the context of personal relationships.

Small group church models influenced by South Korean pastor Paul Yong Cho and others have been prevalent in contemporary Brazilian theologies over the last two decades.[72] Some models propose cell groups formed of a maximum of twelve, as does that of Colombian Charismatic apostle Cesar Castellanos. His model, called G12, became popular in Brazil in the late 1990's. He influenced former Brazilian Baptists and now Charismatic apostle Rene Terra Nova (M12), who leads a megachurch in Manaus, in the state of Amazonas.[73]

Another Charismatic leader who has influenced Baptist pastors in Brazil over the last decade is Abe Huber. His *Modelo do Discipulado Apostólico* (Apostolic Discipleship Model, or MDA) cell group methodology is based on one-on-one discipleship, which clearly influences the *Igreja Multiplicadora* model. The Brazilian Mennonite Robert Lay, propagated the G5 model in the 1990s, with groups of five people. During that decade, the Bahia State Baptist Convention hold conferences to promote this model, to mention. North American Joel Comiskey of the cell church model is a church growth leader followed by the leaders of Central Baptist Church, in Belo Horizonte, Minas Gerais States, as are other leaders and indigenous church growth models that have been transforming the face of Evangelicalism in the country by multiplying disciples through cell groups and small groups in large and small cities.

---

72. The small relational groups mirror Brazilians' preferred way of communicating and being; it is something fundamentally indigenous.

73. Terra Nova was born in the city of Serrinha, in the state of Bahia. He was raised in Serrinha and Feira de Santana. The leader studied at the BBC's Northern Baptist Theological Seminary (Recife). He left the denomination in the 1990's. His church claims to have 75,000 members in four different states. He is the leader of the church model called *Visão Celular no Modelo dos 12* (Cell Vision in the Model of 12), with churches and pastors following it around the country and abroad. The model is a derivation of Castellanos' format. Terra Nova leads trips to South Korea to Cho's church. Terra Nova, "Biografia."

Denominations such as the largest one, *Assembleia de Deus* (Assemblies of God), and the indigenous *Igreja Pentecostal Deus é Amor* (Pentecostal Church God is Love) still follow a growth model based on lay leadership of new congregations in urban and rural areas. The Neo-Pentecostal churches still maintain a hierarchy led by pastors, bishops, and apostles. The dynamics of the growth of both models—church-based and cell-based—is a phenomenon still to be studied.

A Baptist influence over the *Igreja Multiplicadora* is that of Steve Smith and Ying Kai's book *T4T—A Discipleship Revolution*. Even though popular in IMB circles around the world, is not used in Brazil as extensively as it could be, given the prestige of Southern Baptist missionaries in Brazil.[74] In their book, Smith and Kai propose one-on-one training for evangelism and discipleship.[75] For them, the key to church growth is one-on-one discipleship and investment in lay leaders for small groups and house churches. This vision has been followed by the NMB in the *Igreja Multiplicadora* movement. Another strong influence is author Waylon Moore, whose books are being released by the NMB, following the author's participation in the movement's 2015 conference in Brazil.[76]

Igreja Multiplicadora: Institutional Self-Theologizing

The literature produced by the NMB is a contemporary example of self-theologizing in evangelism and discipleship. In total, there are presently seven books and one pamphlet available, as detailed in this section. These books are written exclusively by indigenous leaders, all of whom are involved in evangelism and discipleship in churches or in the missionary organization itself. As mentioned before, the primer is *Igreja Multiplicadora*, organized by Brandão. The follow-up book is *Relacionamento Discipulador* (Discipling Relationship), by Diogo Carvalho, who leads evangelism efforts in the organization.[77]

A third book is *De Volta aos Princípios* (Back to the Basics), by Fabrício Freitas, Executive Director of Evangelism for the Board.[78] Freitas primarily deepens the concepts already presented by *Igreja Multiplicadora*.

---

74. Smith and Kai, *T4T: A Discipleship Re-Revolution*.
75. See more about the T4T model in Chapter 7.
76. Moore, *Multiplicando Discípulos*, 2015.
77. Carvalho, *Relacionamento Discipulador*.
78. Freitas, *De Volta aos Princípios*.

Freitas includes an in-depth bibliography covering international authors in the church growth movement. This reveals his scholarship and intent of being conversational with the broad community of evangelicals around the world.

Aprofundando Raízes (Deepening Roots), by Roosevelt Arantes, explains the principles and attitudes that form the discipling relationship.[79] A discipling relationship is the core principle of the *Igreja Multiplicadora*. Arantes covers the topic thoroughly with biblical and practical backgrounds. The NMB seeks to produce original literature by the board personnel and Brazilian Baptist pastors. There is merit in furnishing local leaders with resources, methodologies, and ideas for reflection, but overall, these books lack critical discussion on the impact of the Gospel in the lives of people, specifically Brazilians and their local cultures.

Other titles in the series deal with specific areas of the church. *Pequeno Grupo Multiplicador* (Small Multiplying Group), by Márcio Tunala, teaches about the details of the multiplying small group.[80] *Escola Bíblica Discipuladora* (Discipling Bible School), by Marcos Paulo Ferreira, presents the Sunday school inside the church model.[81] *Evangelização Discipuladora de Crianças* (Discipling Evangelization of Children), by Jaqueline da Hora Santos, develops strategies for evangelism and the discipleship of children.[82] A church leader or member would find these books more specific and less repetitive than the ones mentioned earlier. All of them reinforce the strategies of *discipling relationships* and *multiplying small groups*, as do most recent books in the series by Dave Earley, which focus on the leaders of small groups and training them to become better leaders.[83]

The concept of the *discipling relationship* is central to *Igreja Multiplicadora*. As Brandão explains, it goes beyond the vision of evangelism versus discipleship.[84] A discipling *relationship* means that one intentionally shares the good news and influences non-believers and believers daily. *Multiplying small groups* grow out of *discipling relationships*. The idea is for there to be an ongoing cycle.[85]

---

79. Arantes, *Aprofundando Raízes*.

80. Tunala, *Pequeno Grupo Multiplicador*.

81. Ferreira, *Escola Bíblica Discipuladora*.

82. Santos, *Evangelização Discipuladora de Crianças*.

83. Earley's titles are *Transformando Membros em Líderes* and *8 Hábitos do Líder Eficaz de Pequenos Grupos*.

84. Brandão, *Igreja Multiplicadora*, 70–71.

85. The influence of IMB missionary David Allen Bledsoe on the *Igreja*

Christ Challenges Culture

Igreja Multiplicadora emphasizes the need for small groups for the growth of the church in Brazil. The collectivistic sociocultural trait of the country is the foundation for this translation approach. In this self-theologizing process, the Gospel finds itself literally at home; in other words, the indigenizing principle is at work in evangelism and discipleship. This reality resonates with Eugene A. Nida's analysis makes of the Protestant approach in his book, *Understanding Latin Americans*. Nida understands that three pillars sustain the Protestant work in Brazil: (1) working with the masses, (2) the upper-lower and lower-middle classes as the key vectors of growth, and (3) identification with the masses. Nida gives two explanations for why evangelical Christianity is experiencing such growth in Latin American: humility, instead of arrogance and a proud approach to the culture and "giving leadership to others by participation and the challenge to follow."[86] This last feature is at the heart of the *Igreja Multiplicadora* movement, especially in its multiplying methodology.

Nida's reflections are very helpful for comprehending the Brazilian culture and the success of small groups in its communities. For him, "A face-to-face society is just what it implies—one in which all the members are known to one another and everybody knows all about everyone else."[87] The author describes Latin American culture as communitarian (a particular mark of which is that decisions are made collectively), centralized, and having conservative values.

In individualistic societies, the guiding idea of evangelism is that each person is responsible and accountable to God for his or her decisions. If anyone shares the Gospel with someone else, even if there are no bonds or personal connections between the two people, the task of transmitting the Gospel is accomplished. However, the official BBC approach discussed in this chapter does not entirely follow this perspective. The door-to-door evangelistic method is not encouraged in the denominational movement.

Multiplicadora movement is evident. He is the author of the book *Evangelismo Via Relacionamentos*, which preceded the denominational books analyzed in this chapter. He leads the Master of Theological Studies program offered by Southeastern Baptist Theological Seminary in partnership with the Brazilian mission boards. Fabrício Freitas is a graduate of this program, and other authors are enrolled in that program. Bledsoe wrote his Ph.D. dissertation on the Universal Church of the Kingdom of God, indigenous and Prosperity Gospel church. An article about his early missionary work in Brazil is Akins, "Incarnational Discipleship and Church Growth," 87–102.

86. Nida, *Understanding Latin Americans*, 94–95.
87. Nida, *Understanding Latin Americans*, 97–98.

Carvalho finds that even though the Doctrinal Declaration of the BBC is deeply soteriological, evangelistic practices in the churches are shallow: "To make disciples means, in one sense, *to lead people to salvation*. However, we will only be able to understand what discipleship really is when we associate it with the process of *intentional relationship* which results in conversion and development along the way."[88]

Brandão, then, summarizes the idea of discipleship starting even before evangelism in the following words:

> It is impossible to fulfill the Great Commission without *relationships* . . . Our attempt is not to defend an Evangelism through relationships methodology as antagonist to an Evangelism "without relationships." Actually, what we are trying to demonstrate is that there is a complementarity, because it is impossible to fully implement the Great Commission without relationships and the proclamation of the Word."[89]

Besides the collectivistic trait, two other traits of the Brazilian people, cordiality and religiosity, make it easier to do evangelism, according to David Mein, Southern Baptist missionary and President of the NBTS (Recife, Brazil) in the 1970s. He adds features such as tolerance and curiosity to the list of national characteristics that favor receptivity to the Gospel.[90] These features favor translation of the Gospel and the transformation of individual lives within Brazilian society. More on the influence of these traits will be dealt with through the analysis of the interviews. However, the very strength of such discipling relationships also means one is likely to encounter cultural features such as the Brazilian way of coping, that can hinder the Gospel witness, as it will be evaluated in the following chapters and in the interviews with the BBC leaders.

Conclusion

This chapter analyzed how Christ challenges culture in the Brazilian Baptist model of evangelism and discipleship called *Igreja Multiplicadora* (Multiplying Church). It stands out as an example of self-theologizing for the sake of accomplishing the Great Commission and is based mainly on the collectivist

---

88. Carvalho, *Relacionamento Discipulador*, 23.
89. Brandão, *Igreja Multiplicadora*, 68.
90. Mein, *O Que Deus Tem Feito*, 9.

culture of the people. Whereas, North American practices of evangelism and discipleship generally are based on individualistic initiatives, the Brazilian Baptist theological approach values community, small groups, and involves hearing, seeing, imitating, and influencing other people.

The collectivistic or communitarian trait of the Brazilian culture, compared to the other three traits dealt with in this dissertation, has more impact on self-theologizing by the authors in the series of books related to the *Igreja Multiplicadora* movement, which are a rich source for future academic endeavors in the field of WCS.

The previous chapters explored how Christ meets, engages, challenges, and changes culture. The following chapters will demonstrate how Christ dialogues, interacts with, and bridges cultures. This cultural dialogue was researched using the oral history methodology in interviews with key leaders of the BBC.

These interviews provide ideas and insights on the translation of the Gospel in Brazil, such as adding complexity to the topic of collectivism and its influence and power in the Brazilian culture. The BBC leaders interviewed are involved in different levels of denominational work around the country and encompass a vast span of ministerial experience in divers roles inside churches, conventions, and regional associations. Their reflections convey the contextualizing mentality of the *Igreja Multiplicadora* model and add other perspectives to this analysis of the translation of the Gospel in Brazil through sociocultural factors.

5

Christ Dialogues with Culture

*BBC Leaders Refining Gospel Translation
from a Biblically Sound Angle*

CHRISTIANITY AND CULTURE DIALOGUE in a particular way in Brazil. How does an investigation of Brazilian socio-cultural work within the BBC facilitate what is known in WCS as "biblically sound translation"? The previous chapter mainly analyzed the *Igreja Multiplicadora* literature produced by the denomination. The inquiry indicated that this self-theologizing effort engaged with specific values of Brazilian culture, the strongest of which is collectivism. In this fifth chapter, the thesis that sociocultural factors play a significant role in the translation of the Gospel in Brazil as discovered and expressed among the BBC is explored further and tested. This happens through a qualitative study of the oral history interviews with eight key leaders of the denomination in the five macroregions of the country. The results point to an affirmation of sociocultural traits found in the literature review and in the *Igreja Multiplicadora* movement and validates the usefulness of the sociological approach for studying the translation of the Gospel in Brazil.

Three questions guided the interpretation of the material collected from the interviews with the eight leaders of the BBC. First, "What is a definition of 'biblically sound translation' that can both serve as a reference to the researcher for the evaluation of the interviews and also resonate within the WCS community"? Second, "What are the practices of biblically sound translation, and how are they expressed through the reflections of the BBC key leaders"? Finally, "How do the findings from their research impact WCS, Brazilian scholars, and the church itself as each seeks to enhance the translation of the Gospel into the national culture"? With the goal of answering these general questions, additional sub-questions are introduced and discussed to analyze the interviews.

What is a Biblically Sound Translation?

What can be considered a biblically sound translation of the Gospel in a given culture? The writings of Walls and Eitel help to answer this crucial question. First, Walls, in his primer, *Missionary Movement in Christian History*, gives a definition which will also guide the evaluation of the oral history interviews. At the end of the chapter, "Translation Principle in Christian History," the author looks at the linguistic and cultural translation done by two early church missionaries. The first one is Wulfila, a leader in the fourth-century Gothic Christian community who undertook a Gothic Bible translation. The second is Patrick, the sixth-century Celtic missionary to Ireland, who remains one of the most important figures in the Irish church to the present day.[1] Walls describes the impact of Wulfila and Patrick on the history of the churches they served and then presents a key statement that, for the purposes of this research, serves as the grounding definition of a biblically sound translation: "The measure of [the translation's] effectiveness is how far the Word once more recognizably takes flesh in the cultures in which [it] work[s], and people behold [God's] glory under human conditions."[2]

Per Walls and Eitel, biblically sound translation means, first, that the Gospel and the Scriptures are transforming the culture, and not the opposite.[3] Second, God's glory in the culture is seen by the translator, church, and surrounding community. Another way of saying this is that through such translation, the person preaching the Gospel, the church around him, and non-believers recognize that God is at work in the lives of Christians, affecting society, and prompting everyone to give glory to the Lord for the lives, families, and culture, as they are experiencing transformation and becoming better. In other words, people are being saved from eternal

---

1. Walls, *Missionary Movement*, 37–42.
2. Walls, *Missionary Movement*, 42.
3. This definition was already discussed in Chapter 2, based on the diagram and probing questions found in the article by Eitel, "Scriptura or Cultura," 74–75.

damnation, and society is benefitting. Drug addicts are being set free. The poor are being assisted. Divorces, abuse, and violence are lessening. The economy is improving. Educational levels are rising. People who used to steal, lie, and break the rules are now good citizens.

Thus, a biblically sound translation implies the ability to engage with culture by finding or building bridges by which to share the good news.[4] It is about keeping in the culture what is biblically positive or neutral, and transforming what is contrary to Christian standards.[5] Through biblically sound translation, the glory of God is seen in the cultural means of the daily lives of people. The inability to do sound translation or lack of awareness of the cultural implications of the Gospel is evident when one does not identify the bridges, barriers, or opposition to the Christian message, or is not able to build bridges inside the culture where the Gospel is being proclaimed and biblical principles are being taught.

Biblically Sound Translation in Leaders' Views and Practices

How can one discover practices of biblically sound translation in the reflections of strategic Brazilian Baptist leaders? This question opens the path for a critical evaluation of the interviews. First, oral history is a methodology that can reveal a vast array of experiences, worldviews, and translation practices. Second, the representative set of interviewees provides geographical and denominational diversity for an in-depth study of the BBC. Thanks to such a diversity of interviewees, this research is unique. The experiences and practices shared by pastors and denominational leaders are like a photograph of the present state of the translation of the Gospel in Brazil. They represent churches of the BBC, state conventions, the NMB, and local associations. Their testimonies give evidence to the Gospel being translated into the local culture inside the diverse regions of the country.

---

4. Another perspective on biblically sound translation is given by John Gration, Professor at Wheaton College Graduate School and former missionary in Congo, Africa. In a seminar with French and Swahili-speaking pastors on contextual theology for tribal cultures, Africa, and the West, Gration asked four questions whose answers lead to biblically sound translation: "(1) What is the Gospel? (2) What is culture? (3) How and where has the Gospel touched or transformed your culture? And (4) How and where has the Gospel not yet transformed your culture?" Ott and Netland, *Globalizing Theology*, 5632.

5. Hiebert reinforces this perspective. He defends the communication of the Gospel that transforms cultures "in the light of God's truth, beauty, and righteousness." Ott and Netland, *Globalizing Theology*, 6018.

Oral History Methodology

The interviews with eight Brazilian denominational leaders followed the oral history methodology. The interviews were conducted according to the guidelines of Donald A. Ritchie.[6] According to Ritchie, the benefits of using oral history are that it "collects memories and personal commentaries of historical significance through recorded interviews."[7] The information collected through oral history is made available to the general public through recording, transcribing, and otherwise making material accessible. Ritchie explains that, "By preserving the recordings and transcripts of their interviews, oral historians seek to leave as complete, candid, and reliable a record as possible."[8]

The methodology required the compilation and interpretation of the historical data given by the interviewees about the translation of the Gospel in contemporary Brazil. It included thorough background research, organizing, preparing questions, and conducting the interviews. The transcripts (see Appendices) were composed according to Leslie Roy Ballard's guidelines.[9] Other books, specialized websites, oral history interviews, and class lectures also modeled the methodological approach, envisioning that scholars in WCS are "history makers" of their place and times.[10] The audio of the interviews are archived at Southwestern Baptist Theological Seminary's Robert Library and Archives for the use of future scholars.

Background of the Interviews

The literature review phase of Chapter 1 considered authors who have written about Brazilian culture. The national emphasis continued throughout the historic and self-theologizing sections (Chapters 3 and 4) and in the

---

6. Ritchie, *Doing Oral History*.
7. Ritchie, *Doing Oral History*, 1.
8. Ritchie, *Doing Oral History*, 8.
9. "Every transcript in every project should include the same introduction, written to place that interview in the context of the project as a whole." Ballard, *History of Oral History*, 210. This work mirrors the stylistic norms contained in the mentioned book.
10. The oral history interviews followed the standard practices of oral history. The interviews, articles, and guidelines contained in the following websites served as a basis for the methodology applied in this project. See "Time Coding & Indexing Oral Histories," "Transcribing Oral Histories," and the "BBC Broadcast/Interview about the Prosperity Gospel in Nigeria."

remaining chapters. The oral history methodology was applied to leaders of Brazilian Baptist churches. The interview format began as a proof case sampling in a local denominational context and became the final format for interviews with BBC leaders.

Initially, there was a phase of tests with preliminary questionnaires and interviews. The first questionnaire was applied to ten pastors serving in churches of the Southern Minas Gerais Baptist Association. This questionnaire was distributed during its business meeting on November 14, 2015, in the city of Extrema in the state of Minas Gerais. The group answered five written multiple-choice questions that helped determine whether sociocultural traits were bridges, barriers, or bridges and barriers. Each question/response allowed space for comments. The first four questions of the questionnaire tested the output of testing the four sociocultural traits (cordiality, collectivism, Brazilian way of coping, and religiosity). The last question specifically probed the local culture of Southern Minas Gerais.

Second, the author conducted three e-mail interviews with two pastors and a seasoned church planter in Southern Minas Gerais.[11] The questionnaire was like the first one. The interviewees wrote as much as they wanted about the topic, giving their insight on the issue at hand from a practical standpoint. They evaluated sociocultural values and regional traits with these two rounds of interviews. The questionnaire proved to be solid and reliable as a quality source of information.

Third, a second model of the questionnaire was applied on July 23, 2016, to fifty-six pastors and church members who were involved or interested in evangelism and discipleship during an *Igreja Multiplicadora* training at Bethel BC (Pouso Alegre). These participants answered a set of four multiple choice questions about the translation of the Gospel in that specific region. The second model was structured similarly to the previous questionnaire, except, in this case, there was no space for comments. The

---

11. E-mail interviews were conducted with Pr. Felipe Hirata, Pr. Genevaldo Andrade Bertune, and church planter Alair José da Silva. Hirata was the senior pastor of FBC Extrema for nine years. He also served the Itapeva congregation for one year. Bertune served FBC Pouso Alegre for thirty-two years. He also led FBC Campanha, another city in southern Minas Gerais, for two and a half years. Finally, in his fourteen years of church planting in Southern Minas Gerais, Alair planted Second Baptist Church [SBC] of Pouso Alegre, the Baptist Evangelical Church of Congonhal, the Baptist church in the district of Barreiro, Ipuiúna city, and Bethel Baptist Church, Pouso Alegre. Interviews were conducted with Pr. Genevaldo (over the phone) and Alair (in person, over the phone, and via e-mail).

author used the results of this preliminary survey to consolidate the questionnaire model that was later used with the eight national leaders.

Fourth, oral history interviews were conducted with three key leaders of the Southern Minas Gerais Baptist Association using the final version of the questionnaire. These conversations served as practice for the final interviews with the national leaders. Marcelo Antonio da Silva, pastor of First Baptist Church, Três Corações and twice the President of the local Baptist Association, was the first interviewee.[12] His interview took place on the morning of October 5, 2016. On the afternoon of the same day, an interview was held with José Alberto Dias Nobre, pastor of Central Baptist Church in Três Corações, the largest church in the region. Nobre is an innovative leader, the main catalyst for church growth in Southern Minas Gerais, and promoter of the *Igreja Multiplicadora* model there.[13] A third interview was done with Wagner Ferreira, pastor of FBC Cambuí and President of the Southern Minas Gerais Baptist Association.[14] Future research may explore these interviews

---

12. Silva is originally from Rio de Janeiro and was living, at the time of the interview, in Três Corações, the city where the soccer player Pelé was born. Despite being from another state, he knows this region very well. He is one of the most respected leaders in the association. Silva has keen insightful to the soul of the Southern Minas people, commenting about its people, culture, and dynamics. He sees some traits as barriers and others as bridges. Silva experienced many adversities in life (he is handicapped) and his ministry in Southern Minas Gerais. He served, what many pastors consider to be, some of the hardest congregations in the area.

13. The interview with Nobre attested to biblically sound translation skills in this challenging area of the state and country. Nobre went to Southern Minas Gerais as a missionary of the NMB in 2000. Under his leadership, Central BC church grew from thirty people to a vibrant community of more than six hundred. In Southern Minas Gerais, where churches average forty to sixty people, Central is considered a megachurch. It has the best church facilities in the region, compared to the ones in the larger cities in Brazil and even those in the US. Nobre is intentional about dealing with the sociocultural traits in a positive manner, meaning that he uses the traits as a bridge to share the Gospel and make disciples.

14. Ferreira was the President of the Southern Minas Gerais Baptist Association at that time. Along with Silva, Ferreira is more inclined to see the local culture as a barrier to the translation of the Gospel in the region. Ferreira says that Southern Minas Gerais can be compared to the 10/40 Window in terms of hardship in ministry. He is an authority on missions in the region. For more than a decade, FBC Cambuí has been promoting an annual Missions Conference. Ferreira has helped dozens of seminary students in the region through an internship and mentorship program in his church. Consequently, many pastors who are serving in Southern Minas Gerais and around the world did internships in his church. He is a mentor and leader by his example, character, and education. At the end of 2016, Ferreira earned a Master of Theology degree at *Seminário Bíblico Palavra da Vida* (Word of Life Biblical Seminary) in Atibaia, São Paulo.

from a regional perspective. Finally, oral history interviews were done with the BBC leaders' engagement in the translation of the Gospel in the country considering the country's sociocultural traits. The same set of questions that was used in the interviews with the pastors of Southern Minas Gerais were also used with the convention leaders.

The interviews with the BBC leaders established the prevalent sociocultural traits in contemporary Brazil, and how these traits affect the translation of the Gospel in a specific region. They considered diverse cultures within the same country rather than simply focusing on a regional culture such as Southern Minas Gerais. By doing this, the author could assess more broadly the translation of the Gospel in Brazil through the expertise, practices, and experience of convention leaders in evangelism and discipleship as they remembered and reflected on their ministry in diverse places. A deeper comprehension of how the translation process occurred in its indigenizing and pilgrim principles demonstrated the bridges and barriers to sharing the good news in Brazil.

Interview Goals and Questions

In accordance with Ballard's advice, the interviewer applied the theoretical framework of WCS and the literature review about Brazilian sociocultural traits to inform the process as an insider agent.[15] The interviewer also adopted James Hoopes' perspective, which suggests that interviews help a researcher find out how someone's ideas led them to their practices and evaluates the significance of those ideas.[16] The goal of the interviews was to test how the sociocultural traits positively and negatively affect evangelism and discipleship. In the end, the research contributes to understanding the state of the translation of the Gospel in Brazil through evangelical churches and the contribution of Brazilian Baptists to this phenomenon.

The initial questions sought to collect basic information about the time and places of ministry in churches and denominational positions of the interviewees. Then, an open-ended question regarding the Brazilian culture was asked. What are the main traits of the people? How do these traits impact the fulfillment of the Great Commission? The pastors were also asked to give examples and mention concrete cases from their own experiences. After this general question, four other questions were posed to

15. Ballard, *History of Oral History*, 111.
16. Hoopes, *Oral History*, 50.

Christ Dialogues with Culture

test the four prevalent traits of cordiality, collectivism, the Brazilian way of coping, and religiosity, and to measure the impact these traits have on the translation of the Gospel in Brazil.[17] In all these questions, the interviewees were asked to provide examples and concrete experiences they had in ministry. The model of the interview was as follows:

"Based on your experience as a pastor and denominational leader, please answer the following questions related to evangelism and discipleship in the local culture. This survey addresses the impact of local characteristics and four major Brazilian sociocultural traits in evangelism and discipleship."

1. How long you have been serving as a pastor and leader of the denomination?

2. Which churches and institutions have you served, and how long have you been serving these churches and institutions?

3. Brazil has its own local culture. Given your experience, please list local cultural traits and discuss how they affect evangelism and discipleship. Provide concrete examples or cases that illustrate those local traits and how they affect the obedience to the Great Commission.

4. One of the important sociocultural traits of Brazilians is cordiality. People are typically gentle and kind, with a character marked by respect for the human person, tolerance, and hospitality. Does cordiality facilitate, make it harder, or is it both a bridge and, at the same time, a barrier for evangelism and discipleship? As you give your opinion, provide examples or tell stories from your experience.

5. Another remarkable trait of Brazilians is collectivism. Brazilians tend to have "strong, cohesive groups (especially represented by the extended family; including uncles, aunts, grandparents, and cousins) which protects its members in exchange for loyalty." Does collectivism facilitate, is it a barrier, or does it both facilitate and constitute a barrier for evangelism and discipleship? Give examples from your ministry experience.

---

17. The questions inquired about bridges and barriers. Michael Green presents some bridges to the communication of the Gospel in *Evangelism in the Early Church*. For him, the Pax Romana, the common language, the Roman road system, and monotheism created a hunger for God in other people. Together, these helped to establish a mindset of early church expansion in the first century. Green, *Evangelism in the Early Church*, 232–33.

6. The Brazilian way of coping also impacts the fulfilment of the Great Commission. Our people resort to creativity, mutual support, and the network of friends and acquaintances as a problem-solving strategy. Does the Brazilian way of coping facilitate, is it a barrier, or does it both facilitate and constitute a barrier for evangelism and discipleship? Give examples from your ministry experience, including ethical dilemmas.

7. One mark of the Brazilian people is their religiosity. The Catholic faith inherited from Portugal, together with the Indigenous and African religious traditions, play a great role in the nature of the people. How does religiosity become a barrier, a bridge, or both a bridge and a barrier for evangelism and discipleship? Feel free to narrate stories and describe general principles or patterns you experienced in ministry.

8. Make any final considerations or add anything you wish to this interview.

Profile of Interviewees

The group of interviewees was composed of eight key leaders from the five macro-regions of the country: the North, Northeast, Central-West, Southeast, and South. The interviewees were selected partially at the suggestion of Geremias Bento da Silva, General Director of the Northeastern Baptist Theological Seminary (NeBTS), in Feira de Santana, Bahia state. Silva was also chosen by the author to be one of the interviewees. He offered advice on four Brazilian Baptist leaders who had experience serving local churches, coordinating denominational agencies, or doing missionary work in the field, and who would be able to add insight to the present research. Three additional names were determined by the author through contacts with denominational leaders of state conventions and associations.

The ministry experience of the interviewees ranges from eleven to forty-three years in the BBC and its denominational agencies. The interviewees either serve or have served as a senior pastor, associate pastor, church planter, and /or leader of denominational agencies at the regional, state, or national levels. The following table summarizes their profile information. Additional considerations are made regarding their length of ministry, geographic-cultural area of service, and the impact of both on the interviewees' expressed ability to do a biblically sound translation of the gospel.

Christ Dialogues with Culture

Name	Years in Ministry	Present Position	Ministry Experience	Date of Interview
Socrates Oliveira de Souza	30	Executive Director of the BBC	Denominational leader in the BBC for 15 years, Senior Pastor and Associate Pastor for 15 years	March 28, 2017
Nilton Antonio de Souza	43	General Director of the CBC	Missionary for the NMB for 39 years, including being Executive Manager for Missions	March 24, 2017
Guilherme Oliveira Nossa	27	President of the Baptist Convention of Rondônia and pastor at SBC of Jaru, Rondônia	Pastor of churches in Minas Gerais state (cities of Belo Horizonte, Ipanema, and the region of Governador Valadares)	May 9, 2017
Hércio Fonseca de Araújo	16	President of the Baptist Convention of Planalto Central (Central-West region) and Senior Pastor at North Lake Baptist Church, Federal District	Associate Pastor at FBC of João Pessoa, Paraíba state for four years	May 15, 2017
Samuel Meira Moutta	11	NMB Executive Manager for Missions	Previously involved with local association and state convention and pastor in the city of São Fidélis, Rio de Janeiro state	March 28, 2017
Valdir Soares	35	NMB Evangelism Manager for the Indigenous People	As a missionary, has been serving as church planter, coordinator for various states and regions, and Executive Secretary of Roraima State Convention	March 29, 2017

Name	Years in Ministry	Present Position	Ministry Experience	Date of Interview
Geremias Bento da Silva	43	General Director of NeBTS, Feira de Santana, Bahia state	NMB Executive Manager for Missions, church planter, pastor in Rio de Janeiro state and Belo Horizonte, Minas Gerais state, director of the Air Broadcasting Biblical School, president of Operation Mobilization in Brazil	March 28, 2017
Reginaldo Pires Moreira	32	Deputy Treasurer at Northeastern Baptist Association, Rio Grande do Sul and Pastor at Consolation Baptist Church, Vacaria	Senior Pastor, Associate Pastor, and denominational leader in São Paulo, Piauí, and Rio Grande do Sul states, Rector of Paulistana Baptist Theological College, São Paulo city, São Paulo state	May 9, 2017

Table 2. Profiles of the Eight Brazilian Baptist Leaders Interviewed

Socrates Oliveira de Souza. Souza is the Executive Director of the BBC. He was interviewed by phone, March 28, 2017. He has been in ministry for over thirty years, serving mainly in Southeast Brazil. His first ministry was as a church planter. "I had a project to bring toward total financial autonomy churches that could not sustain the pastor . . . Because I used to have a professional activity in which I made money, I started . . . with a small church, in a town in the countryside, with thirty-six members at the time. I worked there for five years, and I left the church with a full-time pastor," Souza recalled.

His second ministry was at First Baptist Church [FBC] Caramujo, in Niteroi, Rio de Janeiro state. He states, "I was there for about three years with the same project. When the church was able to support its pastor, I left so that another pastor could take over." After that, Souza worked for about three years as an Administration Minister at the November 22nd Baptist Church in Niterói.

Souza's first denominational position was as Executive Secretary at the Carioca Baptist Convention [CBC], where he served for almost three years.[18] Then, in 2002, he started his tenure as Executive Director of the

---

18. CBC includes churches in the city of Rio de Janeiro, while Fluminense Baptist

BBC. In this capacity, he oversees the Baptist work in the nation. In the past, he has been interim director for the NMB, World Mission Board, NBTS, Recife, Pernambuco state, Equatorial Baptist Theological Seminary (Belém, Pará state), Missionary Union of Baptist Men, and SBTS, Rio de Janeiro, Rio de Janeiro state. He also has been an interim pastor in several churches.

Nilton Antonio de Souza. Nilton Antonio de Souza (hereafter, referred to as "Antonio") is the General Director of the CBC. Antonio was interviewed on the phone, March 24, 2017. He has been in ministry for over forty-three years in the Southern and Southeastern regions. As missionary for the NMB, he served for thirty-nine years in capacities such as Executive Manager for Missions, Executive at the Baptist Convention in Santa Catarina state, Coordinator of the missionaries of South Brazil including São Paulo state, Coordinator for Southeast Brazil, Director of Evangelism at the FlBC, and Church Planter of five churches (with direct involvement), besides overseeing ministries in churches. Antonio also has a teaching ministry at Integrated Center of Education and Missions, in Rio de Janeiro, Rio de Janeiro state, Bauru Baptist College, NBTS, SBTS, Paraná Baptist College, and Minas Gerais Baptist College.

Guilherme Oliveira Nossa. Nossa is the President of the Baptist Convention of Rondônia. He is Pastor of SBC of Jaru, Rondônia state. He was interviewed on the phone, May 9, 2017. He has been in ministry for twenty-seven years in the Minas Gerais (Southeast region) and Rondônia (North) states. His ministry has been in local churches and as a church planter. Initially, he served FBC in Barreiro de Baixo, a neighborhood in Belo Horizonte, Minas Gerais state. Then, he went on to lead FBC of Ipanema, one of the first Baptist churches established in Minas Gerais. Afterwards, he served in church planting in the Governador Valadares area in the same state, and then went to Rondônia state.

Hércio Fonseca de Araújo. Araújo is the President of the Baptist Convention of Planalto Central. This convention includes churches of the Federal District, Goiás, and Minas Gerais states. Araújo is senior pastor of the Baptist Church of Lago Norte, Federal District. He has been in ministry for sixteen years in the Northeastern and Central-Western regions. Araújo was a businessman who turned to pastoral ministry. He first served four years at FBC of João Pessoa, Paraíba state, in the Northeast region. His ministry at North Lake Baptist Church has lasted twelve years. He was Vice-President of the BCPC and became its President in April 2017.

Convention [FlBC] includes the other churches of the state of Rio de Janeiro.

Samuel Meira Moutta. Moutta is the NMB Executive Manager for Missions. His phone interview occurred March 28, 2017. He has been in pastoral ministry for eleven years. As a teenager, he served the denomination in the association and FlBC. Moutta served a Baptist church in the city of São Fidélis for three and a half years. After that, he served as Executive Director for Missions at NMB.

Valdir Soares. Soares is the NMB Evangelism Manager for the Indigenous People. He has been in ministry for thirty-five years. His phone interview was on March 29, 2017. In his present position, Soares has coordinated church planting projects and overseen missionaries for the past four years. His first ministry was in Boa Vista, Roraima, starting on September 20, 1982. He and his wife Alice coordinated missionary work in twelve states. He also planted churches and served as Executive Secretary for three years in Roraima. In 1997, Soares coordinated the missionary work in the North and West-Central regions, based in Cuiaba, Mato Grosso state, and Brasilia, Federal District.

Geremias Bento da Silva. Silva is the General Director of NeBTS. His phone interview was on March 28, 2017. He has been in ministry for forty-three years and served in the Southern, Southeastern, and Northeastern regions. Silva spent the first three years of his ministry as a church planter. He also served for eighteen years at Hope Baptist Church in the city of Rio de Janeiro, first as Assistant Pastor, then as Senior Pastor. His next (five-year) pastorates were at Gamboa Baptist Church, Rio de Janeiro city and FBC in Belo Horizonte, Minas Gerais state.

As a missionary, Silva served ten years at the NMB. He held executive positions in the areas of expansion, missions, evangelism, and discipleship. He has been serving in the Air Broadcasting Biblical School, a radio and training ministry based in Rio de Janeiro state, since 1974. He has been the director of the company since 2007. He has been the General Director at NeBTS since December 27, 2011. Silva is the president of Operation Mobilization [OM] in Brazil.

Reginaldo Pires Moreira. Moreira is the Deputy Treasurer of the Baptist Association of the Northeast of Rio Grande do Sul state. His phone interview took place on May 9, 2017. He pastors Consolation Baptist Church of Vacaria. Moreira has been in ministry for thirty-two years in the Southern, Southeastern, and Northeastern regions of the country. In Rio Grande do Sul, he also served at Baptist Church of Getúlio Vargas for four years and at FBC in Pelotas for two years. He then served the Baptist Church of Vermelha in Teresina, Piauí state, for five years.

After leaving Piauí, Moreira served in pastoral capacities in São Paulo state: first, in the city of São Paulo, at Jardim Primavera Baptist Church (seven years); the Baptist Church in Brooklyn, as Minister of Evangelism, where he implemented the strategy, Explosive Evangelism; and at FBC São Paulo, where he led the midday and prayer services. In the countryside of São Paulo, he led Baptist Congregations in Anhembi for five and a half years, before going to Rio Grande do Sul to serve at Consolation Baptist Church. In denominational positions, Moreira served as Rector of the Paulistana Baptist Theological College in São Paulo, President of the Baptist Pastors Conference in Rio Grande do Sul, President of the Baptist Pastors Conference in the Piauí-Maranhão Baptist Convention, and President of the Executive Council of the Baptist Convention in Piauí.

Major Sociocultural Factors Affecting Translation

The third question of the oral history interviews affirmed that Brazil has its own culture. The author asked interviewees to list national cultural traits and discuss how those traits affect evangelism and discipleship. Concrete examples or cases that illustrate those local traits and how they affect obedience to the Great Commission were additionally asked. In this open-ended question, the terms "bridges" or "barriers" were intentionally not mentioned. The answers given attest that those sociological categories are already used by the interviewees, who mentioned them directly or indirectly.[19]

In analyzing their stories, the interviewer sought to understand whether their answers confirmed or contradicted the sociocultural traits found in the literature review. In the end, the answers confirmed the traits, as detailed in the following section. In addition, the author attempted to understand whether the answers presented signs of biblically sound translation, awareness of translation, or little to no awareness of translation practices. Following this same line of thought, the author sought to assess

---

19. As mentioned in Chapter 1, bridges relate to the indigenizing principle, because they are a path of connection to the local culture. Barriers are related to the pilgrim principle, as they point out aspects of the culture that are dissonant with the Gospel. Preliminary results of local oral history interviews in Southern Minas Gerais indicate that religiosity (mainly Catholicism), collectivism, and cordiality are the top three sociocultural traits mentioned. These three traits are the most prevalent to be considered for the translation of the Gospel in Southern Minas Gerais per the interviewees. Similar surveys can be done in other parts of the country to indicate how local traits impact the work of local evangelists, pastors, and disciples of Christ.

from the interviewees' responses whether the translation principles they used were indigenous principles, pilgrim principles, or both.

Affirmation of the Four Major Sociocultural Traits

Is the Brazilian culture, as described by the interviewees, similar or different to the ones found in the literature review that mention cordiality, religiosity, the Brazilian way of coping, and collectivism?[20] Overall, the answers given by the interviewees affirm the four traits found in the literature review as the following figure shows. First, their comments reinforce that Brazil is culturally diverse.[21] This fact is confirmed in this research by the continental size of Brazil and the composite cultural matrix of the people living within Brazil: Portuguese, African, and Indigenous, besides minority groups of immigrants from around the world, as covered in Chapters 1 and 3. In addition, the interviewees' answers affirm the cordiality and collectivism traits inside this cultural diversity.

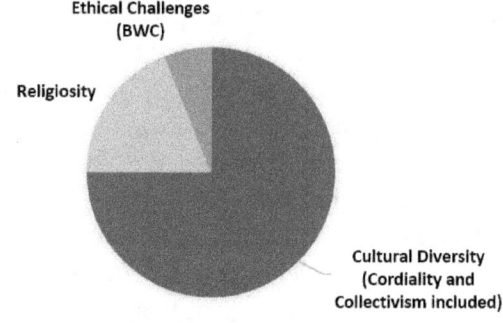

Figure 11. Sociocultural Traits as Classified by the Interviewees

20. These traits had a greater recurrence in the literature review and found more affirmation in the preliminary survey conducted by the author, as detailed in Chapter 1 and the *Igreja Multiplicadora* approach. Cordiality means that Brazilians are emotional and warm in their relationships, intimate and affectionate, and against formalisms and social conventions. In regard to religiosity, as a religious people, Brazilians highly value the "other world" beyond the "street" and the "house," as presented by Matta. The Brazilian way of coping is basically a problem-solving strategy. Brazilians generally resort to a network of friends and acquaintances to find solutions. Finally, collectivism means that the people's self-image is defined more by the "we" than the "I," and members of the society have a high level of interdependence.

21. This perspective is discussed by Freyre in Chapter 1.

Main Brazilian Sociocultural Traits as Seen in Interviews

Interviewee	Trait Mentioned	Literature Review Equivalent Trait	Bridge and/or Barrier
Souza	Cultural Diversity (assumed trait): with varied levels of cordiality and collectivism; people groups and immigrant roots	Cordiality Collectivism	**Bridge** and *Barrier*
Antonio	Cultural Diversity Religious Diversity	Cordiality Collectivism Religiosity	**Bridge** and *Barrier*
Nossa	Ethical Challenges	Brazilian way of coping	**Bridge** and *Barrier*
Araújo	Religiosity	Religiosity	*Barrier*
Moutta	Cultural Diversity Religious Diversity	Cordiality Collectivism Religiosity	**Bridge** and *Barrier*
Soares	Cultural Diversity	Cordiality Collectivism	**Bridge** and *Barrier*
Silva	Cultural Diversity Religious Diversity	Cordiality Collectivism Religiosity	**Bridge** and *Barrier*
Moreira	Cultural Diversity	Cordiality Collectivism	**Bridge**

Table 3. Traits According to Interviewees Defined as Bridge and /or Barrier

Second, the interviewees' answers also reinforce the religiosity trait in Brazilian culture and its impact on evangelism and discipleship. Finally, the interviewees mentioned the ethical challenges present in the country and specific regions, which relates to the Brazilian way of coping.

The tables below summarize the findings, detailed in this chapter and the following ones.

Ranking of Traits

1st	Cultural Diversity—*Cordiality and collectivism* mentioned (besides national /immigrant origins)
2nd	Religious Diversity—*Religiosity*
3rd	Ethical Challenges—*Brazilian way of coping*

Table 4. Ranking of Traits that Appear in the Interviews

Main Traits: Cultural Diversity and Religiosity

Six of eight (75 percent) of the interviewees mentioned the cultural diversity of Brazil, with some pointing to the varied historical origins (Portuguese, Indigenous, African, and other immigrant communities) and the specific main traits of cordiality and collectivism. Three out of eight (38 percent) noted the religious diversity in Brazil. Only one mentioned ethical challenges. The interpretation of the data is guided by their ranking in their recurrence in the open-ended questions. Each of these traits—cordiality and collectivism, which encompasses cultural diversity, and religiosity—are dealt with separately and in connection to one another.

Cultural Diversity through Cordiality and Collectivism

Souza sees immense cultural diversity in the country, a diversity that varies from region to region. The North is more open in terms of cordiality and collectivism, and the people of the country become more closed as one goes further South. For him, depending on this openness or "closedness," one either finds total barriers or more permeable barriers that enable bridges to be built with these traits, or cultural bridges that currently exist and can be used to preach the Gospel. Souza summarizes:

> Brazil is a continental country. When we cross the country from North to South, we find many varied characteristics. For example,

for you to evangelize a person in Rio Grande do Sul, a traditional Gaucho, you can't come and talk about the Gospel to him. We must, first, establish a relationship, and I would say that, while he doesn't call you to drink a mate tea or *chimarrão*, he is not ready for you to talk about the Gospel. So, you need to build relationships, you need to get close to that person to find an opening to speak of Jesus to him.

In the Southeastern or Northeastern regions, according to Souza, people are more open to the Gospel and hospitable:

[I]n Rio de Janeiro, for example, in the countryside, it is easier to invite a person to go to your house, to go to your church. It's much more open ... Similarly, the Northeast people are extremely hospitable. You can arrive at any region of the Northeast and you will be warmly welcomed. You have the possibility of speaking about Jesus immediately to these people.

Souza remembers an experience he had in the city of Juazeiro do Piauí during a campaign for the NMB. The openness of the people was a bridge to present the Gospel and talk about spiritual matters: "We sat at a house door with two boys, who were wearing soccer jerseys of two different soccer teams and we started talking about soccer, and we said, "Look, your team can lose and you can still be a winner. The Bible says in Romans 8:38 we are more than conquerors regardless." Souza shared that in about thirty minutes, the young men received Jesus Christ as their personal Savior and Lord.[22] In effect, the Gospel messenger indigenized the culture of soccer and scored a goal.

As the interviewees pointed out, Brazil, like any other place, is diverse in regional and local cultures. The analysis here is an attempt to address national traits. BBC leaders have considered the cultural diversity. Regional or local approaches should be a fertile field for future endeavors.

Cultural and Religious Diversity as Bridges

Antonio focused his comments on Southern Brazil, reinforcing what Souza mentioned: people in the Southern region are less cordial. Furthermore, Antonio sees an intertwining between religion and immigrant culture, which can be confused by the people themselves. Italian, German, Ukrainian,

---

22. One of the men remains a faithful Christian, according Souza's comments. He made a recent visit to the same region and confirmed this information.

Christ Meets Culture

Estonian, Italians, and Japanese, among others, are tied to their national and religious cultures. "We could almost say that religion is their culture. The parties are related to religion . . . Culture in the Southern part of the country is that typical *Gaucho* culture, with typical clothing and songs. People are into parties and the religious aspects are well rooted in the culture."

When interacting with regional or local cultures, the translator can engage the people through popular music, literature, food, dress, and other external cultural manifestations. As the relationships are developed, the internal values and worldviews of the group are demonstrated. Then, the conversation can come into place, and in-depth translation may occur, as the interviewees detailed.

In general, Antonio's words indicate an awareness of the need of translation, both in indigenous (incarnational) and pilgrim (transformational) perspectives. In this sense, one should look at culture as an iceberg and engage it as better as possible, as pictured on the figure below. His perspective is that these traits are initially a barrier but must be turned into a bridge. The first way for doing it is by reaching out first to the man of the house. "If we fail to reach the man, we won't have permission to access the family," notes Antonio. Second, there is a need for establishing relationships.

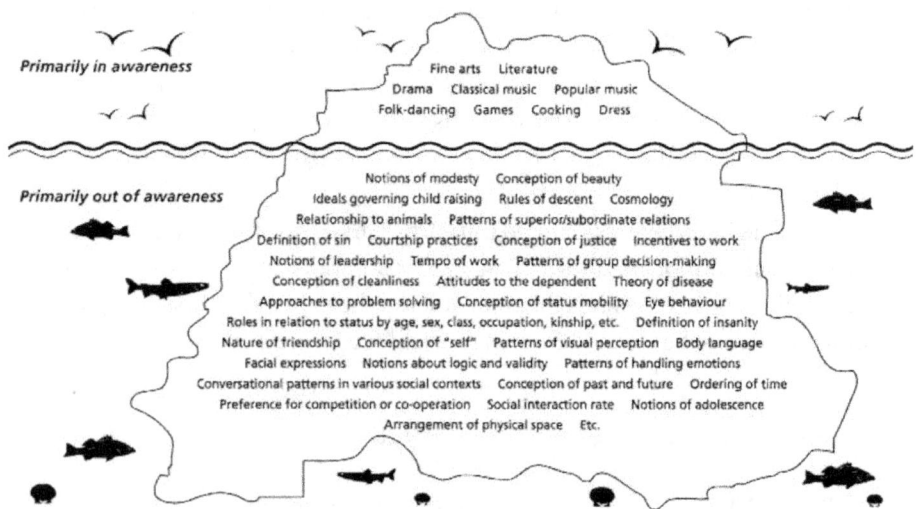

Figure 12. Cultural Iceberg Metaphor[23]

---

23. The cultural iceberg metaphor is valuable to see the need to study the culture and its deep relationships to achieve better results in missionary endeavors. The metaphor is attributed to anthropologist Hall, *AFS Orientation Handbook*.

The translation of the Gospel happens through individuals who incarnate Jesus' unconditional love, service, and teachings, according to Antonio. He highlighted the need to use love languages to connect non-believers and believers. He was adamant that loving people is the key for translating the message of Christ, which is a message of love from God to humanity through Christ: "[W]hen we arrive with the Gospel and discipleship, we should work with a lot of love [and] dedication, willing first to win the person to us and then take them to Jesus." Antonio further explained this method, "Without love, there is no trust. Without trust, there is no education and therefore there is no evangelization." He continues,

> First, we arrive with love, willing to serve and then after they trust us, we can transmit the Word. Another aspect is that, generally, in terms of discipleship, we must be close to the people and close to God. Some people have a life that is so God-oriented, so spiritual, that they can't relate to people. Therefore, they have the message but don't have listeners. Others are so connected to the people; they enter the offices of the mayors, they're even in politics . . . Therefore, they have the listeners but don't have the message. A [missionary] worker needs to have both a deep relationship with God and a relationship with the community, to be a link between God and the community. That goes for the whole country and everywhere in the world. But when it comes to the Southern region, this is very important. I haven't baptized anyone in the South, with very few exceptions, without first having held empirical studies for ten or twelve weeks in their houses, first to strengthen the relationship, and then to help them in many aspects of their lives. And when they trust you, they will hear the message and will accept to go to church to be baptized and become part of another community, almost breaking with their culture.

Antonio sees a difference in the openness of the people in other regions, apparent in details such as people opening their houses to him more readily, which is consistent with what Souza and other interviewees mentioned. He affirms that it is much easier to preach the Gospel "because of this access that people generally give you." In the South, there is a need to "make an appointment for everything. In the North, you are welcome at any time. You are welcome in any situation," he affirms. Another feature that makes evangelistic strategies different between the regions is that, in Northern and Northeastern Brazil, "There is no such a barrier as the man being the leader of the family. In these regions, we make contact and baptize more women than men," Antonio indicates. He adds that towards the Central-West and down toward the Southeast, strategies are necessary for one to enter the communities and families and do "the work of God."

Finally, Antonio highlights the need to live the Gospel, as the *Igreja Multiplicadora* model proposes with its discipling relationship, which engages both the cordiality and collectivism traits. He sustains, "People will want to see life in life and not just speeches. So, we must do a lot more like Paul did, 'Follow my example, as I follow the example of Christ.' When we take the time to get to know and to have a relationship with people, they become open to hear what we have to say."

For Antonio, the translation of the Gospel in Southern Brazil and even the whole country involves individually indigenizing the Gospel to the openness or "closedness" of the culture. In other words, one should become like a Southerner or a Northeasterner in order to reach out to them. If the individuals are more open, Christians should take advantage of this characteristic and share the Gospel. If the individuals are more closed, Christians should attempt to get close to them and share the Gospel. In both cases, words and actions must be connected. In the end, biblically sound translation occurs as core values, rituals, heroes, and symbols of local cultures are addressed and discussed according to biblical principles, so that God's glory is seen in culture as seen in the figure below:[24]

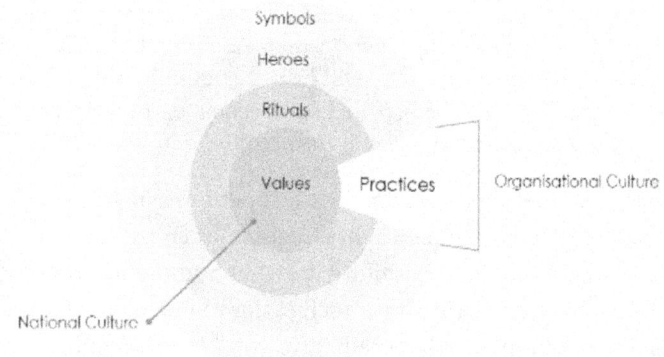

Figure 13. The Levels of Culture Inside a Nation

24. The different levels of culture as proposed by Hofstede aids the assessment of the culture for furthering practices such as comparing, combating, or using symbols, heroes, rituals, and values of the society for the benefit of the Christian message. Hofstede, "Geert Hofstede's Scientific Innovation."

Moreira has a similar approach to Antonio. His definition of culture relates to social strata, which does not prevent him from doing evangelism among any group, including politicians. Moreira has served as chaplain for specific groups. The lack of an appropriate witness of Christian living may be a barrier, he affirms, as Antonio also highlighted. "What I believe is that the problem of people's lack of spiritual character has been preventing very cultured people from paying attention to the plan of salvation or religious education," Moreira said. This also relates to the Brazilian way of coping, given that many believers morally fail and compromise their testimony before the community.

Dangers of Syncretism

In his responses, Moutta combines cultural diversity in the literal sense (a nation composed by diverse cultures) with the varied religiosity that is an outcome of the varied national cultures of origin. He uses particular expressions repeatedly in the interviews (i.e. "a multicultural country of continental dimensions"). He mentions the differences between the Southern, Northeastern, Central-Western, Northern, and Southeastern regions and adds that, within these regions, there is cultural diversity at in-state levels. In the Northeast, "Bahia is different from Piauí. Ceará is totally different from Maranhão. And then, there are differences within each State. Within a State, I have, for example... in the State of Bahia, Salvador [the capital] is one thing, the South of Bahia is something else." Accordig to Moutta, this broad cultural diversity in Brazil makes it difficult to describe the national culture.

Moutta addresses the historical origins of the country and the influence of culture upon the openness and religiosity of Portuguese, indigenous people, and African slaves. There is also the risk of syncretism, a danger that recurs in the comments of the interviewees. This risk is addressed in next chapter, alongside the specific trait of religiosity. Moutta provides the following description of Brazil's religious diversity:

> It was all mixed very deeply into the culture, which is also reflected in the Brazilian religiosity. Besides, there are people more accessible to the Gospel and discipleship, and there are others more resilient. There are more rational individuals who hear and understand and then accept or reject the message of the Gospel, while others mystify a lot and have a mystical vision of the Gospel with Catholicism, with witchcraft, with superstition, and this generates

> great religious syncretism in Brazil. Maybe that explains a little the significant growth of Neopentecostal religions in Brazil because they use exactly this syncretism of Catholic elements together with Spiritism and elements of the Gospel.[25]

He further states,

> So, this cultural, and therefore religious diversity, I think, by itself represents a major challenge in the process of evangelization. When I say challenge, I don't mean impediment. But the evangelist must learn how to identify the person inside his culture as he can be either a reflection of it or the complete opposite. But the Brazilian person's individuality must be understood for the Gospel and discipleship to be most appropriately presented to him or her. But, in general, he is open to the Gospel.

Syncretism, per Moutta is bad translation. In the end, Moutta demonstrates awareness of a biblically sound translation as he affirms that although the varied cultures and religions in Brazil are initially a challenge (or barrier) for the diffusion of the Gospel message, they still should be analyzed and understood in order to become a bridge for cultural translation. A tension and strong correlation between the indigenizing and pilgrim principles is seen, since there is a clear danger of syncretistic practices through the mixed religious symbols. The former religious practices should become like pilgrim practices as the Gospel influences and changes the local culture, places, economies, and societies.

Cultural Diversity of People Groups

Soares appeals to the cultural diversity of Brazil in terms of people groups. He mentions gypsies, indigenous people, *Quilombolas* (those coming from African slaves' communities), riverside communities, and urban groups, with their local, regional, and inter-regional features. He opines, "They are very different from each other, and this also happens from region to region. There are several of these ethnic groups in Brazil that transcend our knowledge in terms of how well prepared we are in terms of methodology for the work of church planting."

---

25. The syncretism of NeoPentecostalism is seen in the appropriation of symbols of Catholicism, Spiritism, Candomblé, and Umbanda, such as Blessed Water, the use of salt to clean spiritual fields, oils, and flowers, among others seen on TV programs and special campaigns. Oliveira, *Messianismo Pentecostal*, 69.

Soares goes on to reflect his own journey, and how the diversity of the Brazilian people tested him. When he left his hometown, Recife, in Pernambuco state, and went to Boa Vista in Roraima state, he found diverse cultures in the new place, with people from states such as Maranhão, Ceará, Rio de Janeiro, Rio Grande do Sul, and some of the indigenous communities. The missionary proposed some ways of doing a "cultural filter," knowing that the Gospel is supra-cultural but needs to be related to the local culture. He explains,

> You must analyze them culturally, and you should know this: Where am I going to mark out, head to the planting of churches, considering the universe of those cultures that are here around me? Even the type of approach . . . addressing a person from the Northeast is different from addressing one from the South. A person from São Paulo is different from one from Rio. I mean, they each come with a backpack on their backs, mind, heart, and their culture. Do you understand? So, we must be very wise about it. We know the Gospel is supra-cultural. We know the Gospel surpasses the power of any adversity so that it can be announced, so that we can evangelize, and so we can make disciples.

Together with Antonio, Soares manifests a biblically sound translation perspective, particularly when addressing the indigenous issue. He acknowledges adversities or barriers to the proclamation of the Gospel in a way that is intelligible to both indigenous peoples and those in non-indigenous contexts. Building bridges means gaining knowledge and expertise regarding the culture and the language (linguistic translation) so that, "We can transmit biblical and theological concepts to these people, so they will assimilate what we are communicating, that is, the communication should be clear and objective to reach these people."

Immigrant Influences on Culture and Religion

Silva, as the other interviewees, sees the cultural diversity of Brazil as its main cultural trait. He avers the indigenous culture is becoming increasingly weaker. This decline can be explained by the oppressive and destructive character of the colonial system, as detailed in Chapter 3. However, the indigenous culture and religion are still evident in some syncretic practices of the Afro-Brazilian religions and even Neopentecostalism.[26] Cultures im-

26. In NeoPentecostal circles, there is a high value given to the main leader of the

ported from Africa and Europe and, more recently, North-American culture (through globalization), have also become established in the country.

Like other interviewees, Silva demonstrates an awareness of translation practices. According to him, biblically sound translation considers the religious environment and involvement of the people and engages them in terms of their needs. "This way, we can understand that whatever we design or intend to do, we need to consider that we have a sum of cultures that demands from us a certain attention, so we can succeed in what we are proposing to do." Silva shares examples of the reality of the regions, starting with the mix between religion and culture in his own home area of Southern Brazil. In that part of the country, the religious environment and involvement of the people is more superficial (nominal) and maintained as tradition in the European evangelical communities. He says, "These things exert influence even over the ones raised in a Baptist home as I was. But some things end up getting impregnated in people's minds." Silva continues sharing his personal testimony:

> I was born and raised in the state of Paraná and left home when I was sixteen years old, but my house has never left me. Even in my childhood . . . I would go to church and the services were in German. At school, on my first days, I also had classes in German. That means the European culture was very strong in the South. I was strongly influenced by the Italian culture. The Italian and the German cultures were the strongest in the South. So, I have been influenced by the language, both German and Italian, and by the food and the religions. The German with Lutheranism and the Italian with the staunch Catholicism—very strong, very traditional.

In the Northeast, where Silva is serving nowadays, one should not hurt the "very mystical religious tradition . . . and . . . the tradition of the land, of the region." In the North, in states such as Amazonas, the riverside culture is unique. The Brazilian Biblical Society offers Bibles and literature in a translation specifically designed to reach the riverside communities of the Amazon, as Silva recounts.

In the case of the Southeast, the most affluent region of the country, Silva points to the variety of cultures and traditions that originated through

---

church. For example, in God is Love Pentecostal Church, David Miranda deviates far from the doctrine of the priesthood of all believers and comes closer to a spiritualist view as he views a leader as "consecrated," the "missionary," who has the power to do exorcism, heal the sick, anoint with oil. "Myths are dangerous, because their role is to inhibit rational thoughts." Leite Filho, *Seitas Neopentecostais*, 94–95.

migration from inside and outside the nation, and to the benefits of this globalized context.²⁷ He notes, "In the Southeast, it is easier to bring forward evangelism, training and discipleship projects."

The cultural and religious diversity in the country indicates a need for diverse approaches concerning evangelism and discipleship. For example, the type of small groups practiced may vary from region to region. In metropolitan areas, while the work with students and business people may be a promising niche, the costs of transportation restrain these ministries making them more conducive to home-based groups. In small cities, the implementation of small groups may take a longer time or even not work out, given that the community is an asset in those places.

Ethical Problems and Religious Festivals as Barriers

Nossa and Araújo's responses to the open-ended questions were different, showing a lesser degree of translation ability. They classify religiosity in the Northeast and the ethical challenges in the North as barriers to preaching the Gospel and making disciples of Jesus Christ in those regions. They opine that such contexts are hostile to the message and show a prevalence of loose moral behavior; thus, the Gospel tends to become a pilgrim.

Nossa affirms the continental size and cultural diversity of the nation. He sees this multicultural ambience as negatively influencing the church. In Rondônia state in the Northern region, he perceives theology as not challenging moral and ethical issues. Nossa posits, the decreasing emphasis of the Old Testament prophets and of Jesus Himself is not seen "in our State though. There is this great permissiveness, and this makes the proclamation of the Gospel very difficult. Perhaps, the church itself begins to adapt to this scheme and to live so calmly, going along with all that." Because of this lack of critical engagement with the culture, the church has lost its missionary vision of the Great Commission given by Jesus Christ, "as if the Gospel would not be as transformative in people's lives," he said.

Araújo, in turn, points to some very particular features of Northeastern Brazil as barriers for translating the Gospel: religious festivities such as the carnival and Saint John festivities in June.²⁸ Araújo has been experienc-

---

27. Wesley Grangberg-Michaelson points out that the new generations are more focused on "authentic spirituality," searching for transcendent reality and immediate spiritual communities." Granberg-Michaelson, *From Times Square to Timbuktu*, 25.

28. In the June festivities, people launch fireworks, kindle fire pits in front of their

ing these religious matters since childhood: "As a Northeasterner, I have followed the Northeastern people of Brazil since I was a kid. We see how these influences we receive prevent us, somehow, from experiencing the Gospel in its entirety . . . I see the predominant Catholic religious issue in the Northeast preventing us from reaching some people."

At the same time, the religious festivities are also a doorway for understanding the local culture and its core values. People who adhere to the spiritual meaning of the carnival are committed Catholics who adopt a works-based salvation mindset. They need a cross-based and apologetic approach. Individuals who participate only in carnival parties and celebrations may be more open to relational evangelism or events-based strategies.

Conclusion

This dissertation argues that sociocultural factors play a significant role in the translation of the Gospel in Brazil as discovered and expressed among the BBC. So far, this research has dealt with how Christ meets, engages, changes, challenges, and, as discussed in the present chapter, dialogues with culture. As the interviewees attest, Brazil is a country with continental dimensions and a varied culture that has been formed by different peoples, immigrant communities, and religions expressions. The cordiality and collectivism of open or closed groups exists to varying degrees around the country.

As discussed in this chapter, for the evangelical church to enhance its practices in Brazil, per the interviewees, there is a need to take advantage of the cordiality of the people to share the Gospel and develop strategies to engage with its collectivism and groups. Chapter 6 examines more closely how Christ interacts with culture, specifically with the major sociocultural traits per the memoirs of the eight interviewees and their opinion concerning the bridges, barriers, and other nuances for the translation of the Gospel in Brazil.

---

houses in the street, eat corn-based food and boiled peanuts, drink liquors made of fruits, all these being religious habits tied to the worship of Saint John the Baptist, a Catholic idol. The indigenous principle helps one eat the seasonal food (1 Cor 8) thanking the Lord for His provision through nature. The pilgrim principle leads believers to avoid making connections with Catholic traditions, such as being part of festivities where there is worship to the Saint and sinful behaviors (Cf. Ps 1:1–2).

6

Christ Interacts with Culture

Bridges and Barriers in the Major Traits
as Viewed by BBC Leaders

CHRIST MEETS, ENGAGES, CHANGES, challenges, and dialogues the Brazilian culture, as seen in the previous chapters. As Christ interacts with culture, new contours and shapes are born, as depicted in this chapter. Inside the cultural diversity of the country, as demonstrated through its historical origins, economic differences between the regions, and other geographical and sociological differences, four primary traits are seen throughout Brazilian culture namely cordiality, collectivism, the Brazilian way of coping, and religiosity. At this point, two central questions are raised in relation to these traits. First, how do these traits impact the translation of the Gospel in modern-day Brazil? Second, what aspects of a biblically sound translation are seen in the memoirs, practices, and sociocultural work of the strategic BBC leaders? This sixth chapter presents answers to these and other questions to deepen the discussion about the significant role of the sociocultural factors in the translation of the Gospel in Brazil as discovered and expressed among the BBC.

Cordiality: Bridge for Evangelism, Barrier for Decision Making

After the open-ended, general question about the culture of Brazil, the focus of the interviews moved to major sociocultural traits prevalent in the literature review.[1] It started with a question on cordiality: "One of the important sociocultural trait of Brazilians is cordiality. People [are] gentle and kind, with a character marked by respect for the human person, tolerance, and hospitality. Does cordiality facilitate, make it harder, or is it both a bridge and at the same time a barrier to evangelism and discipleship? In your response, provide examples or tell stories from your experience." The answers are shown below.

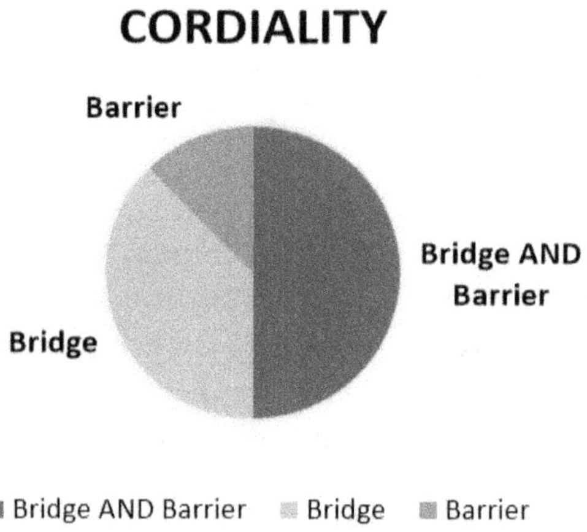

CORDIALITY

■ Bridge AND Barrier   ■ Bridge   ■ Barrier

Figure 14. Cordiality as Both Bridge and Barrier

For four of eight (or 50 percent) interviewees, cordiality is both a bridge and a barrier for evangelism and discipleship. Three out of eight (37.5 percent) see it as a bridge, while one (12.5 percent) sees it as only as a barrier. In terms of translation ability, half the interviewees demonstrated signs of awareness of translation, while the other half presented signs of biblically sound translation practices in their ministry experience. The proportion of indigenous and pilgrim principles mentioned or perceived by the interviewees is balanced. A summary is more detailed is presented on the table below.

1. An analysis of sociocultural traits is found in Chapter 1.

Cordiality

Bridge and *Barrier*

Interviewee	Bridge/Barrier	Indigenizing/Pilgrim Principles Mentioned
Souza	**Bridge** and *Barrier*	Pilgrim
Antonio	**Bridge**	Indigenizing
Nossa	**Bridge** and *Barrier*	Pilgrim
Araújo	**Bridge** and *Barrier*	Indigenizing and Pilgrim
Moutta	**Bridge**	Indigenous
Soares	**Bridge** and *Barrier*	Indigenizing and Pilgrim
Silva	*Barrier*	Pilgrim
Moreira	**Bridge**	Indigenizing

Table 5. Cordiality: Bridges, Barriers, Indigenizing and Pilgrim Principles

Bridge for Relationship, Evangelism, and Discipleship

Antonio, Moutta, and Moreira see cordiality mainly as a bridge for approaching people and translating the Gospel. For Antonio, relationships are a major factor in worldwide evangelism.[2] Antonio exemplifies one who understands the philosophy of evangelism as being based on relationship

---

2. This approach, based on the traits of cordiality and collectivism, is very strong in Brazil, according to the *Igreja Multiplicadora* model and its Discipling Relationship proposal. However, the relationship is mainly a bridge to establish trust, as Antonio affirms. Intentionality in evangelism is defended by Antonio and Soares and Roland Muller, missiologist for Arab Muslim people. Muller proposes that, "Successful evangelists did not use evangelism through friendships as a missionary strategy. All of them used something that I will call 'evangelism based in teaching.' In this case, friendships are real friendships. As the Discipling Relationships [approach] defends, one should live Christianity as a life style, engage in real friendships, find opportunities to teach the Bible, share the Gospel, and confront people to decide for Christ." Muller, *O Mensageiro*, 37–43.

and friendship: "In Brazil, people who convert the most—98 percent—are family members, neighbors, co-workers or colleagues. Ninety-eight percent is the overall average in Brazil. So, this is the result of relationship," he estimates. Cordiality should be used as a bridge to bring people into a relationship with the translator, who preaches the Gospel, integrates persons into the church, and disciples them.[3] Christ becomes like one of them as His disciples reflect Him, live, and share His love. This is a sign of biblically sound translation, even though one can question the linearity of the process. Antonio states:

> If I deliver the message straight away, I may have good results, but I can't get to the discipleship until I transform that new believer into a multiplier. So, we should start winning people through our trust, our friendship. And there's the Brazilian cordiality. The trust that many already have in God, or their relationship with other Christians, with evangelicals—all of that builds our relationship with these people. Now, if we isolate ourselves, don't relate to people and want only to deliver a message, we're going to have our difficulties multiplied.

Moutta sees a connection between nationwide cordiality, which may vary according to the region, individual, and socioeconomic conditions of the people. For him, in the riverside communities of the North and poor areas of the Northeast, people are open to receiving help because of their lack of medical, educational, and health resources, along with the lack of basic quality of life components such as electricity, water, food, transportation, and logistics. In these cases, "Cordiality joins the necessity . . . there is a very favorable environment for evangelization, although we must be careful not to turn this into paternalism, dependency, and hidden interests," Moutta warns.

When one goes to rich neighborhoods in the cities of the Southeast, such as São Paulo or Rio de Janeiro, or in Southern Brazil cities as Caxias do Sul or Porto Alegre, "People are welcoming but not needy. Then the access, the contact, the bond, the relationship with these people become more difficult." An awareness of translation practices is seen in Moutta's affirmation that, "We need to understand all that to identify and use this welcoming trait in favor of evangelism and discipleship."

---

3. The Parable of the Sower (Matt 13) can be used for teaching about this duality in the Brazilian culture, utilizing the rocky soil, where the seed springs up quickly but does not prevail, as the barrier perspective, and the good soil, where the seed produced a crop, as the bridge approach.

Finally, Moreira perceives cordiality as building bridges. The Gospel becomes indigenous, indeed something personal, as cordiality connects to concepts such as love, hospitality, tolerance, pleasantness, and mercy. He tells of some strategies from his present ministry that illustrate this approach. He invites people to dinners and birthday parties, where he sings songs and presents Christ, and he opens his house to receive people in times of need. He further shares,

> I remember that, when I was a pastor at the Baptist Church of Vermelha in Teresina, Piauí, my wife was traveling. In the building where I lived, there was a guy who I would hardly see, but I found out he was going to get married . . . He said: "I'm indeed receiving my relatives, but I can't host everyone." Then I said: "My apartment is available." I gave him the house keys. People would come and go. They would do whatever they wanted . . . Of course, occasionally, we would hear: "Would you like a beer? A whiskey?" I would say: "Thank you very much." . . . At the end of the afternoon he said: "Pastor, I'd like you to be at my wedding." . . . At the wedding party, the guys came to me and said: "You could only be a Christian. Opening the doors of your home, handing over the keys, and letting us do whatever we wanted . . . only someone who has Jesus in his life [does that].

Barriers for Evangelism—When "Yes" Means "No"

Cordiality, for Silva, is seen inside and outside the country: "Brazilian people are cordial. We see the Brazilian difference right away . . . when Brazilians meet, even when they are out of the country, we can tell there's a different culture there." Hospitality, as demonstrated by Moreira, is also mentioned by Silva. Yet, for him, in terms of evangelism, cordiality becomes a barrier when there is no sincerity in evangelistic dialogues—that is, when "yes" means "no," both in word and in behavior:

> Brazilians have a hard time saying 'no.' They usually say 'yes.' And even when they say 'yes,' they often do not go this direction. They say 'yes' because of this culture. That's how they were raised. When you arrive at someone's house to talk to people about the Gospel, most of the time, at least 90 percent of the time we arrive to make contact, people are open, they are always opening their doors. They listen, and they might even say 'yes,' but in practice, sometimes that does not happen. I have had the privilege to participate

in many evangelism operations in our country, and I noticed that. People say 'yes,' but in practice they end up saying 'no.' If we ask someone in Brazil if he believes in God and wants to go to heaven, he will immediately say that he believes and wants to go to heaven, but the lifestyle that he's living shows he is doing the opposite of what he's saying.

Other interviewees pointed out that cordiality and collectivism are closely related, which can create obstacles for sharing the good news. The ease with which people receive, embrace, and are around others creates difficulty when this trait is confused with the acceptance of an invitation to go to church or with the message itself. A sociocultural trait can become an adverse agent to the Gospel as easily as it seems to be an indigenizing agent. This capacity to interpret the culture critically can be identified as biblically sound translation ability. Silva declares, "I understand that cordiality is essential to the relationship, but to the definition of a religious matter, sometimes cordiality is very shallow. It is just words that do not come from the bottom of their hearts."

The comprehension of this dubiety leads, first, to relying on the work of the Spirit of God on people's heart. The believer does his part in proclaiming the good news and trust in the Spirit's power to overcome a barrier. Second, faith is exercised in these endeavors. Third, the missionary will be intentional in sowing the seeds to as many people as he can, so that the harvest is expanded in its results.

Cordiality: Bridges and Barriers Interconnected

Souza, Nossa, Araújo, and Soares classify cordiality as both a bridge and a barrier for translating the Gospel in Brazil. Souza, for example, sees the "natural feature of Brazilian cordiality" as a bridge to establish initial contact and have a conversation the first time he meets people.[4] However, cordiality can also be a barrier since people are open to saying "no" in a sincere tone or to justify their denial of the Gospel with the Catholic mentality of good works or tradition. Souza argues, "So, while this cordiality, this Brazilian trait is a facilitator in the relationship aspect, it also makes him say he does not want to change his position or attitude in a very friendly

---

4. Soares reflects on living close to his father: "I remember my dad, there in Recife, saying this: 'My son, your friend is my friend. The food you eat is the food he will eat. Then, the doors are open.'"

way." This demonstrates an awareness of translation practices, in that Souza perceives the pilgrim principle in action.

The same perspective is shared by Nossa. He gives the example of Minas Gerais and Rondônia states, where people tend to open their houses but not their hearts: "We would enter easily [into the houses], but there was always that mistrust in listening intently to the message of the Gospel." In its turn, Rondônia is one of the most Evangelical states of the country, where there is the Evangelical Day, a state holiday. There, despite people's cordiality, Nossa asserts, "The Gospel itself did not enter the hearts of the people. You see cordial people on one side, but those who reject the Gospel on the other side."

Another issue to be considered is the potential barrier cordiality becomes for the translator who presents the Gospel. Nossa indicates there is a barrier "in the sense that we are afraid to offend the person who is welcoming us so well." Soares pinpoints the same danger: "Sometimes, when you become too cordial, very friendly, you miss the timing to communicate the Gospel to that friend, to your father, to your friend from school or university and so on." Nossa's discourse indicates awareness of translation, since he evaluates the pilgrimage of the Gospel inside the culture, but does not present signs of building bridges over these barriers.[5] The following diagram can help the translator build bridges using evangelism styles proposed by Muller.[6]

Evangelism Styles

Life Style ←→ *Friendship* ←→ *Based on Teaching* ←→ *Proclamation* ←→ *Confrontation*

Figure 15. Scale of Evangelism Styles

The evangelism styles are diverse in their approach. However, all of them include, at some point, the proclamation of the Gospel, confrontation, and teaching. In this sense, cordiality is the bridge in the lifestyle and friendship evangelism styles, but it always ends in real Gospel engagement.

5. Soares sees differences in the regions of the country: "For example, in Brasilia, the suburb cities are different. There are a lot of people from the Northeast of Brazil there. But when you go to Plano Piloto [a richer neighborhood], there is a significant difference. People are closed. People focus on their work, their own survival. And it also makes evangelization more complicated."

6. Proclamation also uses media and literature. Muller, *O Mensageiro*, 43.

If not, it is merely social interaction and relationships. These basic human needs are fully satisfied by the Christian living, but only by those who already are saved by God's grace.

Araújo affirms practicing both Nossa's and Souza's patterns:

> The tolerance in our country ends up creating an opening for people to have lives [that are] somehow completely distant from what the Gospel and the Christian example require. On the one hand, we have cordiality in terms of receiving people, reaching hearts, but at the same time that it is a facilitator, it can become a hindrance from the point of view that people do not take the Word of God seriously and as the truth for their lives.

Soares demonstrates biblically sound translation skills when he opines, "The biggest barrier that we must overcome is not to look at them as difficulties but taking them as an opportunity." This opportunity can involve evangelistic insistences. He states, "We must understand that our main point is not to totally use their kindness, but our main point, our intention is to put Christ the Lord in the life of every one of them."[7] He goes on telling another story:

> I remember one gentleman when I arrived at the mission field, which was a negative experience for me. His wife was a Christian and he received us with great cordiality. But, from that day in 1982 until 2017, this gentleman has not yet made the decision to accept Christ. When, recently, I was with him in Boa Vista, Roraima, he was very cordial. But the time to admonish and to confront him has not passed. Now, being in another position, having left the State and come back, I may have the chance and must provoke this chance to talk about the Gospel of Jesus Christ. Then, I was thinking: "Man, it is one more chance to tell Dagoberto that Jesus loves him and that He died for each one of us and that He wishes we are all saved."

---

7. The Brazilian Study Bible defines these biblically sound translation practices in a note about the Jerusalem Council and the discussions about circumcision (Acts 15:1). "The Gospel is so simple that it can come out of a culture and enters in another one. Always when a group tries to bind it to a specific culture, [the group] suffocates [the Gospel], and the group ends up dying (those Judaists became the sect of the Ebionites, which ended up disappearing). To enter in a culture, however, is not an excuse to adopt cultural traits conflicting with the exclusive Lordship of Christ; that would be syncretism. The Gospel, while fits in any culture, also becomes its judge." Sayão. *Bíblia Brasileira de Estudo*, 1534.

Cordiality as Bridges among Indigenous People

Regarding the indigenous groups of Brazil, Soares understands that they value relationships, but they do so in different ways than other people groups. Love and hospitality are expressed by going to a party, hunting, farming, and making crafts together. He also shared some specific strategies that can be used in indigenous contexts. First, cordiality should be applied first with leadership, namely the indigenous leader, the chieftain. Soares expresses,

> Then he starts opening doors so that you can have relationships with the others. I don't mean that if the chieftain accepts the Gospel, everyone else will accept it too. But it does happen sometimes. If an influential family accepts the Gospel, such as the chieftain of another leader; it opens doors, so we can reach other families.

Second, orality is key. Indigenous people have an oral and not a written tradition. Oral narratives and story-telling help to contextualize the message for a family. Soares shares an example alluding to the filtering system formulated by Keith Eitel, "That's why I talked about the need to have a relationship, a contact with these families. Then you can start a cultural filter." Soares sustains the Bible and not the culture should be the filter: "You take a story from the Bible and share with them. It is a matter of confrontation between the cultural issue and the confrontation with the word of God."

Third and finally, teaching happens inside this relationship chain simultaneously and intentionally. Soares explains:

> This reminds me of an experience I had with the Xerente people, with three indigenous leaders . . . with four indigenous leaders. We had a very nice relationship . . . it was nice to talk and eat at their house. They would also eat with us, participate in events. This created an enormous affinity. They respect me, and I respect them. Consequently, this has significantly changed my life and theirs too. Cordiality within the indigenous context is very strong because it also becomes an extended family. Many times, we have a concept regarding indigenous people that they only want things for themselves. This is a reality. The indigenous people look at the non-indigenous ones as a prey. They are always in search of something. But when you have parameters, these things tend to decrease, and they begin to understand. So, what is our role as a non-indigenous group and what is theirs?

Christ Meets Culture

The indigenous culture is closed to immigrant cultures in the southern region or the higher social strata of the society and requires an investment of time and effort. Yet, once the trust is earned, the mission field is opened to the whole group.

Collectivism: Strategic Trait in Brazil

The second specific sociocultural trait discussed is collectivism.[8] The following question was posed:

> Brazilians are part of strong, cohesive groups (especially represented by the extended family, including uncles, aunts, grandparents and cousins), which continues protecting its members in exchange for loyalty. Does collectivism facilitate, is it a barrier to facilitating, or is it both a barrier to and a bridge for evangelism and discipleship? Give examples from your ministry experience.[9]

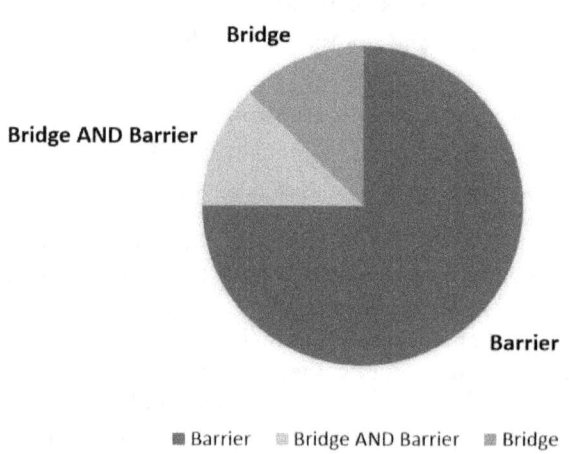

Figure 16. Collectivism as Mainly a Barrier with Few Bridges

---

8. "While Americans herald rugged individualism, self-reliance, and solitude as important components of a national identity, Brazilians favor cooperation, interdependence, and connectedness." Vincent, *Culture and Customs of Brazil*, 81.

9. One personal example from the author was when, in a test center for driving license exams, the people in the waiting room were talking with one another, sharing information about affordable places for driving theory and practice classes.

Christ Interacts with Culture

For six of the eight (75 percent) interviewees, collectivism turned out to be a barrier for evangelism and discipleship. One (12.5 percent) saw it as a bridge, while the other one (12.5 percent) saw it as both a bridge and a barrier as the picture above depicts. In terms of translation ability, half the interviewees demonstrated a lack of it, while two presented signs of awareness of the need for translation in their ministry experience. Two (25 percent) show biblically sound translation practices in their memoirs and comments. The pilgrim principle is in some way mentioned by five of eight (64 percent interviewees); one of them (13 percent) sees the indigenous principle at work, while other (13 percent) sees both the indigenous and pilgrim principles at work, as shown on the table below.

	Collectivism	
	Barrier	
Interviewee	Bridge/Barrier	Indigenizing/Pilgrim Principles Mentioned
Souza	*Barrier*	Pilgrim
Antonio	**Bridge**	Indigenizing
Nossa	*Barrier*	Pilgrim
Araújo	*Barrier*	Pilgrim
Moutta	**Bridge** *and Barrier*	Indigenizing and Pilgrim
Soares	*Barrier*	Pilgrim
Silva	*Barrier*	Pilgrim
Moreira	*Barrier*	Pilgrim

Table 6. Collectivism: Bridges, Barriers, Indigenizing, and Pilgrim Principle

Collectivism as Bridge

Antonio considers collectivism to be a bridge for translation practices. His ideal is that Christians intentionally remain part of their original group so they can share the message in their terms and context. Biblically sound translation, in this sense, means to take advantage of the collectivistic lifestyle as a gateway by which Christ changes lives and transforms communities. He believes that families are a starting point in ministry, as he did in his first missionary experience in the Southern region. "Any community ministry is most welcome . . . I started teaching English, music classes, musical education to children, and that's how I started reaching families. First serving these families and, once they trusted me, they would listen to me."

Second, the collectivistic mindset is favorable to train soul-winners. Per Antonio, the pastor is the master trainer for the members of the church to become translators of the Gospel: "We must win this person, teach him, and then continue to do so, make him commit to the work of God, and he will be the point of contact with his community, his family and his people."

Third, Antonio proposes a natural missionary strategy: new converts should remain in their communities as much as possible, from engaging in soccer games with friends, to inhabiting rural regions and slums, in order to become missionaries among their peers. This is the same strategy proposed by Donald McGravan in *The Bridges of God: A Study in the Strategy of Missions*. In regions with higher collectivism, family tradition may be both a barrier to religious conversion and a channel through which the Gospel can infiltrate the family (οἶκος) ties.[10] This starts from the home and spreads throughout the smaller community, clan, tribe, people group, and so on.[11] Antonio adds:

> The person loses all his relationship with his family and friends, and then when we say 'now you are getting your family, you will win your friends' . . . his family will not come. So, we cannot remove the person from his life . . . The more I can keep the person who converted in his place . . . [the more] I will have a mission field open through him and his family. Then, the person will begin

---

10. Hiebert explains in the conversion experience, one will accept or reject the faith. In other words, it will be either confirmed or rejected faith. Hiebert, *Transformando Cosmovisões*, 357.

11. According to McGavran, the People Movement concept and its terminology, of unreached people groups is valuable in considering hard soils such as the ones in the states of Southern Brazil, especially Rio Grande do Sul.

to conquer the neighborhood, far or near but I cannot kill that possibility of establishing a mission field.

Moutta shares a similar vision with Antonio. He turns the obstacle into a bridge. For him, strong collectivism is "negative for evangelism because it creates barriers. It does not allow you to enter. However, when you enter, "you win everyone," he says. Moutta further notes that on the other side, when collectivism is weaker, entering the group is easier, "but when you do, you do not have the impact of multiplication, that effect on a family, because there is not the idea of a group."

The following assertion attests to a biblically sound translation perspective: "There are positive and negative points, and we need to be aware of them in the process of evangelization and discipleship." This strategic approach is an advantage point of the *Igreja Multiplicadora* and all other small groups methodologies in Brazil and other collectivistic societies. To build relationships and create community is an innate bridge-making ability for these native people.

Moutta affirms that there is a Rio Grande do Sul (Southern Region) state pride: "They are very collectivist in the sense of the *Gaúchos*. We, the *Gaúchos*." For example, if missionaries from the Bahia or Rio de Janeiro states go to Rio Grande do Sul, they are considered outsiders, or intruders. For this reason, it is indispensable to win trust first. It is the idea of group minds and group decisions.[12] The discipling relationship and multiplying small group of the *Igreja Multiplicadora* are key in this context.

> You are kept apart until you win the trust and your space with that family. Once you conquer that space, their trust, their friendship and their heart, then you opened it . . . and once you open it for one of them, then you open it for everybody, because there's only one group. When someone converts, and that family is not from

12. The local culture in Southern Minas Gerais, where the author served for two years, revealed rich aspects for this analysis. For example, family values are very strong in Southern Minas Gerais. Sons and daughters go to their parents' home at least once a week to have lunch or dinner. This regional feature highlights the community-oriented mindset in this region. On the one hand, the indigenizing principle works because the family is an institution created by God, and the people of Southern Minas Gerais value it. On the other hand, many fathers in the local church influence their children's religious behavior. Some sons and daughters are not good Christians, but their fathers want them to be members of Evangelical churches anyway. Sometimes, parents cover up bad behaviors and may become angry if church leaders propose disciplining their children. In this case, the pilgrim principle must be applied. Even if the head of the family does not like it, the church leadership should take care of the spiritual life of all members of the church.

an evangelical line, there's rejection in the whole family. But when this work starts to be done, and that person who converted generates good fruit and good testimonies, there is a chance the family will be converted too.

The Religious-Collectivistic Mindset as a Barrier

Most of the interviewees connect collectivism with the religiosity trait. Statements such as, "My family has this religious tradition and I cannot abandon it" are common in their memoirs and comments.[13] There is a tendency to lack translation strategies or provide a soft awareness of this need on the interviewees reflections.

When describing the Religious-Collective group mindset, Souza opines: "Oh no, my father had that religion, I'm not going to change." For him, collectivism affects the development and growth of the church. Souza understands that people are not willing to unbind or divorce themselves from their families, because they "do not want the spirituality factor to result in breaking a relationship with the entire family." He shares two personal stories regarding this perspective:

> I was working with a group of teenagers integrated with the church, in the Royal Ambassadors, Girls in Action, and they would say, "Look, pastor. I cannot come anymore. My mom said I can no longer come to church because we are from another church, so we are not going to come here anymore. My mom will not let me come." Or in teenager groups, training groups. That is very common. Or, sometimes, a wife says, "Look, my husband forbids me. I cannot belong to this church."[14]

The second story is the testimony of Pr. Vanderlei Batista Marins, who was the President of the BBC from 2016–2017. In both stories, Souza shares the pilgrim principle in action:

> It was a widely-known case in a family when one of the teenagers converted. By the time he got home, his grandmother was at the door putting a shirt in a bag and saying, "Look, because I am kind,

---

13 Luke 14:25–35 concerns a passage which can be used to prepare churches for these specific challenges. Jesus warned His followers about the cost of discipleship, which may involve losing family ties, being abandoned, or persecuted by their families.

14. Royal Ambassadors and Girls in Action are missionary organizations for young men and women teenagers in Baptist churches.

this one is for you not to get cold tonight. Here in this house, there is no place for a Christian." You see, the sixteen-year-old teenager converts and goes home after having accepted Jesus. As soon as he gets home, he is kicked out, and the only thing he gets is a shirt from his grandmother.

Similarly, Nossa affirms the Religious-Collective group mindset is a barrier to the translation of the Gospel. His key statement that identifies this belief is, "I already taught my children that way; I cannot change my life's path. Otherwise I will end up betraying my children." This quotation comes from a story when he lived in the countryside of Rondônia state, his present ministry. He went to visit a terminal cancer patient. Nossa shared the Gospel with the man and asked if he wanted to accept Jesus Christ as his Savior and Lord. The man answered, "Look, you spoke the truth. There is no way to argue or reject it. No one can reject what you said. I don't doubt that. But I cannot accept Jesus."

The reason for denying salvation was the Catholic tradition he had taught his children. "I will betray their loyalty [if I accept Jesus]. And I will be loyal to them until I die." For Nossa, that was an extenuating experience: "I felt like, on that occasion, I arrived late. Afterward it felt like I had been beaten. I was all sore imagining that soul heading to eternity without Jesus, without salvation precisely because of such a silly and ordinary thing."

Araújo locates the same issue of collectivism inside families but describes it in different terms, and with a higher awareness of the need for translation practices inside the local church. The Christian faith can be a threat to the rules and truths by which families live and to their history; furthermore, it can become a motive for prejudice within the family. Biblically sound translation in this case means that the local church is a new support community. Araújo suggests, "The church can be both faithful to the Word of God and, somehow, fully support this person . . . [providing] assistance, so he can feel sheltered by the church. This way, their faith will not be affected."

Soares's key statement for the Religious-Collective mindset is: "I was born a Catholic, I will die a Catholic." His personal example is the source of his thoughts and reflections on the issue, which highlights the pilgrimage of the Gospel in hostile cultures, such as Muslim countries:

> I remember when I converted, my mother rejected me because I came from a Catholic family. My father was a Catholic, my aunts were Catholics . . . it was a generation . . . I did not have

any perspective for the future if it was not through Jesus. [I was] A person who used to drink, smoke, was involved with prostitution . . . But I was a good son, a good friend, and I respected my parents and so on. Therefore, during many years, I had to deal with a sequence of persecution, rejection by my family. And when I received the call to the ministry, it was even worse . . . If you think of it, it is almost as if a Muslim decides to become a Christian.

Soares finds bridges for dealing with these closed environments: perseverance, patience, and long-term witness. "Now that time has been passing, it is showing . . . before my dad died, he confessed Jesus as his only and sufficient Savior. Many of my uncles have already converted . . . some aunts have also converted . . . my cousins, sisters and so on." The Catholic culture is deeply rooted in the Brazilian culture and is by default bonded to collectivism.

Two final interviewees see the Religious-Collectivistic mindset as a barrier, prompting the Gospel to flee from culture. First, Silva observes when people are confronted with the Word of God and asked to make a decision, they respond with, "My grandfather, my great-grandfather, my grandmother, and my parents, all followed this religion, and I am going to die following it too." He identifies traces of patriarchal and matriarchal forces inside communities, "even when we get married and go away from our parents . . . but the first opportunity we must be able to be close, we will be close."

Silva sees the importance of family, especially in his wife's family. Though her parents have passed away, the focus of conversations in family meetings ends up being "her parents, what they did, what they failed to do, what they left in terms of culture, education, care and safety too."[15]

> My family, per my parents, should all be living around their house. My family . . . It is like a light bulb, and we are attracted to them by the light. It also ends up creating a certain difficulty in making decisions. When we are faced with something, we think the same way mom and dad would do . . . if I take or when I take a certain path I think I should take. But the family tradition, as well as the cultural and religious tradition, weigh on my decision . . . It is been changing a little, I believe because of globalization, but it is still very strong in our country.

Moreira asserts, "My father was Catholic, my mother was Catholic, my family was Catholic, and I will die Catholic." These Religious-Collectivistic

---

15. This global movement is seen in terms of birth rates and its impact on families, in how people are having fewer children, including in the global South. Jenkins, *Next Christendom*, 103.

words are a barrier, especially in Southern Brazil, that cannot be overcome, both in Catholic and Lutheran circles. Therefore, how can such a barrier become a bridge? By showing love for and interest in that family, Moreira suggests. In the end, the perspective of the interviewees on collectivism reveals that the *Igreja Multiplicadora* literature lacks a discussion of the barriers of the sociocultural trait, as discussed by the BBC leaders.

Religiosity: Natural Barrier

Another sociocultural trait discussed with the interviewees was religiosity. The question asked of them was:

> The Brazilian people is marked by religiosity. The Catholic faith inherited from Portugal, together with the Indigenous and African religious traditions, play a great role in the nature of the people. How does religiosity become a barrier, a bridge, or both a bridge and a barrier for evangelism and discipleship? Feel free to narrate stories, or expound general principles or patterns you experienced in ministry.

For five of the eight (63 percent) interviewees, religiosity is both a barrier and a bridge for evangelism and discipleship. Two (25 percent) see it as a bridge, while one (12 percent) sees it as a barrier. Five of the eight (63 percent) interviewees demonstrate signs of translation awareness while the other three (37 percent) present signs of biblically sound translation practices in their ministry experience. Six of the eight (75 percent) interviewees perceive the indigenous principle, while two (25 percent) mention the pilgrim principle. In general, the interviews were similar in their approach and line of thought, dealing with syncretism, nominal Evangelicalism, and the problem of the NeoPentecostal churches.

RELIGIOSITY

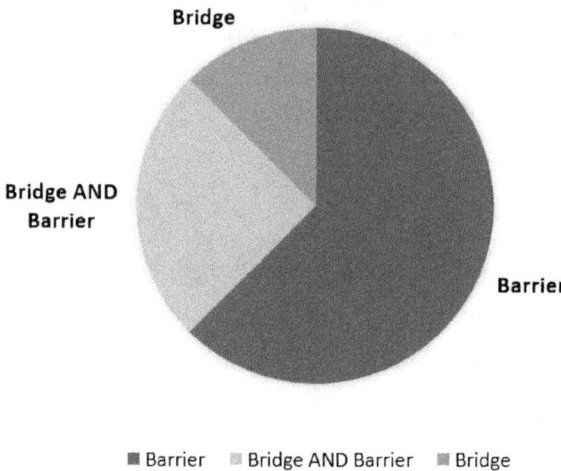

Figure 17. Religiosity: Barrier with Bridges

Religiosity

Barrier

Interviewee	Bridge/Barrier	Indigenizing/Pilgrim Principles Mentioned
Souza	**Bridge** *and Barrier*	Pilgrim
Antonio	**Bridge** *and Barrier*	Indigenizing
Nossa	*Barrier*	Pilgrim
Araújo	*Barrier*	Indigenizing
Moutta	*Barrier*	Pilgrim
Soares	*Barrier*	Pilgrim
Silva	**Bridge** *and Barrier*	Pilgrim
Moreira	**Bridge** *and Barrier*	Pilgrim

Table 7. Religiosity: Bridges, Barriers, Indigenizing and Pilgrim Principles

Brief Overview

Given the weight of the issue in the present research, some background and additional information on the topic is helpful before discussing the interviews.[16] Southern Minas Gerais can be taken as an initial example and illustration. People may attend church as an obligation or tradition rather than for spiritual nourishment. The pilgrim principle is seen in action in that portion of the state in relation to this strong local feature: *Mineiros* are very religious. In this case, religiosity leads to coldness in one's spiritual life. How do people react to the call to costly discipleship? Why do people from Southern Minas Gerais get involved in church without exercising their spiritual gifts? These are challenges for ministries in that area.[17]

Around Brazil, religiosity is not always seen as a dynamic and personal relationship with God. This perspective is very common in Catholic circles. Even in Baptist churches, there are people who only go to church on the Lord's Supper day, as seen in Catholics who only attend church to receive the sacraments. Indeed, there are many similarities between the Catholic church and its habits and some believers in Evangelical churches. In contrast with a genuine spiritual life, there is the perception that there is no need to be accountable to the fellowship of believers. Some believers trust in the idea is not necessary to go to church as frequently as one should.

---

16. Chapter 6, "Religion," in *Culture and Customs of Brazil*, contains rich information for people studying the phenomenon of the growth of Evangelicals in Brazil. "Brazil has the world's largest Roman Catholic population and ranks as the second largest Christian country in the world" (71). One of the down sides of the book is the fact that Vincent gives more weight and importance to Candomblé, Spiritism, Umbanda, and Messianism than to Protestantism. In fact, the spiritualist religions are fertile in a soil which inherited the indigenous habits and the African influence. At the same time, Messianism is a vibrant expression of faith in a land where exploitation, colonialism, and poverty continue to be felt. The small space given to non-Catholic Christians is a flaw, since Protestants are the strongest power in the religious arena nowadays. Protestants, especially Pentecostals and Charismatics, even though they are not the majority numerically, possess influence in the political arena and in the daily lives of people in the slums, offices, streets, and media. Milleret includes religion in the chapter entitled, "Social Customs" (93–94). This is a very insightful approach, since most of the festivities detailed are religious by nature. "Living in community and believing in miracles are characteristics that make Brazilians a hopeful and energetic people who treat others with enthusiasm, humor, and, generosity" (94). It is a reason for the expansion of the Charismatic and Pentecostal movement in Brazil, marked by a joyful and enthusiastic attitude.

17. These observations are based on the ministry of the author in the region and on narratives of colleagues from churches in the area.

The Catholic faith still influences Brazilian society in many ways. The Catholic church hosts many street celebrations for Lent and Easter.[18] Religion and culture are in constant exchange, as are their vocabulary and expressions. For example, Brazilians will say that a very hard situation is a *via crucis*. This is a Latin expression that means "the way of the cross," and refers to Christ carrying his cross to Calvary. Other popular expressions are *Ave Maria* and *Nossa Senhora*, which are invocations of Saint Mary. On the same way that people in other countries with other Christian influences will say "oh, my God" and similar expressions, Brazilians will call out to the name of the main idols of the Catholic pantheon.

The Brazilian people are religious by nature. They seek God for basic needs, such as health issues or financial problems. They appeal to their faith as a way of coping with the challenges of a society in which the law is disrespected and basic needs are not always met. One example of appealing to one's faith as a way of coping is the use of a vocabulary of faith in God, such as "God helps me" and "by faith in God" as a resource for filling the gaps of the human and societal flaws and uncertainties.

The media explore this trait in television and radio networks, news programs, soap opears, and other formats. Brazilian broadcasting groups sell air time, stations, and products related to Catholic, Pentecostal, Neo-Pentecostal, and other churches and religions. Popular singers sing songs with religious lyrics. For example, one of the core songs of Roberto Carlos, one of the most famous singers of the country, is entitled, *Jesus Cristo* (Jesus Christ). The so-called Gospel music transforms faith into a product. People who are already evangelized or influenced by Christian values listen to this kind of music. Even popular secular artists sing Gospel songs to open or close their concerts.

Brazil is indeed a very religious country. Brazilians have a very strong predisposition to be involved in religion, as detailed on Chapter 1. This spiritual predisposition has the potential to become a strong bridge for translating the Gospel in the country. This idea will be proposed in this chapter and in the conclusion. The implicit barrier is that many people already have religious traditions, including the ones inside Evangelical

---

18. As it happens in Serrinha, Bahia state, where the author lives, some question may be asked additionally: "Should Evangelicals engage in evangelism on those days? Would such engagement trigger persecution or rivalry? In what kind of popular celebrations can a Baptist church engage without becoming syncretic? How does the translation process happen during those times? In which cases can one see the pilgrim and indigenizing principles in action"?

churches (nominal Evangelicals) and NeoPentecostals, most of which end up syncretized, which is a blatant sign of a kind of translation that is not biblically sound. This is true with non-religious people and other world religions, such as Islam, which are arriving in Brazil and Latin America, as the following graphic attests.

Size and Projected Growth of Major Religious Groups in Latin America and Caribbean, 2010-2050

	2010 ESTIMATED POPULATION	% IN 2010	2050 PROJECTED POPULATION	% IN 2050	POPULATION GROWTH 2010-2050	% INCREASE 2010-2050	COMPOUND ANNUAL GROWTH RATE (%)
Christians	531,280,000	90.0%	665,500,000	88.9%	134,220,000	25.3%	0.6%
Unaffiliated	45,390,000	7.7	65,150,000	8.7	19,770,000	43.6	0.9
Folk Religions	10,040,000	1.7	14,310,000	1.9	4,270,000	42.5	0.9
Other Religions	990,000	0.2	1,170,000	0.2	180,000	18.4	0.4
Muslims	840,000	0.1	940,000	0.1	100,000	12.5	0.3
Hindus	660,000	0.1	640,000	< 0.1	-20,000	-3.5	-0.1
Jews	470,000	< 0.1	460,000	< 0.1	-10,000	-3.0	-0.1
Buddhists	410,000	< 0.1	450,000	< 0.1	40,000	8.6	0.2
Regional total	590,080,000	100.0	748,620,000	100.0	158,540,000	26.9	0.6

Source: The Future of World Religions: Population Growth Projections, 2010-2050. Population estimates are rounded to the nearest 10,000. Percentages are calculated from unrounded numbers. Figures may not add to 100% because of rounding.

PEW RESEARCH CENTER

Figure 18: Projection of the Growth of Religions in Latin America

The subtle but real coming of Islam should not be ignored in the Brazilian religious scenario. The religiosity of the people appears to be one of the reasons for the growth of other religions, including Islam. Some personal reminiscences illustrate that local leaders' awareness of Islam is increasing incrementally. During the last decade, while studying and working as a journalist in Salvador, the author first learned of the Muslim presence in the city. Between 2006 and 2008, Pr. Gerson Perruci, Missions Manager for the Bahia Baptist Convention and the NMB mission strategic coordinator, mentioned this trend in informal conversations at the office of the Convention in Salvador, where the author served in the communications area. On November 9, 2014, Silva preached the Sunday morning service at SBC Feira de Santana and mentioned "the coming of the Muslims" to Brazil. Later, in 2016, this writer saw an Islamic mosque in the Jardim São Jorge neighborhood of São Paulo as large as any other Catholic or Protestant building on the street. Indeed, Islam is coming and will be a major issue in the future in Brazil and Latin America.

Christ Meets Culture

The Dangers of Syncretism and Nominal Christianity

Four interviewees (Moreira, Souza, Antonio, and Silva) see religiosity as both a bridge and a barrier to evangelism. First, for Moreira, Brazilian religious diversity leads people to syncretism, as exemplified in the mixture between Catholicism and the Afro-Brazilian cults, which is a barrier for "the true church to preach the Gospel . . . that, for me, is something undeniable," he asserts. Moreira's comments come from a personal religious experience. For twelve and a half years, he was an adherent of Kardecist and Umbandist Spiritism. Both religions have Catholic influences. His memoirs describe this syncretic pantheon.

> When I reached a certain stage in the Afro-Brazilian cult, after leaving the place where the person at this stage stays, I had to go to seven Catholic Churches . . . The priest gave the host to me and to the other members of *terreiro* (where the Afro cult is celebrated), and we participated in the mass. When the mass is not held in a church, the priest goes to *terreiro* and celebrates the mass there, gives us the host . . ."I remember that one day I questioned a *Preto Velho* (African cult entity) about eternity, if there was heaven and hell, and he quoted the Bible to me. He said: "Look, Reginaldo. The text of Jacob's ladder says that the angels were going up and down on the head of the son of man. These angels are the *orixás* (deities) and the son of man is us." And he pointed me to the text of the Pythia of En-Dor, where a demon disguised himself as Samuel and appeared to Saul, to say there was a séance in the Bible. After that, he quoted a text from John that says: "Test the spirits to see whether they are from God." All those things confused me, even though I didn't think those things were from God . . . I would hear biblical quotes, and I would see mysticism in Catholicism, Kardecist Spiritism, and Afro religions. I would think: "Is this from God?" And then I would see, next to terreiro, something like: "*Exu* (African cult deity) that has two heads, he shakes his foot. One is from Satan and the other from Jesus of Nazareth." These things would make me question both Catholicism and the Afro cult, which was a non-Christian religion. Bible quotation, hymn singing.

The turning point in Moreira's life came through his grandmother, who was a Christian and prayed for him. She would tell him he was going to hell. He shares, "The day I gave my life to Christ, I broke all those things. I became a new creature, and my grandmother's prayers were the door that God used for the evangelization of my life." His testimony and book attests his ability to practice a biblically sound translation.[19] The Gospel is indigenized in a religious culture as it becomes the religious choice of the people and does not mix with other religions and symbols that are contrary to the Word of God. When there are syncretic practices, the Gospel initiates its pilgrimage out of religious expressions.

Spirituality as a Way of Life and a Barrier

Second, for Souza, Brazilian religiosity is both a bridge and a barrier because "Everyone is religious. Everyone believes. Everybody has their own individuality in religion." Religiosity, such as the Brazilian way of coping, is a complex matter for the translation of the Gospel, because it "ends up bringing values that are, sometimes, difficult to overcome." For example, Bible teachers should invest time to make people stop believing in certain superstitions and previous teachings such as if someone has an accident, he should knock on wood three times. Or not pass under a ladder. Other superstitions are making the sign of the cross on one's face when passing in front of a cemetery or a Catholic Church, and using amulets for protection, all of which come from Catholic, Indigenous, and Afro religions:

> At my first place of ministry, there was a lady who converted when she was around 70, 75 years old. For a long time . . . she was raised a Catholic, so sometimes she'd say: Pastor, I have asked the Lord and the Virgin Mary to bless you. She would use that expression often. She did . . . She believed that Jesus was her only Savior, but [had] her historical religious training . . . She had this: It was God and the Virgin Mary, Our Lady. This religiosity sometimes brings a difficulty even in terms of the language of the new believer.

Finding Bridges in Improbable Places

Third, for Antonio, Afro-Brazilian and Christian religiosity, at first, facilitate the preaching of the Gospel. First, they do so because they contain symbols, concepts, and figures common to those faiths, such as God, Jesus, heaven, and hell. Second, he argues that the religious variety helps people to differentiate between "an Evangelical, a Catholic, a Spiritualist, an Umbandan, or an Eastern religion."

---

19. Moreira, *Grandes Verdades sobre o Espiritismo*.

The diversity of denominations inside the Brazilian Evangelical community, however, can become a barrier or create confusion instead of being a bridge for cultural translation. Antonio says, "In Santa Catarina, I had to say I was Baptist. If I told them I was an Evangelical, I would not be welcome, because Evangelicals in this region do not set a good example. They even exploit people. I would have problems with communication and relationship with traditional families." The identification as a Baptist helped Antonio to be more accepted.[20] He was able to explain more about the denomination: "People wanted to know what it was like to be a Baptist. They already knew some Evangelicals and had the wrong idea."

The biblically sound translation seen in Antonio's memoirs resides in statements such as: "I need to use and explore religiosity," and "Peter was kind of a prophet, and he would come and soon show the realities, the wrong things among the people. But it was such a persuasive and intellectual approach, that he convinced people of the truth."

Another example of biblically sound translation by Antonio is his mention of Paul at the Areopagus in Athens (Acts 17) [21]: "When the Apostle said that God did not dwell in hand-made temples, he found a way to enter and deliver a relevant message to the people. He saw there was an altar to the unknown God. He took that hook in the culture of the people and in religiosity and brought it to Christianity."

One more biblically sound translation practice is given by Antonio. Indigenous people, such as the Guarani, expect salvation to come from the sea on a big boat, or from the river, as do the Xerente.

> When I was in a Xerente tribe, on a day of a storm, there was an indigenous lady asking me to pray for her husband who had left by boat to go shopping. She was asking God to protect him so that he did not have any problems with his boat on the river. So, the concept of salvation changed completely with the power of evangelization. It used to be on the river. Now salvation is Jesus. Dying in a river is a disgrace. Dying with Jesus is happiness.

---

20. As a Brazilian Baptist, this writer agrees with Antonio regarding the respectability of the denomination in the country. In the last few years, Baptists have been on the news because of their work through the NMB with drug addicts in the rehab project *Cristolândia* in cities such as São Paulo (partnership with FBC São Paulo), and Salvador (partnership with Dois de Julho Baptist Church). New Alliance BC and Mount Horeb BC in Serrinha also maintain a rehab center in the city.

21. An analysis of this passage appears in Chapter 2.

For Antonio, a key for interacting positively with other religions is "to take the culture, study it, and find out how we can get into that culture with what is culturally acceptable to the truths of the Bible." It is biblically sound translation in a pure form that breaks taboos and traditions which are contrary to the Gospel. A final bridge presented by Antonio is for interacting with people in the Northeast, where there is a terrible drought. If one preaches that Jesus Christ is the water of life but is not sensitive to the secular problem, he may miss the opportunity to share the "message that would be so propitious, but so negative, if [there is no] solution to the problems the people there live with."

Tradition-based and Nominal Christianity Explored

Silva shares the view that religiosity is both a barrier and bridge for the translation of the Gospel. Brazilian people, for him, are gullible people, open to hearing about spiritual matters: "The big problem is that, often, religion is more a traditional thing than a life experience. On the other hand, there are very few true Christians. Nominal Christians are the majority." Silva further exclaims, "There are many nominal Christians who hide behind a religion that was imported or imposed on them . . . So, religiousness is much more effective in our country than a truly Christian life." Regarding the Northeast, where he serves today, African-Brazilian religions are strong in Bahia state: "I had never seen so many symbols of African religions as I see here in Bahia. It is very present. It seems to me that the symbols of African religions here are stronger than the symbols of the Catholic religion that came from Portugal."

Nossa also appeals to nominal religiosity, both in Catholic and Evangelical circles, as a barrier. He was raised in the Catholic tradition, being hateful towards Evangelicals, following his grandparent's teachings: "I remember when I was a kid, there was an Assembly of God church near my grandmother's house. I would not pass in front of the church because I strongly believed it was a devil's thing." For Nossa, many Brazilians have a Catholic tradition, but their faith is not based in the Bible but the teachings of the priests.

Agreeing with Souza, Nossa feels that discipleship is difficult given Catholic influences, such as that the Bible is considered to be less a holy book that is God-given, and more as a book that tells a religious story than the authoritative Word of God. One bridge to religious people suggested by Nossa is to use the Catholic version of the Bible to teach people from traditional Catholic families.[22] Nossa concludes, "We notice that people do not have any knowledge of God . . . [they have] the verbal tradition and not what the word of the Lord builds on people."

Soares also builds on the indisputable religiosity of Brazilians. For him, Catholic traditions, festivities, and saints are still very strong, and people are afraid to confront this reality, as he himself experienced as a young man: "Then, going to mass was everything and not going was an affront. I was rejecting God himself. And it was brought through generations." According to Soares, religiosity in some sense darkens the mind.

> You have no idea what a person is within a Catholic context. For them to understand that this is not the message of the Word, the message that God wants. You are surrounded by religious doctrines which we receive during breakfast, lunch, dinner, at school, at the university and so on. Then, I remember how many times I rejected the Gospel. How many times I have ripped up leaflets and said those people were stupid and did not understand anything about enjoying life, living life. I was a fool. But thank God, my eyes were opened.

In the case of the Quilombolas or Indigenous people, this religiosity is also very strong, attests Soares, and has ramifications for ancestral relatives, witch doctors, myths, and others. For him, if there is already a linguistic translation, then cultural translation is a second mile that one must walk with the Indigenous people. Soares explains, "These things make the understanding of the Gospel more difficult. It demands a lot of time, even if you are working with an indigenous community that speaks Portuguese and understands your language. But they don't cease to be indigenous people." How can one explain "who Christ is, why He came, died, and has risen from the dead, what it means to have eternal life in Jesus Christ?"

Soares demonstrates biblically sound translation practices, given statements such as, "These are barriers, but I always say they are also opportunities." For him, "there is nothing better in life than to see a young indigenous Christian man and hear him say he wants to live a life with Christ Jesus. It is priceless . . . even more [so] when he becomes a multiplier

---

22. An advanced example of this practice is given by Daniel R. Sanchez in his study of the Catholic rosary. Sanchez suggests that the Gospel found in the prayer chain and introduces Christ as the way, the truth, and the life. Sanchez, *Gospel in the Rosary*.

of that message." This is the revival movement described by Mark Shaw, McGavran, Antonio, and Soares:

> They become that person who will communicate the Gospel to their own people, with no cultural barriers, with no language barriers. Nothing. It is a huge transformation. That is why it is worth it to invest in indigenous and non-indigenous matters because we do not know what will happen in the future. Remember the experience that happened to Phillip, with that Prince there in Africa [Acts 8.26–40]. It turned out to be a great blessing. The Gospel arrived and reached many in that region. The dream is an investment with return. We do not know the dimensions of announcing the Gospel of Jesus Christ overcoming the religiosity matter. May God give us wisdom and grace.

NeoPentecostals and Syncretism: Genuine Faith in Jeopardy

Two final interviewees complement one another in their comments and memoirs. Araújo considers religiosity only as a barrier. Araújo phrases the pilgrim movement in a religious scenario: "We cannot acculturate something that confronts the truth of God. We have a pattern that is absolute and that does not fit other religious cultures. We have all these influences, but we cannot give in." For Araújo, the religious base in Brazil becomes a hard soil for the seed of the Gospel to penetrate and grow: "For them to have receptive hearts to accept this Gospel and the teaching of the Word of God."

Some Pew Research Center interpretations of the most recent Brazilian census help to understand these transitions in religious trends in Brazil, specifically among Catholics. The religious change movement among Catholics from childhood to the present is a vector for the growth of Evangelicals: 81 percent of Brazilian adults were raised Catholic, and only 61 percent are currently Catholic. This means that 20 percent of them left their childhood religion.[23] Why did they leave the Roman Catholic Church? The following graphic summarizes the answers related to Latin Americans:

---

23. Pew Research Center, "Religião na América Latina."

Latin Americans' Reasons for Leaving the Catholic Church

Median % of converts from Catholicism to Protestantism who say ... is an important reason they are no longer Catholic

Seeking personal connection with God	81
Enjoy style of worship at new church	69
Wanted greater emphasis on morality	60
Found church that helps members more	59
Outreach by new church	58
Personal problems	20
Seeking better financial future	14
Marriage to non-Catholic	9

Q41a-h

Respondents were asked whether each of these items was an important reason for leaving Catholicism.

PEW RESEARCH CENTER

Figure 19. Reasons for Latin Americans Leaving Catholicism[24]

However, Araújo sustains when there is an attempt ("even within our churches") to fit the reality, syncretism infiltrates the so-called Christian church "[w]hich, in fact, becomes an impediment for true evangelism to be practiced in the life of these people. I think that one of the impediments to the growth of the genuine Gospel in Brazil is this religious syncretism." The danger of syncretism in the Evangelical church is a wake-up call given by Moutta, too. In his interview, he presents a well-informed overview of the history of religion in Brazil. He covers the Catholic state in the beginning of the country; the persecution of other religions by the Catholic church; the syncretism of Catholicism with African spiritism; and the Evangelical missionary movement and the Catholic population as a mission field.

According to Moutta, there is an intertwining between African-Brazilian, Catholic, and Evangelical beliefs, which creates the syncretism seen in Neopentecostal churches. "What is the barrier for evangelization today? The Catholic church? Not really. When you remove the marks [of Evangelicalism], you lose a bit of your identity. We do not know who is who," he affirms. Another striking statement by Moutta is: "Today I do not really know which the biggest challenge is—whether it is to evangelize Catholics, people from

---

24. Pew Research Center, "Religião na América Latina."

the African religion, or Evangelicals. I think that we will reach a point of having to evangelize the Evangelicals, especially the NeoPentecostals."

The good news is that even in syncretic contexts, it is still possible to practice a biblically sound translation, as Moutta builds bridges over the dark river. It "is favorable in the sense that there is a sense of God, there is a feeling of searching for God, a supernatural search, a search for answers." There are positive trends, but also negative ones on Brazil's religious horizon, according to Moutta:

> The great majority of Brazilian people are not agnostic, a people closed to religiosity. Absolutely not. It is a gullible people, a people open to religion, who likes to discuss, to seek religious responses, and I think this is a great opportunity. Muslims are aware of this. This openness, this faith . . . these are gullible people. Muslims are trying to grab a slice of our population, due to this openness, this opportunity. So, I see that the religiosity of the Brazilian people is, today, an opportunity for us. Now, this picture will change over the next few years if there is no divine intervention and direct action of the church . . . The growth of the LGBT movement, the Communist movement, the growth of a very militant leftist party in Brazil that becomes anti-Christian. It favors the Spiritism religion, it favors even Islam, which is a giant contradiction, but it is anti-Christian. Everything that is done in the name of Christ or Christianity becomes negative, pejorative, becomes a laughing thing, becomes the reason for persecution. This, for us, is a threat . . . if that grows in Brazil, then we will have more complex barriers . . . they will be more difficult to leave atheism and Postmodernism.

Nonreligious on the Rise

However, statistics predict some roadblocks in this positive trend of Christianity. The number of Brazilians belonging to other religions is increasing. In 1970, 2 million Brazilians were part of other faiths. By 2000, the number was 6 million; as of 2010, 10 million, 5 percent of the Brazilian population.[25] This reveals that the country has the ninth-largest number of religiously unaffiliated, totaling 15.4 million people in another source.[26] The portion of Brazilian agnostics, atheists, and others with no religious

---

25. Pew Research Center, "Religião na América Latina."

26. Payne, *Pressure Points*, 56. For more information on religious change in the nation and the Spiritist movement, among others, see the Pew Research Center's July 2013 report.

affiliation has been increasing. In 1970, these numbers were fewer than 1 million. In 2000, they were 12 million; in 2010, topped 15 million (8 percent). In Latin America, the population without any religious affiliation should have the largest percentage increase (44 percent), growing from 45 million (2010) to 65 million (2050). The number of members of folk religions will grow (43 percent) from 10 million to 14 million.[27]

Some of the interviewees' insights explain the growth of this nonreligious group. For Souza, NeoPentecostalism and its Prosperity Gospel have turned people away from Christianity in Brazil:

> The big problem for us is the image that has been created because all Christians end up being compared to these leaders. And we have found that many people are disappointed with God. Why? Their pastors make promises on behalf of God. God made no such promises. These are material promises, promises regarding financial gain. And when these people do not receive these things, they get disappointed, not with the church, but with God. This is an area where the Gospel can grow, but it's hard to work with those people who are disappointed with God—not with the true God, but with the god that these churches have shown them.

The Brazilian Way of Coping: Challenge Deeply Rooted in the Culture

The final sociocultural trait discussed with the interviewees was the Brazilian way of coping. The following question was asked of them. "The Brazilian way of coping also impacts the fulfillment of the Great Commission. Our people resort to creativity, mutual support, and the network of friends and acquaintances as a problem-solving strategy. Does the Brazilian way of coping facilitate, create a barrier, or both facilitate and create a barrier to evangelism and discipleship? Give examples from your ministry experience, including ethical dilemmas."

Almost all the interviewees said that the Brazilian way of coping is a bridge and a barrier for evangelism and discipleship. Only one of them saw it as a bridge alone. All of them demonstrate an awareness of translation (i.e., the need to counteract evil, and some present a biblically sound translation capacity, evidenced by detailed strategies for engaging and transforming the culture). The interviewees mainly perceived the pilgrim

---

27. Pew Research Center, "Latin America and the Caribbean."

principle while interpreting the impact of this sociocultural trait on the translation of the Gospel, since the Gospel either makes itself at home and sinful attitudes go away—or the opposite.

The Brazilian Way of Coping

Bridge and *Barrier*		
Interviewee	Bridge/Barrier	Indigenous/Pilgrim Principles Mentioned
Souza	**Bridge** and *Barrier*	Pilgrim
Antonio	**Bridge** and *Barrier*	Pilgrim
Nossa	**Bridge** and *Barrier*	Pilgrim
Araújo	**Bridge** and *Barrier*	Pilgrim
Moutta	**Bridge** and *Barrier*	Pilgrim
Soares	**Bridge** and *Barrier*	Pilgrim
Silva	**Bridge** and *Barrier*	Pilgrim
Moreira	**Bridge**	Indigenizing and Pilgrim

Table 8. Brazilian Way of Coping: Bridge, Barrier, Pilgrim, and Indigenizing Principles

Before analyzing the interviews, some explanation about the Brazilian way of coping is helpful. Vincent gives a simple but complete explanation about the *Jeitinho Brasileiro*. It is "an adaptation for coping with society."[28] The Brazilian way of solving problems is to rely on friends and acquaintances, as the author indicates, and it underlines the social skills and relations that are vital and indispensable in the country. These abilities are necessary for a system filled with bureaucracy and some ancient customs. Hofstede explains that, in cultures like the Brazilian one, people "feel threatened by ambiguous or unknown situations and have created beliefs and institutions that try to avoid these." In some cases, there are ethical dilemmas. These are perceived and discussed by the eight leaders of the BBC.

28. Vincent, *Culture and Customs of Brazil*, 90.

A fast-paced routine, guided by informality, is visible in the traffic and in how people do business in Brazil. Observe this example that comes from the streets. When there is no GPS, drivers rely more on information from other drivers or pedestrians instead of planning their destination at home using a map, to mention. This is one example of *Jeitinho Brasileiro*, the Brazilian way of coping.

Bridge for Evangelism, Barrier for Christian Living

Almost all pastors see both bridges and barriers in the Brazilian way of coping. The only one who perceives only bridges is Moreira, as he connects this ethical trait with the collectivism trait. For him, people cope with life challenges by forming groups to share life, hang out, and have fellowship. These groups are sometimes exclusive, with people preventing the entry of new people. In his experience, the key to accessing these groups is to pray, ask God for wisdom, and be a good witness, while being creative in presenting Christ and utilizing apologetic reasoning. Moreira recalls, "I had a very complicated friend and one day he asked: 'Pastor, what if you die and there is no heaven or hell? How is that going to be?' I told him: 'If there is no heaven and hell, I have not lost anything. But if they exist, you are doomed." His comments indicate the indigenization of the Gospel to the cultural context.

Moutta sees the Brazilian way of coping as a bridge for evangelism and a barrier for Christian living. It is a bridge for two reasons: first, it eases access to people's schedule and daily lives and, second, it increases the flexibility of ministry. First, "You can talk to a person at a time that is not as favorable, the person looks for you to ask for your opinion, advice and he is open to it."

Second, the Brazilian way of coping aids evangelists in being more sensible to environments and contexts and to adapt their approach accordingly.

> You arrive in a house to conduct a Bible study, for example, and you have the script ready, but when you get there, the situation is totally adverse. Either someone has died, or the husband left the house, or the child is hospitalized because of drugs and you, as an evangelist, do not have to follow that predetermined script. You need to use your Brazilian way of coping in a good way. You need to use this flexibility so that you can adapt to an unusual situation.

For Moutta, however, the Brazilian way of coping is a barrier, a serious problem for Christian living when it makes the Gospel masquerade as merely a matter of ethics. The example he gives is one of an evangelist who decides to do a Bible study with someone during work hours. "It becomes, in fact, a barrier and a deterrent because you contaminate the basis of values and one of the principles of the Word of God. You build on top of a sandy base, and open breaches for syncretism, for a nominal religion, and for a nominal Evangelicalism."

Third, Nossa contemplates the Brazilian way of coping, and how it has the potential to open doors for evangelism as one finds ways to treat people well, to relate to them, and preach the Gospel and make disciples. However, it works more as a barrier in family life, business, and in one's personal life with God. He theorizes, "We start getting used to this 'fix' in our spiritual life as well, in our personal relationship with the Lord. It is as if we also wanted to transfer it to this type of relationship." For him, the lack of credibility for what is being said compromises the message and the messenger: "It is like dragging our heels, as if we were dealing with something in a way that does not please Jesus Christ."

Soares also see the Brazilian way of coping resulting in creativity to reach people who have not been reached yet. Yet, the first problem is that the Gospel is not meant to make things easier. He argues, "It is not about changing behavior. It is about changing attitudes. It is a life transformation to change external knowledge." Second, he comprehends that some Evangelical groups, in indigenous and non-indigenous circles, connect Brazilian creativity with Brazilian religiosity, i.e., syncretism, and use certain strategies to negotiate the Gospel, something he finds unacceptable: "In the light of the Word of God, we are betraying our Jesus who died on the cross in the Calvary to save us." He adds that people who look for welfare in mysticism go to cities such as Alto Paraíso, Goiás state, but "The welfare that brings pleasure to all human beings is the Gospel of Jesus Christ."

Regarding the indigenous context specifically, Soares sees that it is increasing as the communities leave the jungle and go to the cities. They assimilate everything that happens there. They learn things, including the Brazilian way of coping. He shares,

> I was in Tabatinga, and I went to a place like a market where indigenous people would sell flour, banana, nuts, just for survival since there is no way for them to compete in a non-indigenous market. There is no way. The opportunities are rare. So, what happened? I

wanted to buy some nuts, and I asked: "How much are these nuts here?" Then, the person said: "Look, I can't answer now." "But after I peel all these nuts here, I will tell you how much." So, I mean, they gave the price not for what it was, but because of who I was. Do you understand? What happened? They learned the trick of selling differently depending on the buyer.

Soares takes these experiences as teachable moments. However, many indigenous groups choose NeoPentecostalism with its sometimes confusing ethics and syncretic theology. Soares concludes, "There is still a long way [for them] to understand the concept of God, the concept of Christ, the concept of redemption, or the concept of eternal life. Many have already understood, but the majority has not."

Critical Issues for Teaching, Discipleship, and Ecclesiology

The other four interviewees see the Brazilian way of coping as a barrier for discipleship and Christian witness in the society. Souza, for example, argues that the church is to keep the ethic of the Gospel regarding taxes and other legal obligations: "Jesus said: 'Give back to Caesar what is Caesar's and to God what is God's.' So, I cannot negotiate, I can't argue with the determinations of the Lord." In the same way, believers should think accordingly and pay their taxes. Souza further observes, "But is there not a 'fix,' pastor? Can we not do that? No, we cannot. The Bible says no. I think this is one of the worst things we have in our country." The attempt to circumvent values and principles or fix something is not ethical. "Unfortunately, we're bringing that into our churches," he laments.

Another typical situation Brazilian pastors and churches face relates to marital status and church membership. An example is new converts who have been living together for years or decades and do not get married. Another is the case of women who receive alimony or spousal support, live with a new partner but do not want to marry solely because they do not want to lose the financial benefits they are receiving. Souza had a case like the last one in his ministry and he challenged the new convert to live a transformed life.

> How are you going to teach your daughter to live a life of faith, of truth, of real values if you are a fraud? To society you are married to your husband, have a son, but in terms of law enforcement, for the Army, you do not have a spouse. It is terrible for us to live. We

cannot live that way. [The Brazilian way of coping] is a trait that makes a lot of the proclamation of the Gospel more difficult. It makes discipleship much more difficult.

In his turn, Araújo provides concise and precise definitions on the topic. "The Brazilian way of coping is a way to conquer what you wish. And usually, the means that are used are the most dishonest ones . . . to find the shortest route." He localizes the practice in some parts of the country, such as Rio de Janeiro and Bahia states, due to the Portuguese influence. For him, the solution is to present the irresistible Gospel, the authoritative Word of God, which has a liberating effect, in the sense that it confronts and moves people away from sinful behavior: "So, when we arrive with the proposal of the Gospel, of a straight life, of working to earn what you want, of not having anything hidden from God, that somehow confronts this behavior."

Antonio's comments are along the same lines. He affirms that the Brazilian way of coping is a barrier for Gospel translation since it prevents believers from giving a good testimony, from representing Christ well in the world, and even experiencing the real transformational power of the Gospel. The Brazilian way of coping is perceived when people go to church only to solve marriage or family crises or seek God for financial solutions, as many people in NeoPentecostal churches do. Antonio notes that these churches hold only worship services, form rickety Christians, and do not offer Sunday School or other teaching ministries, as seen in Baptist churches. He maintains, "People go to church, but so many others leave. Why? They go to solve their problems. Once the problems have been solved, they say goodbye to the church, to those communities where they do not find themselves due to lack of a strong base, a lack of commitment to the Word of God."

A permanent solution to the Brazilian way of coping is presented by Antonio and Araújo and builds upon John 9:35–38. Antonio remembers that this passage presents the church preaching the Gospel of the kingdom, teaching, and healing the sicknesses of the people. Teaching, then, is part of the cure for these ethical illnesses. "I need to show these people that we are fully under the authority of the Scriptures. I need to share with these people and make them understand the Scriptures to have a real commitment . . . with God." God has the right answers and fixes for human problems. Antonio reflects on the issue:

> Now, culturally, we use the "Brazilian fix" a lot and when the Gospel begins to be preached, taught through quick "fixes," it does not

work. We will use the "Brazilian fix" for everything because we do not have the power, we don't have what God has. We should connect these people to God, so that they seek God in their difficulties and problems.

Finally, Silva goes beyond the ethical challenges of the Brazilian way of coping and the critique of Neopentecostalism to see how the sociocultural trait impacts Baptist churches and their ecclesiology. First, he echoes the other interviewees' perception that the Brazilian way of coping may harm relationships, friendships, and an appropriate Christian witness. Second, the Brazilian way of coping impacts churches as they are becoming superficial. Silva exclaims: "It's like we have a supermarket with various types of worship, celebration, faith, where people go and pick one. This one is good for me, this one here doesn't work for me, it does not suit my reality." [29] For him, some leaders are lowering the bar and not offering spiritual quality to the believers: "Our churches can be filled with people who are there singing and celebrating but are not being true worshippers. The church is not the priority. Faith is not the priority. God is not the priority. The priority needs to be adjusted to my reality and not to the biblical truth or the qualification of the teaching of the Word."

Conclusion

In this chapter, the major Brazilian traits were analyzed according to the interviewees' perspectives, memoirs, and experiences. In summary, they see cordiality as a bridge for evangelism, relationship and discipleship but a barrier for decision making. Regarding collectivism, it is mainly a barrier with few bridges and some of the leaders understand that it is a barrier that should become a bridge. The Religious-Collectivistic mindset was depicted as a barrier. The interviewees discussed the problems of syncretism, including inside the Evangelical community through Neopentecostal practices and nominal Christianity. Finally, the Brazilian way of coping is seen as a bridge for evangelism and a barrier for Christian living, a critical issue for teaching, discipleship, and ecclesiology. Christ meets, engages, changes, challenges, dialogues,

---

29. As J. D. Payne and John Mark Terry remember, the church does not exist to sell a product to the consumer or deliver a new service to him. They add that there is no competition (as there might be between corporations) between congregations, since there is only one church, a family, the body of Christ made up of priests on mission until the Parousia. Payne and Terry, *Developing a Strategy for Missions*, 2.

and interacts with culture. The final chapter summarizes how Christ bridges with cultures. It addresses the findings of the research regarding how socio-cultural factors play a significant role in the translation of the Gospel in Brazil as discovered and expressed among the BBC.

7

Christ Bridges Cultures

Brazilian Baptist Pathways in an Era of World Christianity

THIS DISSERTATION ARGUES THAT sociocultural factors play a significant role in the translation of the Gospel in Brazil as discovered and expressed among the BBC. It presents how Christ meets, engages, changes, challenges, interacts, and dialogues with culture. As Mark Noll reflects,

> What I should have been thinking about . . . was the relationship between authentic Christian faith and the effects of environment on that faith. How were believers moving the culture, avoiding the culture, transcending the culture, reflecting the culture? These questions, I see more clearly now than at that time, concerned not just the "application" of Christian faith but its very essence.[1]

This concluding chapter offers a summary and provides final considerations about the role of the major sociocultural Brazilian in the translation of the Gospel according to the opinion of the eight interviewees. It adds value and insight to the evaluation of bridges, barriers, and other nuances for the translation of the Gospel in Brazil. This chapter draws together the preceding arguments and makes conclusions about what has been presented. First, it forms analytical considerations regarding the findings of the research on the cultural translation of the Gospel in the country and presents strategic steps to encourage and enhance that development. Stephen B. Bevans proposes, "Faith is not a personal possession, but

---

1. Noll, *From Every Tribe and Nation*, 89.

something to be shared."[2] Second, this chapter ponders the reflections of the interviewees and WCS scholars on challenges to Christian expansion in Brazil and around the world. Finally, this chapter suggests future research perspectives on Christianity and the Baptist movement in Brazil as part of the World Christian family. Jin Yung Park argues that World Christianity corrects the prevalent bias toward a "Western framework that has long been dominant."[3]

Evangelicals Growth and the Brazilian Religious Movement

This research aims to provide theoretical and biblical steps for people to become like Jesus in His redemptive mission, as the authors of *Understanding World Christianity* visualize the goal for scholarship and theological education.[4] The reflections and research findings in this endeavor agree with the idea that ministry needs to begin with theology for the sake of accomplishing the Great Commission.[5]

This dissertation builds on the assumption that churches must reflect on their contexts to comprehend how they can share the Gospel, teach people to obey the Lord, start new churches, and leave new leaders ready to receive the ministry baton.[6] The same vision was expressed by interviewees such as Nossa, Araújo, Moutta, and Antonio, in the final remarks of their interviews. As Antonio recommends, the preaching of the Gospel should be done with a sense of urgency and with strategic intelligence.

Reasons for Studying the Phenomena

In Chapter 1, three reasons were given for carrying out this research. First, World Christianity is shifting towards the south of the globe. Second, Brazil has been a protagonist in this Christian and missionary growth, alongside other African and Asian countries. The nation is the second largest Christian country on the globe, with an evangelical population which continues to grow. Third, the originality and newness of this research lies in the

---

2. Bevans, "Ecclesiology," 116.
3. Park, "Journey of the Gospel," 2.
4. Burrows, *Understanding World Christianity*, 73.
5. The enormous missionary activity in the Majority World is not enough yet. More workers are needed for the harvest. Payne, *Pressure Points*, 42.
6. Payne, *Pressure Points*, 56.

survey of the translation of the Gospel inside the BBC with an emic insight from a WCS perspective. So what?

As Mark Noll puts it, last Sunday, more people were gathered at Assemblies of God churches in Brazil than in US Assemblies of God and the Church of God in Christ, the two largest Pentecostal denominations in the country.[7] Moreover, the cultural reality of Brazil and other Latin American countries is influenced by Catholicism as a cultural system which goes beyond theology or church life.[8] What does this mean? It reveals that Brazil is a very religious country and will continue to be among the leading Christian countries.

By 2050, Brazil is expected to have the second-largest Christian population, following the US and preceding Nigeria. In Latin America, the forecast is that Evangelicalism will grow by 25 percent, from 531 million (2010) to 666 million (2050).[9] Therefore, what kind of Protestantism is coming down the road?[10] Will cell churches or small-group-based churches have a visibly higher growth rate than other traditional and historical groups? Will the increase of the unaffiliated and other religions, such as Islam and Spiritism continue?[11] Future research should explore this issue and evaluate the impact of these changes on the religious scenario in Brazil.

Neopentecostalism as a Challenge

The trends of Pentecostalism and NeoPentecostalism inside Brazilian Protestantism are not encouraging, as Souza and other interviewees affirmed. This group grew from about 6 percent of the population in 1991 to 13 percent in 2010. At the same time, one should ask, "How are historical Protestant denominations such as Baptists growing"? The intriguing and challenging fact, which also spurred this author's curiosity about the topic, is that the historical Protestant denominations have remained at about 3 to 4 percent

---

7. Noll, *From Every Tribe and Nation*, 130.
8. Payne, *From Every Tribe and Nation*, 149–51.
9. Pew Research Center, "Future of World Religions."
10. Twenty years ago, Campos anticipated four possible scenarios for Christianity in Brazil: Pentecostalized Protestantism, Protestantized Pentecostalism, the decline of the Pentecostal movement, and the decomposition of the present religious field. Most of his forecasting has been confirmed to a certain extent, especially in terms of a Pentecostalized Protestantism, meaning its decline in a secularized society.
11. Pew Research Center, "Appendix A: Methodology."

of the population during the same period, while an "unclassified" group of Protestants went from less than 1 percent in 1991 to 5 percent in 2010.

Why are Pentecostals growing numerically? The Pew analysis confirms that neither fertility rates or immigration are the reason, since Protestants and Catholics have about the same fertility rate, and less than 1 percent of Brazilians are foreign born.[12] The primary factor, according to a survey done in 2006 by Pew Research Center, is that nearly half (45 percent) of Pentecostals come from Catholicism. In this sense, the growth of Protestantism in Brazil is largely a question of religious switching. As Mark Noll asserts, "When the niches and needs are so varied, Pentecostalism works by constant adjustment on the ground."[13] The groups which are growing go along with the suggestions given by the interviewees to engage people's hunger, thirst for God, and spiritual matters that teach the truth. Another niche which can continue to be explored by Brazilian Baptists is rural areas, given that Catholics are more likely to live in those areas.[14]

In those rural and small communities, persecution still exists. It occurs at a reduced rate and is not as difficult as it was at the beginning of the Baptist work in Brazil. What should the church do amid the persecution and isolation that their members may suffer? Some answers by the interviewees suggest promoting support groups inside the church that reflect upon the cost of discipleship (Luke 14:25–35) and to be mindful of utilizing potential of insiders. Moutta explains,

> We had a case of a missionary who was staying at a riverside community in the Amazon and a priest decided to ban him from that area. The members of this community have driven our missionary away. But he had already won a young man close to the community, and that teenager continued to work. There is a church there now with more than 100 members started by that teenager who could not be sent away because he was, in fact, part of the community. But these cases are rare nowadays. The priests are open. There is a somehow peaceful dialogue that favors this respect.

---

12. Pew Research Center, "Brazil's Changing Religious Landscape."
13. Noll, *From Every Tribe and Nation*, 152–54.
14. Pew Research Center, "Brazil's Changing Religious Landscape." In the region where this writer lives, there are many small churches and church plants that are dependent on a mother-church in rural areas. FBC Serrinha maintains five campuses. The main congregation is at downtown Serrinha. There are two campuses in the city of Teofiândia and other two campuses in the rural communities called Vira-Mão and Candeal.

Brazilian Baptists' Strategies for Growth

What is the role of the Brazilian Baptist Convention in the growth of Christianity in Brazil and around the world through biblically sound translation practices? What can the denomination do to achieve better results than it has experienced? Will the missionary mindset also include its backyard, or is world missions the only way of accomplishing the mission? Surely, both are mandatory. What will be the strategies to make this happen? The following section summarizes the bridges proposed by the interviewees, other authors, and this writer.

Strategic Planning

Before entering the discussion, one should define his strategy inside the church of Jesus Christ. J. D. Payne and John Mark Terry affirm that mission strategy starts with the attempt to see "what the Lord would desire to be accomplished among a particular people, population segment, village, tribe, or city."[15] It is not business strategy. It is not war strategy. It is mission strategy. In the end, mission strategy is a process to describe what a group understands God wants them to do to make disciples of all nations; it starts with evangelism and demands a theology of mission based on conversion.[16] Hiebert asserts that conversion refers to a deep cultural transformation.[17] Planning does not need to be done in the same way as the Holy Spirit, but strategic planning is doing the human part and "leaving the process and results to the Lord."[18] The discernment comes from prayer and Spirit-guided "preparation, development, implementation, and evaluation of the necessary steps involved in missionary endeavors."[19] There is a need for

---

15. Payne, *Developing a Strategy for Missions*, 4. "Unless a team is specifically called by God to a resistant people, it should begin where the Holy Spirit has been working, ripening the field for the harvest" (47). In other words, it may imply going after an unreached people group, in other words, a people with less than 2 percent evangelical (5).

16. Payne, *Developing a Strategy for Missions*, 5–6.

17. For Hiebert, there are three levels of conversion. First, there is a transformation in one's behavior and rituals, such as stopping drinking alcohol and smoking, baptism, and regularly attending church. Second, conversion implies changing beliefs and belief systems, as evidenced by true repentance and confession of sins, following Jesus, and knowing the Bible. Finally, conversion affects one's worldview, which means adopting a Christian worldview. Hiebert, *Transformando Cosmovisões*, 357.

18. Payne, *Developing a Strategy for Missions*, 8–9.

19. Payne, *Developing a Strategy for Missions*, 43.

strategic planning, especially at the local church level. The BBC, NMB, and state conventions are trying to disseminate this mentality. However, there is still a long way to go. Denominational leaders necessitate to move towards the ground level of the churches and their local members, and pastors need to return to traditional evangelistic and missionary zeal and improve it by fostering a strategic planning mentality in the local churches.

The BCC's strategic planning is called Vision Brazil 2020. It is promoted by the NMB and based on the *Igreja Multiplicadora* strategy.[20] The vision is for Brazilian Baptists to generate a movement of intentional multiplication of disciples and churches, while striving to become a church of ten million people by 2020, with Baptists making up 2 percent of the population. Yet, is there strategic planning happening inside state conventions and associations? For the BaBC, the answer would be yes, with goals for local associations.[21] Parachurch organizations have offered training for local churches.[22]

Interviewees' Recommended Strategies

What are the main findings of the interviews for WCS, Brazilian scholars, and the church itself as they seek to enhance the translation of the Gospel into the national culture engaging with sociocultural traits? Overall, there is a cultural and religious diversity in Brazil that entails severe challenges for translation. The cultural diversity includes colonial, indigenous, and immigrant cultures, paired with cordiality and collectivism, religiosity and religious diversity, besides ethical challenges.

---

20. The vision is described on Visão Brasil 2020. The initiative is paired with an annual conference of *Igreja Multiplicadora*, macroregional, state, and regional conferences, and trainings held by NMB in partnership with state conventions and associations.

21. The headline of *O Batista Baiano* (The Baiano Baptist), newspaper of BaBC was "Planejamento Estratégico é Aprovado na 93a Assembleia da CBBa." There is also an official website "Planejamento Estratégico da Convenção Batista Baiana."

22. During the first semester of 2017, Vaso Novo Publishing Company promoted the 1st Journey of Strategic Planning and Church Growth, with the goal of offering 66 hours of training in Bahia's main cities such as Salvador, Feira de Santana, Vitória da Conquista, Ilhéus, and Jequié. It is based on the church planting model Training for Trainers (T4T) by Ying Kai. Information from e-mail communication with the author, who observed one of the trainings in Feira de Santana on June 23, 2017.

Training, Mentoring, and Scholarship

Some reflections about the present research indicate paths for developing strategies. First, how do quantitative (years of ministry) and qualitative experiences (level of involvement with local churches and denomination) increase translation capacity? Second, in what measure does geographical experience (where they served or in which position) deepen a person's critical view of translation? Another consideration which can reflect the interviews and the data gathered is that there is a need for mentoring and training by those seasoned and informed ministers on biblically sound translation.

Soares suggests, "We have a lot to do in our country. Especially regarding the preparation of leaders, so that the Gospel can reach the unreached within our country and in the world... To do so, we need men and women of God, commissioned and prepared, who can go to the field to deliver the message." Training and mentoring go together. Finally, mentoring and training are part and parcel of scholarship, as this dissertation attempts to expand the study of the translation of the Gospel in Brazil so that the advancement of the Christian faith happens in the country. "Zeal without knowledge is not a good thing, for the one who makes haste will miss the way (Prov 19:2)."[23]

Exploring Cordiality and Engaging Collectivism

In continental Brazil, cordiality varies from region to region and according to the urban or rural scenario, big cities, and small cities. It is an open door for evangelism and a challenge for decision-making and discipleship, as it may drain active decision-making and discipleship. For the interviewees, cordiality is both a bridge and barrier. It is a bridge for evangelism through relationships and discipleship. However, it is a barrier for people follow Christ since it helps people become friendlier; yet, they end up saying "no." In this same way, it may be a barrier for evangelism in that people may say "yes" to invitations to follow Christ or attend a church meeting, but they mean "no.

Second, collectivism is a barrier for evangelism in closed groups, but it can become a bridge when disciples of Christ relate to the bridge-people of the groups. Some strategies are presented to reach collectivistic groups by the interviewees, particularly Soares and Antonio. In the religious-collectivistic

---

23. Payne, *Pressure Points*, 41.

mindset, some barriers can be turned into bridges, according to the interviewees. In Indigenous groups, initially one should establish relationships with the leadership (chieftain) and then, build genuine relationships with the members of the tribe. One should use oral narratives and story-telling to contextualize the message through family and cultural stories. Finally, one should teach inside the relationship simultaneously and intentionally.

In general, collectivistic and religious societies favor the formation of closed groups. To overcome those barriers, one suggested strategy is to establish relationships and friendships. Inside closed families, demonstrate love for and show interest in them. Regarding family tradition, which may block Christian conversion, invest in long-term witnessing with patience and perseverance. When believers face opposition, churches must promote support groups inside the fellowship. Finally, in contexts of persecution and isolation, remember the cost of discipleship (Luke 14:25–35), as Jenkins proposes when reflecting on the persecution Middle East Christians endured for centuries.[24]

Additionally, Antonio suggests that families are a starting point in ministry within collectivistic cultures. Think about community ministries to serve families through music, languages, sports, and other activities. Second, train soul-winners. Collectivism favors the formation of disciples who reproduce inside their groups. Finally, try a courageous mission's strategy: new converts should remain in their communities as much as possible to work in their mission fields. This is the same suggestion given by the authors of *Reaching the City: Reflections on Urban Mission for the Twenty-first Century*.[25]

Understanding and Challenging Religion

Third, religiosity is both a bridge and a barrier, as it enables syncretism, even among the evangelical community, as Neopentecostals mix different religious symbols and concepts. There is also the danger of nonreligious people coming out of the church because of a consumer-driven worldview. How can one overcome these challenges? Here are some ideas given by the interviewees.

---

24. Phillip Jenkins, "Is this the End for Mideast Christianity?"
25. Fujino, *Reaching the City*, 436–37.

Religious-Collectivistic Mindsets: Barriers x Bridges

Barriers	Bridges Suggested by Interviewees
Closed groups	Establish relationships and friendships
Closed families	Connect by showing love and interest
Family tradition	Long term testimony, patience, and perseverance
Opposition	Promote support groups inside the church
Persecution/Isolation	Remember the cost of discipleship (Luke 14:25–35)

Table 9. Religious-Collectivistic Mindset: Barriers Found and Bridges Proposed

In situations of syncretism, use Christian concepts already known. In situations of nominal Christianity, highlight biblical distinctives and standards of living. In African Brazilian religious contexts, pray, persevere, and proclaim the Gospel. Among Catholic traditions, read the Catholic Bible aloud to teach people. For people of Indigenous religions, do linguistic/cultural translation and promote a missionary people movement. In the context of NeoPentecostalism and other religions with non-religious people, engage people's hunger and thirst for God and spiritual matters and teach the truth.

Transforming Ethics and Society

Finally, the Brazilian way of coping is understood as both a bridge and barrier. Regarding the ability to form closed groups for coping with challenges, the interviewees suggest one pray for God's wisdom, be a good witness, and be creative in presenting Christ, especially through apologetic reasoning. Take advantage of the easy access to people in their open times to engage with the Gospel and discipleship and have the flexibility to change the schedule and agenda and minister to people in their time of need. Treat people well, relate to them, preach the Gospel, and make disciples.

Regarding ethical problems and shortcuts in marriage, business, finances, abiding the law and rules, which impacts the personal integrity and church theology (syncretism), the strategy is composed of the following steps: Take these experiences as teachable moments. Encourage real commitment to God and the Scriptures, which has the right answers and solutions for human problems. Present the irresistible Gospel, the powerful Word of God, confronting sinful behavior. Teach to heal ethical illnesses (John 9:35–38) and offer Sunday school and other teaching ministries.[26] One question asked by world leaders in missions to North Americans can enrich this Brazilian discussion: "Does the church have a prophetic role in its own society, or does it simply mimic the culture and entertain its members?"[27] Or, as Luiz C. Nascimento asks, "Should Brazilians acquire a critical awareness that enables them to identify and transform cases of injustice?"[28] Paul Borthwick encourages the global church to partner together to serve the poor, instead of only sending money.[29] Miriam Adeney, offers other principles, as follows:

- Know when to do charity, when to do development, and when to do advocacy. In the long run, most efforts should focus on long-term development.
- Sustainable development is best. Programs are not much good if they are not affordable after the Western money or support is gone.
- Value-added development is best. For example, processing crops into oil and flour brings more income than selling the crops.
- Participatory development is best. This requires spending a lot of time with people and listening to them. They may not want what you want. Poor people need to be repeatedly asked what they think.
- Integrated development is best to maintain significant improvements.
- Christian development is best. Humans need God and development is not complete until they meet him.[30]

The author, based on the interviewees' insights and his emic experience, recognizes some venues for sharing the Gospel in the Brazilian culture. The following steps may be taken linearly, but they overlap and

---

26. The following survey adds insight for future research. Pew Research Center, "Religion and Morality in Latin America."
27. Borthwick, *Western Christians in Global Mission*, 914–15.
28. Nascimento, "Religion and Immigration."
29. Borthwick, *Western Christians in Global Mission*, 1776.
30. Borthwick, *Western Christians in Global Missions*, 1780–86.

enhance one another as the translation cycle continues and contextualization occurs:

1. Consider the local culture of the city and region. The context where the church is inserted is the starting point.

2. Study the local church reality to discover how evangelism, discipleship, and biblical principles happen and can be enhanced.

3. Consider and evaluate church growth models—and above all their biblical principles and strategies to discover how they connect with the local reality

4. Involve and engage the church, leaders, and individual cultures to build strategies suited for the local reality with the goal of accomplishing the Great Commission.

5. Always have on mind the mission field starting in the region and reaching the ends of the earth. It brings new air, motivates, and moves the church in its ongoing mission.

Future Research

Some future research possibilities are given in this section considering the results of this investigation. First, how does the translation and versions of traditional foreign hymns reflect the translation of the Gospel in Brazil in historical evangelical churches? How do pastors and church planters share the Gospel personally and from the pulpit? What do they preach? What do their printed sermons and articles say, and how does the way they serve the local people reveal their translation practices? What are they doing? What are they emphasizing? These may give evidence of the translation of the Gospel into the local culture in different forms.

Second, local research is promising, such as the one in Southern Minas Gerais, as tested using the oral history methodology, or in the city of Salvador, the capital of Bahia state. There are examples of the variety of research possibilities in this country. For example, Salvador is a place with a strong Catholic and African heritage. There, it is said that there is one Catholic church for each day of the year, and that rudiments of Catholicism, such as calling the Lord's Supper "Holy Supper," influence Baptist practices. In the same city, idols of the African religion are seen in the central lake of the city and its religious sacrifices are offered in the crossroads. The history, food, music, and skin color of the people pay tribute to the former colonial center of slavery in Brazil.

Another question to be asked in this local approach is: What is peculiar to being Baptist in Salvador or in the state of Bahia? This was the place where the first Southern Baptist missionaries William Buck Bagby and his wife, Anne, planted the first Brazilian Baptist Church in 1882. Which cultural aspects are favorable and contrary to the proclamation of the Gospel in a contextualized way in that city and this state? Some indications can be found as one matches the Baptist features with the Brazilian culture for determining areas of disparity and congruency in their relationship. Since Southern Baptists transplanted the structure of the church to a different society and culture, there were conflicts and changes along the way. New developments still happen, such as the controversy about the pastoral ordination of women, social Gospel, and other debates now ancient to the SBC in the US but still alive in Brazil.

Other questions can guide this regional research and be modified according to the place they occur: How does the Baptist church exist and subsist in a city with strong Catholic and African-Brazilian religions roots? What Baptist distinctives are more remarkable and compelling in this region of Brazil? What local and cultural features should Baptists take into consideration when preaching the Gospel and discipling the indigenous people? How can the BBC appropriate and utilize its good reputation?

This research can also analyze why Brazilian Baptists, who arrived in Brazil in 1882, did not grow in Brazil as, for example, the indigenous Assembly of God, which was born inside FBC of Pará in 1911. Likewise, research can discuss the aspects of the Brazilian culture which help Pentecostal and Prosperity churches be the major groups in Brazil. In the first half of the last century, Baptists and Presbyterians were the most prominent Protestant groups. Why did this shift happen? This research indicated some reasons, but there is space left for deeper investigation, specifically about of the stagnation of the Baptist work in Brazil and to provide additional insights for its growth.

There are further questions that can be posed: Why did the Pentecostals, Charismatics, and NeoPentecostals explode, yet, the mainline denominations did not follow the same pattern? The outcome of such research will be beneficial for Brazilian Baptists. However, the hope is that pastors, denominational leadership, local church members, and academic circles may reflect on the issues and improve the translation of the Gospel in the country. Finally, a provocative avenue of research is to survey translation on the recipient's side. What attracts people to an evangelical church? What is the role of personal evangelism and small groups in the Brazilian church? In the end, the field for WCS is ripe for harvest in Brazil.

Final Remarks

Culture indeed presents both bridges and barriers to the translation of the Gospel. According to the findings of this research, biblically sound translation means that one not only perceives these barriers, but also has the ability to turn them into bridges for translating the Gospel in such a way that it transforms lives and cultures for the glory of God. As Silva stated, "we have created many barriers, but God overcomes barriers and opens opportunities for transformation of lives." Or, as Moreira says, "There are no cultural aspects, there is no other way that can prevent God's acts." These interviewees, for example, demonstrate biblically sound translation skills, as seen also in the *Igreja Multiplicadora* collectivistic church model promoted by the NMB of the BCC.[31] The hope is that the glory of God will be shown even more when people who bear His image are saved and transformed more and more into His likeness and lead others to the Messiah. Christ meets culture, and the Christian movement in history continues.

---

31. "Churches that are most likely to move forward effectively are those who embrace a radically biblical approach to sending missionary teams to function in apostolic ways when it comes to making disciples, planting churches, and appointing pastors in those churches." Payne, *Pressure Points*, 22.

Appendix

Barriers Turned into Bridges

Interviewees' Strategies for Engaging and Transforming the Culture

Four Steps to Cultural Translation in Brazilian Indigenous Groups

1. Establish relationships first with the leadership (Chieftain).
2. Then, establish genuine relationships with the members of the tribe
3. Utilize oral narratives and story-telling to contextualize the message through family and cultural stories
4. Teach inside the relationship simultaneously and intentionally

Table A1: Soares' Suggestions on Reaching out to Indigenous Brazilian Communities

Three Steps to Cultural Translation in Collectivistic Groups

1. Families are a starting point in ministry. Think about community ministries to serve families through music, languages, sports, and other activities
2. Train soul-winners. Collectivism favors the formation of disciples who reproduce inside their own groups

Appendix

3. Try a courageous missionary strategy: new converts should remain in their communities as much as possible to work in their own mission fields

Table A2: Antonio's Suggestions on How to Reach Collectivistic Groups

Religious-Collectivistic Mindsets: **Barriers x Bridges**

Barriers	Bridges Suggested by Interviewees
Closed groups	Establish relationships and friendships
Closed families	Connect showing love and interest
Family tradition	Long-term testimony, patience, and perseverance
Opposition	Promote support groups inside the church
Persecution/Isolation	Remember the cost of discipleship (Luke 14:25–35)

Table A3: Religious-Collectivistic Mindset: Barriers Found and Bridges Proposed

Religiosity: **Barriers x Bridges**

Barriers	Bridges Suggested by Interviewees
Syncretism	Use Christian concepts already known
Nominal Christianity	Highlight biblical distinctives and standards of life
African Brazilian religions	Prayer, persevere and proclaim the gospel
Catholic traditions	Use the Catholic Bible to teach people
Indigenous religions	Do linguistic/cultural translation and promote missionary People Movement
NeoPentecostalism	As with Catholics and other religions, engage people's hunger and thirst for God and teach the truth

Table A4: Religiosity: Barriers Found and Bridges Proposed

***Brazilian Way of Coping:* Barriers x Bridges**

Barriers	Bridges Suggested by Interviewees
Forming closed groups for coping with challenges	Pray for God's wisdom, be a good witness and creative in presenting Christ, including apologetic reasoning
	Take advantage of the easy access to people in their open times to engage with the gospel and discipleship
	Have the flexibility to change the schedule and the agenda and minister to people in their times of need
	Treat people well, relate to them, preach the gospel, and make disciples
Ethical problems and shortcuts in marriage, business, finances, abiding by the law and rules, impacting personal integrity and church theology (syncretism), ethics, and practices	Take these experiences as teachable moments
	Encourage real commitment to God and the Scriptures, which have the right answers and fixes for human problems
	Present the irresistible gospel, the powerful Word of God, confronting sinful behavior
	Teach to heal cure ethical illnesses (John 9:35–38)
	Offer Sunday School and other teaching ministries

Table A5: Brazilian Way of Coping: Barriers Turned into Bridges

Bibliography

Andrade, Maristela Oliveira de. "A Religiosidade Brasileira: O Pluralismo Religioso, a Diversidade de Crenças e o Processo Sincrético." *CAOS—Revista Eletrônica de Ciências Sociais*, no. 14 (2009) 106–18.

Arantes, Roosevelt. *Aprofundando Raizes: Dinamica e Elementos do Relacionamento Discipulador*. Rio de Janeiro, JMN, 2016.

Araújo, Hércio Fonseca de. "Interview Transcript." May 15, 2017.

Arias, Mortimer. "Contextual Evangelization in Latin America: Between Accommodation and Confrontation." *Occasional Bulleting of Missionary Research* 2, no. 1 (1978) 19–28.

Augustine, Saint. *Letters*. Vol. 2, 83–130. Translated by Sister Wilfrid Parsons. Washington, DC: Catholic University of America Press, 2008.

Azevedo, Fernando de. *Brazilian Culture: An Introduction to the Study of Culture in Brazil*. New York: Macmillan, 1950.

Azevedo, Israel Belo de. *As Cruzadas Inacabadas: Introdução à História da Igreja na América Latina*. Rio de Janeiro: Gêmeos, 1980.

Ballard, Leslie Roy. *History of Oral History: Foundations and Methodology*. Lanham, MD: AltaMira, 2006. Kindle.

Barfield, Thomas J. *The Dictionary of Anthropology*. Oxford; Malden, Mass: Blackwell, 1997.

Barlach, Lisete. "O Jeitinho Brasileiro: Traço da Identidade Nacional?" *Revista Gestão & Políticas Públicas* 3, no. 2 (2013) 228–45.

Baylor University Institute for Oral History. "Time Coding & Indexing Oral Histories." *Baylor University*, April 13, 2017. http://www.baylor.edu/content/services/document.php/66437.pdf.

———. "Transcribing Oral Histories." *Baylor University*, April 13, 2017. http://www.baylor.edu/content/services/document.php/ 66438.pdf.

Bebbington, David W. *Baptists Through the Centuries*. Waco, TX: Baylor University Press, 2010.

———. *Evangelicalism in Modern Britain: A History from the 1730s to the 1980s*. London; Boston: Unwin Hyman, 1989.

Bechard, Dean Philip. "Paul Among the Rustics: the Lystran Episode (Acts 14:8–20) and Lucan Apologetic." *The Catholic Biblical Quarterly* 63, no. 1 (2001) 84–101.

Beckwith, Carl L. *Ezekiel, Daniel: Reformation Commentary on Scripture Series*. Downers Grove: InterVarsity, 2012.

Bibliography

Bell, Lester Carl. "Factors influencing doctrinal developments among the Brazilian Baptists." Th.D. diss., Southwestern Baptist Theological Seminary, 1957.

Benson, John E. "Understanding Liberals and Conservatives." *Dialog* 53, no. 1 (2014) 69–78.

Beozzo, Jose Carlos and Susin, Luiz Carlos. *Brazil: People and Church(es)*. London: SCM, 2002.

Berg, Mike and Paul Pretiz. *Spontaneous Combustion—Grass-Roots Christianity, Latin American Style*. Pasadena, CA: Carey, 1996.

Bezerra, Elvia. "Ribeiro Couto e o Homem Cordial." *Revista Brasileira* 44 (2005) 123–30.

Blaising, Craig A. "The Day of the Lord Will Come: An Exposition of 2 Peter 3:1–18." *Bibliotheca Sacra* 169, no. 676 (2012) 387–401.

Bledsoe, David A. *Evangelismo Via Relacionamentos*. Rio de Janeiro: Convicção, 2012.

Blount, Brian K. *Revelation: A Commentary*. Louisville: Westminster John Knox, 2009.

Bobsin, Oneide. *Uma Religiao Chamada Brasil*. Sao Leopoldo: Faculdades EST, 2008.

Bock, Darrell L. *Acts. Baker Exegetical Commentary on the New Testament*. Grand Rapids: Baker, 2007

Bosley, Harold. "Theology and Social Experience." *The Journal of Religion* 22, no. 4 (1942) 371–81.

Borthwick, Paul. *Western Christians in Global Mission: What's the Role of the North American Church?* (Kindle Edition), Kindle Locations, 914–15.

Brandão, Fernando. *Igreja Multiplicadora: 5 Princípios Bíblicos para Crescimento*. Rio de Janeiro: Convicção, 2013.

Brodie, Thomas L. *The Quest for the Origin of John's Gospel: A Source-Oriented Approach*. New York: Oxford University Press, 1993.

Bryant, Robert A. "Romans 12:1–8." *Interpretation* 58, no. 3 (2004) 287–90.

Bucher, Glenn R. "Toward a Liberation Theology for the 'Oppressor.'" *Journal of the American Academy of Religion* 44, no. 3 (1976) 517–34.

Burrows, William R., et al. *Understanding World Christianity: The Vision and Works of Andrew F. Walls*. Maryknoll, NY: Orbis, 2011. Kindle.

Cahill, Mark. *One Thing You Cannot Do in Heaven. One Thing You Cannot Do in Heaven*. Rockwall, TX: Biblical Discipleship, 2005.

Camargo, Cândido Procópio F. de. *Católicos, Protestantes, Espíritas*. Petrópolis: Vozes, 1978.

Campos, Leonildo Silveira. *Teatro, Templo e Mercado: Organização e Marketing de um Empreendimento Neopentecostal*. Petrópolis: Vozes, 1997.

———. "O Discurso Acadêmico de Rubem Alves sobre 'Protestantismo' e 'Repressão': Algumas Observações 30 Anos Depois." *Religião & Sociedade* 28, no. 2 (2008) 102–37.

Carvalho, Diogo. *Relacionamento Discipulador: Uma Teologia da Vida Discipular*. 2nd ed. Rio de Janeiro: JMN, 2016.

Center for the Study of Global Christianity, "500 Years of Protestantism." *Center for the Study of Global Christianity*, 14 February 2017. http://www.gordonconwell.edu/ockenga/research/documents/136e0d3b6-d706-4bcf-a892-87a608c59104-18.pdf.

———. *Christianity in its Global Context, 1970–2020*. South Hamilton, MA: Center for the Study of Global Christianity, 2013.

Chafer, Lewis Sperry. "The teachings of Christ incarnate [3]." *Bibliotheca Sacra* 108, no.432 (1951) 389–413.

Chesnutt, Andrew R. *Born Again in Brazil: The Pentecostal Boom and the Pathogens of Poverty*. New Brunswick, NJ: Rutgers University Press, 1997.

Bibliography

Clement of Alexandria. *Christ the Educator. The Fathers of the Church.* Vol. 23. Washington, DC: Catholic University of America Press, 1954.

Coleman, Robert. *The Master Plan of Evangelism.* Huntingdon Valley, PA: Christian Outreach, 1963.

Comunicacao Social, IBGE. "Censo 2010: Número de Católicos Cai e Aumenta o de Evangélicos, Espíritas e sem Religião." *IBGE*, August 22, 2014. http://censo2010.ibge.gov.br/noticias-censoview=noticia&id=3&idnoticia=2170&busca=1&t=censo-2010-numero-catolicos-cai-aumenta-evangelicos-espiritas-sem-religiao.

Convenção Batista Baiana. "Planejamento Estratégico da Convenção Batista Baiana." *Convenção Batista Baiana,* June 30, 2017. http://cbbaiana.org/html/index.php/quem-somos/planejamento.

Convenção Batista Brasileira. "Manifesto de Santos." *Convenção Batista Carioca,* August 20, 2016. https://batistacarioca.com.br/manifesto-de-santos/.

Cook, Matthew. *Local Theology for the Global Church: Principles for an Evangelical Approach to Contextualization.* Pasadena: World Evangelical Alliance Theological Commission, 2010.

Corten, André. *Between Babel and Pentecost: Transnational Pentecostalism in Africa and Latin America.* Bloomington, IN: Indiana University Press, 2001.

Costa, Esdras Borges. "Protestantism, Modernization and Cultural Change in Brazil." Ph.D. diss., University of California, Berkley, 1979.

Costa, Sirgisberto Queiroga da. "Church Multiplication: A Grounded Theory Study of the Missiological Paradigm of Multiplying Presbyterian Churches in the Synod of Brasilia." Ph.D. diss., Reformed Theological Seminary, 2005.

Craig, William Lane. *Reasonable Faith: Christian Truth and Apologetics.* Wheaton: Crossway, 2008. Kindle.

Dean, William D. "Can Liberal Theology Recover?" *American Journal of Theology & Philosophy* 30, no. 1 (2009) 24–47.

Dever, Mark E. *Nine Marks of a Healthy Church.* Washington, DC: Center for Church Reform, 1998.

———. *The Deliberate Church.* Wheaton: Crossway, 2005.

———. *The Gospel and Personal Evangelism.* Wheaton: Crossway, 2007.

Donelson, Lewis R. *I & II Peter and Jude: A Commentary.* Westminster: John Knox, 2010.

Duc, Arthur W. "Attraction and Retention Factors in Three Pentecostal Churches in Curitiba, Brazil." Ph.D. diss., Trinity International University, 2001.

Dunham, Robert E. "Acts 17:16–34." *Interpretation* 60, no. 2 (2006) 202–4.

Duraisingh, Christopher, ed. *Called to One Hope: The Gospel in Diverse Cultures.* Geneva: World Council of Churches, 1998.

Dyrness, William A. and Garcia-Johnson, Oscar. *Theology Without Borders: An Introduction to Global Conversations.* Grand Rapids: Baker, 2015. Kindle.

Earley, Dave. *Transformando Membros em Líderes: Como Ajudar os Membros de seu Pequeno Grupo a Liderar Novos Grupos.* Translated by Ingrid Neufeld de Lima. Rio de Janeiro, JMN, 2016.

———. *8 Hábitos do Líder Eficaz de Pequenos Grupos.* Translated by Haroldo Janzen. Rio de Janeiro, JMN, 2016.

Eitel, Keith E. "Scriptura or Cultura: Is There a Sola in There?" *Southwestern Journal of Theology* 55, no. 1 (2012) 63–76.

Bibliography

Elkins, Richard E. "Conversion or Acculturation? A Study of Culture Change and Its Effects on Evangelism in Mindanao Indigenous Societies." *Missiology* 22 (1994) 168–76.

Erickson, M. J. *Christian Theology*. Grand Rapids, MI: Baker, 1998.

Fee, Gordon D. *Revelation: A New Covenant Commentary*. Cambridge: Lutterworth, 2013.

Feldmeier, Reinhard. *The First Letter of Peter: A Commentary on the Greek Text*. Translated by German by Peter H. Davids. Waco, TX: Baylor University Press, 2008.

Ferreira, Damy. *Evangelismo Total*. Rio de Janeiro: Juerp, 1990.

Ferreira, Marcos Paulo. *Escola Biblica Discipuladora: Formando Lideres Multiplicadores*. Rio de Janeiro: JMN, 2015.

Fonteles, Maria das Graças Sá Roriz. "The Insertion of Protestantism in Brazil: A Contemporary Look." *Ciências da Religião: História e Sociedade* 7, no. 1 (2009) 174–88.

France, R. T. *Matthew: An Introduction and Commentary*. Tyndale New Testament Commentaries. Nottingham, Engand: InterVarsity, 2008.

Franco, Affonso Arinos de Mello. *Conceito de Civilizacao Brasileira*. Sao Paulo: Companhia Editora Nacional, 1936.

Freitas, Fabricio. *De Volta aos Principios: Vivendo o Jeito Bíblico de Ser Igreja*. 2nd ed. Rio de Janeiro: Conviccao, 2016.

Freyre, Gilberto. *O Mundo que o Português Criou*. Rio de Janeiro: José Olympio ed., 1940.

———. *New World in the Tropics: The Culture of Modern Brazil*. New York: Knopf, 1959.

Friesen, Ivan. *Isaiah: Believers Church Bible Commentary*. Scottdale, PA: Herald, 2009.

Fujino, Gary. *Reaching the City: Reflections on Urban Mission for the Twenty-First Century*. Pasadena, CA: Carey, 2012. Kindle.

Garlington, Don. "The Salt of the Earth in Covenantal Perspective." *Journal of the Evangelical Theological Society* 54.4 (2011) 715–48.

Garrard-Burnett, Virginia and David Stoll. *Rethinking Protestantism in Latin America*. Philadelphia: Temple University Press, 1993.

George, Sherron K. "Brazil: An 'Evangelized' Giant Calling for Liberating Evangelism." *International Bulleting of Missionary Research* 26, no. 3 (2002) 104–9.

Gloer, Hulitt. *1 & 2 Timothy-Titus: Smyth & Helwys Bible Commentary Series*. Macon, GA: Smyth & Helwys, 2010.

Goldingay, John. *Isaiah: Understanding the Bible Commentary Series*. Grand Rapids: Baker, 2012.

Gonçalves, Alonso. "De Uma Teologia Canned para uma Teologia Brasileira." *Revista de CiberTeologia* 43 (2013) 59–69.

Gonçalves, Antônio de Campos. "Evangelism in Brazil Today: Its Significance and Results." *International Review of Missions* 48, no. 191 (1959) 302–8.

Gouveia, Valdiney V. and Miguel Clemente. "O Individualismo-Coletivismo no Brasil e na Espanha: Correlatos Sócio-Demográficos." *Estudos de Psicologia* 5, no. 2 (2000) 317–46.

Granberg-Michaelson, Wesley. *From Times Square to Timbuktu*. Grand Rapids: Eerdmans, 2013. Kindle.

Green, Michael. *Evangelism in the Early Church*. Grand Rapids; Cambridge: Eerdmans, 2003, Kindle.

Grimshaw, Michael. "'Redneck Religion and Shitkickin' Saviours?': Gram Parsons, Theology and Country Music." *Popular Music* 21, no. 1 (2002) 93–105.

Guedes, Rivanildo Segundo. *Uma Igreja com a Nossa Cara*. São Paulo: Fonte Editorial, 2010.

Bibliography

Gutiérrez, Benjamin F. and Dennis Smith. *In the Power of the Spirit: The Pentecostal Challenge to Historic Churches in Latin America.* Louisville: Presbyterian Church (U.S.A.), AIPRAL; CELEP, 1996.

G1 Brasil. "Número de Evangélicos Aumenta 61% em 10 anos, Aponta IBGE." G1, August, 22, 2014. http://g1.globo.com/brasil/noticia/2012/06/numero-de-evangelicos-aumenta-61-em-10-anos-aponta-ibge.html.

Hall, Edward T. "Cultural Iceberg." *Estudar Fora,* June 26, 2017. https://www.estudarfora.org.br/sem-fronteiras-choque-cultural

Hall, Edward T. *AFS Orientation Handbook.* Vol. 4. New York: AFS Intercultural Programs INC, 1984.

Harland, Philip A. *Dynamics of Identity in the World of the Early Christians.* New York: T & T Clark International, 2009.

Herndl, Carl G. and Danny A. Bauer, "Speaking Matters: Liberation Theology, Rhetorical Performance, and Social Action." *College Composition and Communication* 54, no. 4 (2003) 558–85.

Hesselgrave, David J. *Communicating Christ Cross-Culturally: An Introduction to Missionary Communication.* Grand Rapids: Zondervan, 1991.

Hickman, Jared. "The Theology of Democracy." *The New England Quarterly* 81, no. 2 (2008) 177–217.

Hiebert, D Edmond. "Presentation and Transformation: An Exposition of Romans 12:1–2." *Bibliotheca Sacra* 151, no. 603 (1994) 309–24.

Hiebert, Paul G. *The Gospel in Human Contexts: Anthropological Explorations for Contemporary Missions.* Grand Rapids: Baker, 2009.

Hofstede, Geert H. "Brazil." *Geert Hofstede,* October 30, 2014. http://geerthofstede.com/brazil.html.

———. "Cultural Dimensions." *Geert Hofstede,* April 1, 2017. https://geerthofstede.com/cultural-dimensions.html.

———. "Geert Hofstede's Scientific Innovation, The Dimension Concept." *Geert Hofstede,* June 26, 2017. https://geert-hofstede.com/cultural-dimensions.html.

Hofstede, Geert H. and Gert Jan Hofstede. *Cultures and Organizations: Software of the Mind.* New York: McGraw-Hill, 2005.

Holanda, Sérgio Buarque de. *História Geral da Civilização Brasileira.* São Paulo: Difusão Européia do Livro, 1960.

———. *Raízes do Brasil.* Rio de Janeiro: José Olympio, 1936.

Hollenweger, Walter J. "Evangelism and Brazilian Pentecostalism." *The Ecumenical Review* 20, no. 2 (1968) 163–70.

Hoopes, James. *Oral History: An Introduction for Students.* Chapel Hill: The University of North Carolina Press. Kindle Edition.

Hutchinson, Mark, and John Wolffe. *A Short History of Global Evangelicalism.* Cambridge: Cambridge University Press, 2012.

Jardim, Lauro. "O IBGE e a Religião—Cristãos são 86,8% do Brasil; Católicos Caem para 64,6%; Evangélicos já são 22,2%." *Veja,* July 18, 2013. http://veja.abril.com.br/blog/reinaldo/geral/o-ibge-e-a-religiao%E2 %80%93-cristaos-sao-868-do-brasil-catolicos-caem-para-646-evangelicos-ja-sao-222/.

Jenkins, Philip. *The Next Christendom: The Coming of Global Christianity.* 3rd ed. Oxford: Oxford University Press, 2011.

———. "Is this the end for Mideast Christianity?" Baylor Magazine, June 29, 2017. http://www.baylor.edu/alumni/magazine/ 1302/index. php?id=871130.

Bibliography

———. *The New Faces of Christianity: Believing the Bible in the Global South.* New York, Oxford University Press, 2008.

Jipp, Joshua W. "Paul's Areopagus Speech of Acts 17:16–34 as Both Critique and Propaganda." *Journal of Biblical Literature* 131, no. 3 (2012) 567–88.

Johnson, Todd M., Kenneth R. Ross and Sandra S. K. Lee. *Atlas of Global Christianity 1910–2010.* Edinburgh: Edinburgh University Press, 2009.

Junta de Missões Nacionais. "Visão Brasil 2020." *Junta de Missões Nacionais*, June 30, 2017. http://www.visaobrasil2020.org.br/.

Kalu, Ogbu U. *Interpreting Contemporary Christianity.* Grand Rapids: Eerdmans, 2008.

Keener, Craig S., *The IVP Bible Background Commentary—New Testament.* Downers Grove: InterVarsity, 1993. WORDsearch CROSS e-book.

Keener, Craig and M. Daniel Carroll R. *Global Voices: Reading the Bible in the Majority World.* Peabody, MA: Hendrickson, 2012. Kindle.

Kiuchi, Nobuyoshi. "Living like the Azazel-goat in Romans 12:1B." *Tyndale Bulletin* 57, no. 2 (2006) 251–61.

Köstenberger, Andreas J. "The Challenge of a Systematized Biblical Theology of Mission: Missiological Insights from the Gospel of John." *Missiology* 23, no 4. (1995) 445–64.

Kynes, Bill. "The Church: A Hidden Glory (1 Timothy 3:14–16)." *Themelios* 35, no. 1 (2010) 30–36.

Landes, Ruth. "Fetish Worship in Brazil." *The Journal of American Folklore* 53, no. 210 (1940) 261–70.

Latourette, Kenneth Scott. *A History of Expansion of Christianity.* Vol. 2, *The First Five Centuries.* London: Eyre & Spottiswood, 1938.

Leite Filho, Tácito da Gama. *Seitas Neopentecostais.* Vol. 3. 2nd ed. Rio de Janeiro: JUERP, 1991.

Leonard, Emile G. *O Protestantismo Brasileiro.* São Paulo: ASTE, 1963.

Lessing, R. Reed. "Yahweh versus Marduk: Creation Theology in Isaiah 40–55." *Concordia Journal* 36, no. 3 (2010) 234–44.

Lewis, Donald M. *Christianity Reborn: The Global Expansion of Evangelicalism in the Twentieth Century Studies in the History of Christian Missions.* Grand Rapids: W. B. Eerdmans, 2004.

Long, Paul Brown. "Disciple de Nations: Training Brazilians for Inter-Cultural Mission." Ph.D. diss., Fuller Theological Seminary, 1981.

Luo, Wei. "Ezekiel in Revelation: Literary and Hermeneutic Aspects." Ph.D. diss., The University of Edinburgh (United Kingdom), 1999.

Martin, David. *Tongues of Fire: The Explosion of Protestantism in Latin America.* Cambridge, MA: B. Blackwell, 1990.

Matheny, Paul D. *Contextual Theology.* Cambridge: Clarke, 2012.

Matta, Roberto da. *Carnavais, Malandros e Heróis: Para uma Sociologia do Dilema Brasileiro.* Rio de Janeiro: Zahar, 1983.

———. *O Que Faz do Brasil, Brasil?* 10th ed. Rio de Janeiro: Rocco Digital, 1986.

McGavran, Donald A. *The Bridges of God: A Study in the Strategy of Missions.* New York: Friendship, 1955.

Mein, David. *O Que Deus Tem Feito.* Rio de Janeiro: Juerp, 1982.

Mission to the World, Presbyterian Church of America, ed. *Looking Forward: Voices from Church Leaders on Our Global Mission.* Enumclaw, WA: WinePress, 2003.

Moo, Douglas J. *Encountering the Book of Romans (Encountering Biblical Studies) A Theological Survey.* 2nd ed. Grand Rapids: Baker, 2014.

Bibliography

Moore, Waylon B. *Multiplicando Discípulos: O Método Neotestamentário para o Crescimento da Igreja*. 4th ed. Translated by Adiel Almeida de Oliveira. Rio de Janeiro: Convicção, 2015.
Moreau, A. Scott, Evvy Hay Campbell, and Susan Greener. *Effective Intercultural Communication (Encountering Mission) A Christian Perspective*. Grand Rapids: Baker, 2014.
Moreira, Reginaldo Pires. *Grandes Verdades sobre o Espiritismo*. São Paulo: Fontele, 2017.
Muller, Roland. *The Messenger, The Message, The Community*. Atibaia: Pregue a Palavra, 2013.
Newbigin, Lesslie. *Foolishness to the Greeks: The Gospel and Western Culture*. Grand Rapids: Eerdmans, 1986.
———. *The Gospel in a Pluralist Society*. Grand Rapids: W. B. Eerdmans, 1989.
———. *A Walk Through the Bible*. Louisville: Westminster John Knox, 1999.
Nicholls, Bruce J. *Contextualization: A Theology of Gospel and Culture*. Downers Grove: InterVarsity, 1979.
Nida, Eugene A. *Understanding Latin Americans*. Pasadena: Carey, 1969.
Niebuhr, H. R. *Christ and Culture*. San Francisco: Harper San Francisco, 2001.
Noll, Mark. *From Every Tribe and Nation: A Historian's Discovery of the Global Christian Story*. Grand Rapids: Baker, 2014. Kindle.
———. *Turning Points: Decisive Moments in the History of Christianity*. 3rd ed. Grand Rapids: Baker, 2012.
Mark, Noll, et al. *Evangelicalism: Comparative Studies of Popular Protestantism in North America, the British Isles, and Beyond, 1700–1900*. Oxford: Oxford University Press, 1994.
Marshall, I. Howard. *The Pastoral Epistles*. London: T&T Clark, 1999.
Moreira, Reginaldo Pires. "Interview Transcript." May 9, 2017.
Moutta, Samuel Meira. "Interview Transcript." March 28, 2017.
Nascimento, Luiz C. "Religion and Immigration Towards a Transformative Prophetic Spirit." Ph.D. diss., Princeton Theological Seminary, 2012.
Nogueira, Affonso Henriques de Azevedo, et al. "Dimensões de Culturas Nacionais e Padrões Culturais: um Estudo Comparativo entre Empregados de Empresas de Previdência Privada do Brasil e dos Estados Unidos." *Anais do 2 Encontro de Estudos Organizacionais*. Recife: Observatório da Realidade Organizacional, PROPAD/UFPE, 2002.
Nossa, Guilherme Oliveira. "Interview Transcript." May 9, 2017.
O Batista Baiano. "Planejamento Estratégico é Aprovado na 93ª Assembleia da CBBA." *Convenção Batista Baiana*, June 30, 2017. http://www.batista.org.br/arquivo/obbmaiago2016_.pdf.
O'Donovan, Wilbur. *Biblical Christianity in African Perspective*. Carlisle: Paternoster, 1996.
Ogden, Schubert M. "What Is Theology?" *The Journal of Religion* 52, no. 1 (1972) 22–40.
Oliveira, Betty Antunes de. *Centelha Em Restolho Seco: Uma Contribuição para a História dos Primórdios do Trabalho Batista no Brasil*. Rio de Janeiro: B.A. de Oliveira, 1985.
Oliveira, Zaqueu Moreira de. *Desafios e Conquistas Missionárias*. Rio de Janeiro: Convicção, 2007.
———. *Messianismo Pentecostal*. Recife: Kairós, 2013.
———. *Perseguidos, Mas Não Desamparados*. Rio de Janeiro: Juerp, 1999.

Bibliography

———. "Persecution of Brazilian Baptists and its Influences on Their Development." Ph.D. diss., Southwestern Baptist Theological Seminary, 1971.

———. *Princípios e Práticas Batistas: Uma Abordagem Histórica*. Recife: Kairós, 2014.

———. *Um Povo Chamado Batista: História e Princípios*. Recife: Kairós, 2014.

Oliveira, Zaqueu Moreira de and Ramos André. *Panorama Batista em Pernambuco*. Rio de Janeiro: Juerp, 1964.

Ortiz, Renato. *Cultura Brasileira e Identidade Nacional*. 5th ed. São Paulo: Brasiliense, 2006.

Ott, Craig and Harold A. Netland. *Globalizing Theology: Belief and Practice in an Era of World Christianity*. Grand Rapids: Baker, 2006.

Payne, J. D. *Pressure Points: Twelve Global Issues Shaping the Face of the Church*. Nashville: Thomas Nelson, 2013. Kindle.

Payne, J. D. and John Mark Terry. *Developing a Strategy for Missions (Encountering Mission) A Biblical, Historical, and Cultural Introduction*. Grand Rapids: Baker, 2013. Kindle.

Park, Jin Hyung. "Journey of the Gospel: A Study in the Emergence of World Christianity and the Shift of Christian Historiography in the Last Half of the Twentieth Century." Ph.D. diss., Princeton Theological Seminary, 2009.

Pereira, Sergio O. "Society-Individual and Postmodern Condition: Understanding the Explosion of Pentecostalism in Brazil." Ph.D. diss., University of Notre Dame, 2000.

Pew Research Center. "Appendix A: Methodology." *Pew Research Center*, June 17, 2017. http://www.pewforum.org/2015/04/02/appendix-a—methodology-2/.

———. "Brazil's Changing Religious Landscape." *Pew Research Center*, June 19, 2017. http://www.pewforum.org/2013/07/18/brazils-changing-religious-landscape.

———. "Latin America and the Caribbean." *Pew Research Center*, June 19, 17. http://www.pewforum.org/2015/04/02/latin-america-and-the-caribbean/.

———. "Religião na América Latina: Mudança Generalizada em uma Região Historicamente Católica." *Pew Research Center*, November 13, 2014. www.pewresearch.org/wpcontent/uploads/sites/7/2014/11/PEW-RESEARCH-CENTER-Religion-in-Latin-America-Portuguese-Overview-for-publication-11-13.pdf.

———. "Religion and Morality in Latin America." *Pew Research Center*, June 19, 2017. http://www.pewforum.org/interactives/latin-america-morality-by-religion.

———. "Spirit and Power." *Pew Research Center*, September 11, 2017. http://www.pewforum.org/2006/10/05/historical-overview-of-pentecostalism-in-brazil/.

———. "The Future of World Religions: Population Growth Projections, 2010–2050." *Pew Research Center*, June 19, 2017. http://www.pewforum.org/2015/04/02/religious-projections-2010-2050/.

Pike, Kenneth. *Language in Relation to a Unified Theory of the Structure of Human Behavior*. The Hague: Mouton, 1967.

Prado Júnior, Caio. *Formação do Brasil Contemporâneo*. Rio de Janeiro: Livraria Martins Editora, 1942.

Raine, Philip. "The Catholic Church in Brazil." *Journal of Interamerican Studies and World Affairs* 13, no. 2 (1971) 279–95.

Ramirez, Paulo Niccoli. *Sérgio Buarque de Holanda e a Dialética da Cordialidade*. São Paulo: EDUC, 2011.

Read, William R. and Frank Avery Ineson. *Brazil 1980: The Protestant Handbook; the Dynamics of Church Growth in the 1950's and 60's, and the Tremendous Potential for the 70's*. Monrovia, CA: MARC, 1973.

Rega, Lourenco Stelio. *Dando um Jeito no Jeitinho*. Sao Paulo: Mundo Cristao, 2000.

Bibliography

Ribeiro, Darcy. *O Povo Brasileiro—A Formação e o Sentido do Brasil*. 2nd ed. São Paulo: Companhia das Letras, 1995.
Ritchie, Donald A. *Doing Oral History*. New York: Oxford University Press, 2014. Kindle.
Rodrigues, Jose Honório. "As Características do Povo Brasileiro." *Journal of Inter-American Studies* 2, no. 4 (1960) 355–77.
Sanchez, Daniel R. *Gospel in the Rosary: Bible Study on the Mysteries of Christ*. Fort Worth: ChurchStarting.net, 2003.
Sanneh, Lamin. *Disciples of All Nations: Pillars of World Christianity*. New York: Oxford University Press, 2007.
———. "Renewed and Empowered: the Christian Impact." *Ogbomoso Journal of Theology* 15 (2010) 11–33.
———. *Translating the Message: The Missionary Impact on Culture*. Maryknoll, NY: Orbis, 1989.
———. *The African Transformation of Christianity: Comparative Reflections on Ethnicity and Religious Transformation in Africa*. Temple: Arizona State University, 1998.
Santos, Jaqueline da Hora. *Evangelizacao Discipuladora de Criancas: Formando uma Nova Geracao de Discípulos*. Rio de Janeiro: JMN, 2016.
Santos, Valdeci da Silva. "Discipling Brazilian Cities: Incarnational Ministries of Historical Protestantism in Greater Metropolitan Vitoria, Espirito Santo." Ph.D. diss., Reformed Theological Seminary, 2000.
Sayão, Luiz A. *Bíblia Brasileira de Estudo*. São Paulo: Hagnos, 2016.
Schwaller, John Frederick. *The History of the Catholic Church in Latin America: From Conquest to Revolution and Beyond*. New York: New York University Press, 2011.
Schwarcz, Lilia Moritz. "Sérgio Buarque de Holanda e Essa Tal de 'Cordialidade.'" *Ide (São Paulo)* 31, no. 146 (2008) 83–89.
Schwarz, Christian A. *Natural Church Development: A Guide to Eight Essential Qualities of Healthy Churches*. Carol Stream, IL, ChurchSmart Resources, 1996.
Shaull, Richard and Waldo Cesar. *Pentecostalism and the Future of the Christian Churches*. Grand Rapids: Eerdmans, 2000.
Shaw, Mark. *Global Awakening: How 20th-Century Revivals Triggered a Christian Revolution*. Downers Grove: InterVarsity, 2010.
Shedd, Russell P. *Adoração Bíblica*. São Paulo: Vida, 2001.
———. *Lei, Graça e Santificação*, 2nd ed. São Paulo: Vida Nova, 1990.
Shenk, Wilbert R. *Enlarging the Story—Perspectives on Writing World Christian History*. Maryknoll, NY: Orbis, 2002.
Selka, Stephen L. "Ethnoreligious Identity Politics in Bahia, Brazil." *Latin American Perspectives* 32, no. 1 (2005) 72–94.
Silva, Geremias Bento da. "Interview Transcript." March 28, 2017.
Smith, Steve and Ying Kai. *T4T: A Discipleship Re-Revolution*. Richmond: WIGTake, 2011.
Soares, Valdir. "Interview Transcript." March 29, 2017.
Souza, Nilton Antonio de. "Interview Transcript." March 24, 2017.
Souza, Socrates Oliveira de. "Interview Transcript." March 28, 2017.
Spike, Robert W. "Evangelism and Culture." *The Christian Century* 76, no. 26 (1959) 775–77.
Stevenson, Kenneth, et al. *Ezekiel, Daniel: Ancient Christian Commentary on Scripture Series*. Downers Grove: InterVarsity, 2008.
Strelan, Rick. *Strange Acts: Studies in the Cultural World of the Acts of the Apostles*. Berlin: Walter de Gruyter, 2004.
Sumner, Robert L. *Evangelism: The Church on Fire*. Chicago: Regular Baptist, 1960.

Bibliography

Tavares, Thiago Rodrigues. "A Religião Vivida: Expressões Populares de Religiosidade." *Sacrilegens* 10, no. 2 (2013) 35–47.

Terry, Mark, and J. D. Payne. *Developing a Strategy for Missions: A Biblical, Historical, and Cultural Introduction*. Grand Rapids: Baker, 2013. Kindle.

Tennent, Timothy C. *Theology in the Context of World Christianity: How the Global Church is Influencing the Way We Think About and Discuss Theology*. Grand Rapids: Zondervan, 2007.

Tertullian and Robert D. Sider. *Christian and Pagan in the Roman Empire*. Washington, DC: Catholic University of America Press, 2001.

Thurston, Naomi. *Studying Christianity in China Constructions of an Emerging Discourse*. Vol. 8, *Theology and Mission in World Christianity*. Leiden: Brill, 2018.

Tillich, Paul and R. C. Kimball. *Theology of Culture*. New York: Oxford University Press, 1959.

Torres, Joao Camilo de Oliveira. *Historia das Ideias Religiosas no Brasil*. Sao Paulo: Grijalbo, 1968.

Tunala, Marcio. *Pequeno Grupo Multiplicador: Compartilhando o Amor de Deus por Meio de Relacionamentos*. Rio de Janeiro: Convicção, 2014.

Triandis, Harry C. "Individualism-Collectivism and Personality." *Journal of Personality* (2001) 907–24.

Vásquez, Manuel Arturo A. *The Brazilian Popular Church and the Crisis of Modernity*. Cambridge: Cambridge University Press, 1998.

Victory in Christ. "Victory in Christ." *Victory in Christ*, August 20, 2016. http://www.vitoriaemcristo.org/_gutenweb/_site/g w-programa-de-tv/.

———. "Programa Vitória em Cristo (20/08/2016)—A Ação de Deus na Trajetória da Nossa Vida—Parte II." *Victory in Christ*, April 4, 2017. https://www. Youtube.com/watch?v=WgD2TB5nhGc.

Vincent, Jon S. *Culture and Customs of Brazil*. Westport, CT: Greenwood, 2003.

Visão Brasil 2020. "Visão Brasil 2020." *Junta de Missões Nacionais*, June 30, 2017. http://www.visaobrasil2020.org.br/.

Von Sinner, Rudolf. "Pentecostalism and Citizenship in Brazil: Between Escapism and Dominance." *International Journal of Public Theology* 6, no. 1 (2012) 99–117.

Wagley, Charles. *An Introduction to Brazil*. New York: Columbia University Press, 1971.

Walls, Andrew F. *The Cross-Cultural Process in Christian History: Studies in the Transmission and Appropriation of Faith*. Maryknoll, NY: Orbis, 2002.

———. *The Missionary Movement in Christian History: Studies in the Transmission of Faith*. Maryknoll, NY: Orbis, 1996.

Woo, Rodney Matthew. "Paul's Contextual Approach for Evangelizing the Jews and the Gentiles Against the Background of Acts 13:16–41 and Acts 17:22–31." Ph.D. diss., Southwestern Baptist Theological Seminary, 1992.

World Atlas. "Which Countries Have the Most Christians Around The World?" *World Atlas*, May 9, 2018. https://www.worldatlas.com/articles/ which-countries-have-the-most-christians-around-the-world.html.

Yeo, K. K. *Musing with Confucius and Paul: Towards a Chinese Christian Theology*. Cambridge: Clarke, 2008.

Zabatiero, J. P. T. *Na Força do Espírito. Os Pentecostais na América Latina: Um Desafio às Igrejas Históricas*. São Paulo: Pendão Real, 1996.

———. *Estágios da Fé*. São Leopoldo-RS: Sinodal, 1992.

www.ingramcontent.com/pod-product-compliance
Lightning Source LLC
Chambersburg PA
CBHW062039220426
43662CB00010B/1567